# Japanese Retailing

# Japanese Retailing

Roy Larke

London and New York

First published 1994
by Routledge
11 New Fetter Lane, London EC4P 4EE

Simultaneously published in the USA and Canada
by Routledge
29 West 35th Street, New York, NY 10001

Typeset in Times by
Ponting–Green Publishing Services, Chesham, Bucks
Printed and bound in Great Britain by
Biddles Ltd, Guildford and King's Lynn

*British Library Cataloguing in Publication Data*
A catalogue record for this book is available from the
British Library.

*Library of Congress Cataloging-in-Publication Data.*
A catalogue record for this book has been requested.

ISBN 0–415–08362–1

for Rika

# Contents

# Figures and tables

**FIGURES**

**TABLES**

# Preface and acknowledgements

Japanese retailing is fascinating in its variety and complexity. There has been a lot of previous research on the subject for these reasons alone. Much of the work produced in English tends to be critical, but lacks the detail available in Japanese sources. The standard has improved in recent years as more and more non-Japanese learn Japanese, or take the time to get Japanese sources translated. This is an important advance.

I wanted to write a book that was simple and to the point, but that contained the detail previously omitted. The result is a descriptive and informative account of what retailing in Japan is really like. I have tried to be objective and straightforward, taking a neutral view – neither excessively critical nor praising. The book provides a wide-ranging but detailed background to anyone with an interest in Japanese distribution and retailing, and an introduction for visiting business people or scholars. It is even short enough to read on the plane over.

In the course of writing the book I have drawn on my own experiences as an informed consumer in Japan. I hope a wide range of non-Japanese business and academic readers will enjoy it and can learn from it. I also hope that a few Japanese might take time to read it, and realise how their system is seen from an outsider's *inside* point of view. No doubt some will disagree with the points made here, and they are welcome to do so. I say to both Japanese and non-Japanese alike, when dealing with one another, remember that there is always more than one way of looking at the world. Like any Westerner who has spent time in a country as non-Western and as tightly controlled as Japan, I have been taught this lesson again and again through my own experiences and mistakes.

I owe thanks to a great many people who have helped me over the years preceding the publication of this work. Professor John Dawson, now at Edinburgh University, was my guiding light during the hard years of studying for my doctorate at the Institute for Retail Studies at Stirling University in Scotland. Without his guidance and advice this book would never even have been started. The current Stirling team, especially the present head Professor Leigh Sparks, whose cut-throat editing and friendly advice was always useful, and his colleagues Keri Davies, Steve Burt, Mark Gabbott and Paul Freathy, all took an interest in my work and helped me out with their specialist knowledge whenever I needed it. Other British researchers took the time and trouble to send me long-distance advice while I was 6,000 miles away in Japan. Steve Worthington helped me learn all about credit cards in Japan, and Richard Harrison – a world authority in Japanese language and CALL (computer aided language learning) – advised on all my computing needs and corrected my Japanese on numerous occasions. I would also like to thank Professor Ian Gow, Val Hamilton and Ian Reader for their help with things Japanese.

Japan is a networking society. It is impossible to get anything done without contacts – what the Japanese call *kone*. Professor Masao Uno, a true Japanese gentleman, was my mentor and guide in my years at Waseda University. Other friends also helped develop my knowledge and enjoyment of marketing in Japan, including Professor Toshimi Tanaka, Kenji Arima, Kota Nagashima, Professor Akira Sogo, Ruth Malayang, Katsue Nishibe, to name but a few.

Finally, I must thank the University of Marketing and Distribution Sciences and all the staff there for their support, and for giving me a great job while I wrote the book. Very special thanks to Seiko Sakata for sparing weeks and months of her time helping me to prepare and complete the manuscript. To the hundreds of other Japanese who have helped me and supplied me with the sources I needed, thank you.

Roy Larke
Spring 1994
Kobe, Japan

# Chapter 1

# Retailing in Japan in the 1990s

## An Introduction

It's 5.15 on any weekday afternoon in central Tokyo and you are browsing the upper floors of a large department store. You've spent a day wandering around the many department stores and shopping buildings in the capital. These are some of the best tourist sights the city has to offer. Huge buildings, most over eight storeys, stocked with every imaginable type of merchandise – and all of it very expensive. You've seen everything from minutely embroidered silk kimonos in dazzling colours, and hundreds of types of writing papers from the simple to the handmade, to thousands of unusual, high-tech children's toys. You've seen more famous brands in a single day than ever before. It seems like all the big stores sell Gucci, Cartier, Jean Paul Gaultier, Louis Vuitton, and all at prices higher than anywhere else in the world. Also, there were people buying these items.

You were impressed by the intensity of the service, with shop assistants everywhere. Information desks with efficient, polite young ladies in smart, colourful uniforms. More young ladies in the same uniforms operating the elevators, welcoming each passenger, describing the merchandise on each floor and thanking each passenger when they alight. Yet more young ladies welcoming each customer at the foot of the escalators, while inconspicuously cleaning the moving hand rail.

Your few minor purchases, just a few pieces of Japanese writing paper, ¥300 a sheet,[1] were carefully wrapped, and they got their own carrier bag too. You were asked if they were a gift, which would have meant even more elaborate wrapping and a choice of ribbon, all included in the original price. Not a gift, but they're wrapped anyway.

You spent ¥1,000 for a cup of tea in one of the store's many smart tea and cake houses, and had lunch, costing only a little more than the tea, on the top floor. That was after twenty minutes choosing from among the many different restaurants, making the decision by peering at the plastic replicas of the food that the restaurants keep in their windows.

Now, your legs are tired, and you have not found much that fits into a Western budget anyway, so it's down through the department store and into the subway below. Earlier in the afternoon you passed through the two underground basement food sections on your way into the store. You noticed the boxed gift sets of coffee, biscuits, tea and many others, all prominently displaying the brand and all laid out in their own little concession stands. You also noticed boxed melons for ¥20,000 each, and boxed apples for ¥5,000.

There have been plenty of customers in the store all day, mainly women, and all shopping, for clothes, for accessories and for gifts. But now, leaving the elevator at a new part of the food basement, you head for the door – or at least you try to. The basement is packed with customers. Here the store sells ready-prepared salads, cuts of meat, roasts, marinated foods, sweet and sour foods, fresh fruits and vegetables like a supermarket, only much more intense. There are several fishmongers each specialising in a different type of fish. At one you count fifteen different varieties of shellfish. Another area has a huge tank of live catch. There is a bakery selling dozens of kinds of sweet breads, and another area selling small balls of rice, each individually wrapped and each with a different, colourful filling. Prices are still high, but perhaps just a little more reasonable here.

But it is the people that have changed the place. When you arrived this morning there were a lot of staff, and enough customers to keep a medium sized Western supermarket happy but now the aisles are packed, and the area has become like an outdoor market. You realise that each small corner is run by a different concession and each competes vigorously and noisily to sell their wares. This is an up-market department store? The scene is noisy and crowded, with people buying and selling everywhere, a total contrast from the controlled efficiency of the floors above.

None of this description is unusual. It could be any one of dozens of big department stores in Tokyo, Osaka or Nagoya. The customers in the basement are mainly working wives who, leaving work at 5 o'clock, rush to the department store food basements to get items for the evening meal.

It is just one of the striking faces of retailing in Japan in the 1990s. Admittedly, not many visitors would look at just department stores, although those in the larger cities could certainly provide a day or two of entertainment for the dedicated browser or student of retailing. There are many other interesting, often surprising sights to see among Japan's shops.

## RESEARCH INTO DISTRIBUTION IN JAPAN

Distribution in Japan is different. It is different from what most Western observers expect a distribution system to be. In many ways it is less efficient. Costs are high and Japanese businesses put emphasis on things such as personal relations with suppliers and customers to the point that profits while never forgotten, come second in some cases.

The distribution system is complex. There are very large numbers of wholesale outlets and retail outlets. Both are major employment sectors. The human side of retailing is important, both in the employment sense and in the emphasis that most retail companies put on customer service. Even supermarkets and other 'self-service' formats employ a relatively large number of people on the sales floor.

In addition, although the range of merchandise available in Japan is remarkably large, especially for someone like myself from the UK, most products are made and sold by Japanese companies. The only prominent and major exceptions are famous luxury brands, which Japanese consumers love. Most of these are distributed via Japanese import agents who realised the market potential for these foreign products many years ago.

Japan is virtually self-sufficient in manufactured products. The country imports most of its raw materials and fuels, and a large proportion of its food, but the proportion of imported consumer goods is low compared with the West.

Some would argue that if Japan is able to supply its own needs, then that is precisely what it should do. Consumers in other countries demand Japanese products, so why should the Japanese consumer be any different? Unfortunately, because of the problem of balancing international trade, and because there are times when the Japanese make very sure that their own interests are protected before they allow competition, there are many people outside Japan who would like to see more imports sold in Japan.

In looking for explanations as to why more overseas products do not find their way onto retail shelves, observers naturally turn to the distribution system as a possible cause.

Numerous researchers in the West have taken an interest in the distribution system in Japan. Mostly, this interest arose from the problems just outlined, but some others study the system because, as first mentioned, it is so different. Others simply because there is so much to see.

On the other hand, a very small number of Japanese have also tried to explain aspects of their distribution system in English. In Japanese, the volume of literature relating to distribution is very large indeed. There are numerous sources of data. Every three years, the Ministry of International Trade and Industry (MITI), carries out a Census of Commerce which provides detailed, macro level statistics on the retail and wholesale industries. The main financial daily newspaper, the *Nihon Keizai Shinbun*, or more usually called the *Nikkei*, publishes numerous books and annual statistical surveys relating to retailing and wholesaling alone, and has a separate broadsheet, published three times a week that is dedicated to distribution. All this is in addition to trade and professional publications and surveys that are also quite widely available if you look.

What surprises me is that, despite all these data and all these publications, among the various attempts to explain why distribution is so different, or more usually, so 'bad', very few people – Japanese or Western – have taken the time to describe the basic structure, and the key companies that operate within the system. The detailed information exists, albeit mostly in Japanese, but too many observers, and far too many businesspeople, have dismissed the distribution system as awkward and inefficient without ever knowing about these data.

Much of the system may well be awkward and inefficient, but it takes very little time to know more about the basic structure of the system. This book provides an unashamedly descriptive overview of distribution in Japan. It concentrates mainly on the retail sector and provides many of the data and much of the work that, while available in Japanese, for some reason are hardly ever seen in English.

## AN OVERVIEW OF THE BOOK

The book has two main parts, although they are not fully differentiated. Chapters 2 to 4 provide detailed background information on the overall retail market and the structure of distribution. A lot of this information is similar to that given in previous publications in English, but I believe that, in a single work, it goes into much greater depth. The next three chapters follow on from this to look at particular retail sectors. The book is summarized in Chapter 8.

Chapter 2 was the most difficult to write concisely. It gives a detailed overview of Japanese consumers. It is a highly statistical account, and includes a wide range of data on demographics, income and expenditure. The chapter also provides brief notes on shopping behaviour and consumer behaviour characteristics, particularly the unusual and important characteristic of gift shopping.

Chapters 3 and 4 provide a comprehensive overview of the distribution system. Chapter 3 again uses statistics to detail the structure of the system as a whole, including the role of manufacturers and wholesalers. It covers the main practices and problems within the system that have brought the most attention and complaint, mainly from overseas. Chapter 4 considers in detail the most prominent and the most tangible of these problems, which is the Large Store Law. Throughout these chapters reference is made to how the system and various parts and practices within it are now changing. The restrictive legislation in the Large Store Law is a case in point, with some of the most drastic changes in the law's effects and application coming in the early part of the 1990s. Chapter 4 provides a detailed update on the current situation and speculates on the most likely futures.

Chapter 5 considers the organisation of small-unit retailing. In order to cover the very broad range of topics that this implies, the chapter both describes small independent retailing and corporate chains that are mostly based on small formats, notably speciality store and convenience store retailing, and also looks at shopping centres. Many shopping centres act as another type of organisation for small-unit retailing. While Chapter 3 shows how numerous small stores are, Chapter 5 emphasises their importance from a business point of view.

Chapters 6 and 7 show that, despite the reputation that previous research has built for Japanese retailing, as consisting solely of small stores, there are large formats mixed in. These are split between two main types, with some overlap. They are department stores and conglomerate retail groups. The latter are focused on chains of large general merchandise stores (GMS). Japan is the last country in the advanced world where department stores continue to exist in any considerable number. Until as recently as the late 1980s, most of these companies were prosperous and had strong results. A change in consumer demand patterns has brought problems and difficulties, however. They represent traditional large-format retailing in Japan, and many of their management systems are equally traditional and conservative. Chapter 6 shows how the 1990s will be a time of challenge and rethinking for these companies; most will struggle, even as tourist attractions.

Chapter 7 looks at the new operators of large-format retailing. These are huge conglomerate groups of companies that include several retail operations as well as numerous other businesses. The chapter looks at the general make-up of these businesses and considers the leading groups in some detail. These will continue to be the leaders of the retail industry well into the next century. They have their own problems, but they are quickest to change and adapt, and can rapidly enter or create new markets and instigate new techniques. They are also now very big. In the 1990s the largest of all could even challenge the traditional leaders of the distribution channels, the large manufacturers.

Chapter 8 summarizes and concludes the book. In this chapter I reiterate the most important points, re-emphasizing the need to study and understand the distribution system in Japan, and look at the main immediate trends that will affect the industry over coming years.

## LEARNING ABOUT DISTRIBUTION IN JAPAN

By the end of the book readers will have the broadest possible view of Japanese distribution and retailing in the 1990s. Throughout the book no attempt is made to draw direct comparisons with the West, although similarities are mentioned. It is a mistake to compare distribution in Japan with that in other countries, although that is what a lot of past research, especially research by Japanese, has tried to do. It is like comparing a cat and a rabbit. There are similarities, but the behaviour of one is very different from that of the other. Distribution systems, with all their good points and bad points, develop from within the local culture and in response to local business conditions.

Throughout the book, the discussion is descriptive, and avoids dwelling too much on intangible problems. The objective is to provide broad, accurate accounts of what the situation really is in the distribution system in Japan. Anyone with a good command of written Japanese can build up such a picture quite quickly by using

Japanese sources, but it is not generally available in English. Dodwell Marketing Consultants' periodically produced *Retail Distribution in Japan* is an excellent source of information, and essential for any serious student, but at ¥80,000 a copy it is out of reach of most. It is also neither as detailed nor usually as up to date as the similar Japanese work, *Distribution Company Yearbook* (*Ryūtsū Kaisha Nenkan*), produced annually by *Nikkei* (Nihon Keizai Shinbun, 1992).

The present book provides basic information on all aspects of Japanese distribution and retailing for any student or businessman. It makes good introductory reading, and helps the reader avoid having to go to the original Japanese sources on which it is largely based. Wherever possible Japanese sources were used rather than English ones.

The discussion is up to date and the notes and illustrations are drawn from my own years of experience living in Japan and being a consumer there. The reader should find it interesting, informative and, above all, useful in understanding not what distribution in Japan should be, but what it actually is.

# Chapter 2

# The consumer environment in Japan

The Japanese are a proud, independent race living in a crowded country. Even in casual conversation they commonly emphasise their own 'Japanese-ness' in the phrase *ware ware nihonjin*, 'we the Japanese do . . .' or 'we the Japanese are . . .', as if being Japanese sets a person apart from the rest of humanity. This self-confidence shapes the Japanese consumer. The assertion that Japanese are different extends to their behaviour as consumers.

This chapter details the consumer environment in Japan. Retailing and consumers are complementary forces in any modern economy. Each reacts and develops with the other. There have been few attempts to describe Japanese consumer behaviour in English (Fields, 1983 and 1988a are major exceptions; also see March, 1990; Yoshino, 1971), so this chapter covers a broad area of mainly statistical data in order to provide a general background to the remainder of the book.

Japanese all speak the same language, go through the same highly controlled education system and, with their belief in themselves as Japanese, have similar values and ideals. Japanese consumers are quality conscious, and demand high levels of service (see JETRO, 1983b). They love famous brands, they are affluent and they have a developed sense of social status and position that often dictates their shopping habits. Despite all this, and despite Japanese claims to the contrary, consumers in Japan are little different to those anywhere in the advanced world. Consumer behaviour is often intangible and inconsistent, while retailing is relatively tangible and objective in its function and result. Even Japanese claim that both consumers and the distribution system are difficult to understand and different from the Western case. Observing differences, however, is largely a matter of personal opinion and experience, and this chapter shows that in terms of the data and information available, there should be no difficulty in achieving proper understanding.

Broadly speaking, the chapter considers three major aspects of the consumer environment. First demographics. The Japanese population is large, and the population structure is quite distinctive. There are two major consumer age groups, and several easily distinguished consumer types, differentiated solely by age and sex. Impending changes in demographic structure will be important for the retail trade in the twenty-first century.

Second, consumer income and expenditure. Recent detailed data on consumer spending show general patterns similar to those in most advanced nations. On the other hand, a higher relative importance is attributed to education and social expenses which relates to aspects of behaviour that are very Japanese.

Finally, shopping. In this chapter I briefly consider general shopping patterns and Japanese-isms, especially the significant role of women, the importance of social hierarchy and the special role and significance of gift shopping.

The aim throughout is to give a broad understanding of Japanese consumers and their behaviour.

## A LOT OF PEOPLE LIVING IN A SMALL SPACE

In 1990 the Japanese population was 123 million. While smaller than that of the combined countries of the European Union, after the USA this was the second largest population for any single country in the advanced world. Moreover, this large population is concentrated into a land area only a third larger than the British Isles.

Japan is an archipelago consisting of four main islands and over 6,000 small islands. Figure 2.1 shows the four main islands, Hokkaido, Honshu, Shikoku and Kyushu, along with the twelve major cities and main geographical regions. The main consumer markets are on the central Pacific coast. This includes the southern Kanto, Chubu and Kansai areas, stretching 600 kilometres from Chiba Prefecture in the north to Hyogo Prefecture in the south, loosely corresponding to the main bullet-train route between Tokyo and Osaka.

Three of the seven largest conurbations, Tokyo, Osaka and Nagoya, are on this coast. These areas dominate the social and economic life of Japan (Table 2.1). They include seven cities over

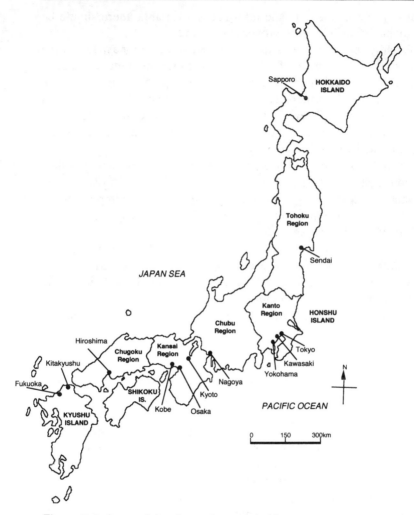

*Figure 2.1* Japan: islands, regions and cities

1 million people, and are home to 50 per cent of the total population.
They account for 49 per cent of all business premises (Sōmuchō,
1992a: 48–50), and almost 90 per cent of savings and deposits (Asahi
Shinbunsha, 1993a). All this is concentrated into about 8 per cent of
the total land area.

Tokyo, the capital, is a huge urban sprawl. As a city it has
tremendous energy, and is the cultural and commercial centre of
the country. It is the only city in Japan that can make any claim at

Table 2.1 Land area, population, households, businesses and retail sales in major urban areas

| City | Land area (sq km) | % of total | Population | % of total | Households | % of total | Private business premises | % of total | Retail sales (¥1 million) | % of total |
|---|---|---|---|---|---|---|---|---|---|---|
| Japan total | 377,737 | 100.0 | 123,957,458 | 100.0 | 43,077,126 | 100.0 | 6,640,101 | 100.0 | 114,839,927 | 100.0 |
| Tokyo area[a] | 11,757 | 3.1 | 31,078,062 | 25.1 | 11,468,937 | 26.6 | 1,529,589 | 23.0 | 30,904,416 | 26.9 |
| Osaka area[b] | 14,526 | 3.8 | 24,250,184 | 19.6 | 8,375,049 | 19.4 | 1,336,250 | 20.1 | 23,518,594 | 20.5 |
| Nagoya area | 5,649 | 1.5 | 6,600,501 | 5.3 | 2,126,068 | 4.9 | 373,074 | 5.6 | 6,343,429 | 5.5 |
| Fukuoka area[c] | 4,317 | 1.1 | 5,664,702 | 4.6 | 2,052,947 | 4.8 | 293,737 | 4.4 | 5,648,336 | 4.9 |
| Sapporo area | 11,691 | 3.1 | 2,670,084 | 2.2 | 1,046,869 | 2.4 | 121,538 | 1.8 | 2,666,180 | 2.3 |
| Hiroshima area | 7,715 | 2.0 | 2,263,976 | 1.8 | 827,516 | 1.9 | 117,910 | 1.8 | 2,067,917 | 1.8 |
| Sendai area | 6,788 | 1.8 | 2,130,636 | 1.7 | 671,465 | 1.6 | 106,952 | 1.6 | 1,907,785 | 1.7 |
| Main area totals | 62,443 | 16.5 | 74,658,145 | 60.2 | 26,568,851 | 61.7 | 3,879,050 | 58.4 | 73,056,657 | 63.6 |

[a] Including Yokohama and Kawasaki.
[b] Including Kyoto and Kobe.
[c] Including Kitakyushu.
Source: Asahi Shinbunsha (1993a)

all to being international, with Japanese and non-Japanese mixing freely together. On the other hand, it is the safest city of its size anywhere in the world.

Within central Tokyo there are six primary rail terminals, which are also the largest shopping areas in Japan, and in terms of sales space, some of largest in the world. Within a square kilometre of the area around Ginza and Nihonbashi, there is over 350,000 square metres of sales space in large (over 6,000 square metres) retail outlets alone and hundreds of smaller outlets too (MITI, 1987b). The other main shopping areas are Shibuya, Shinjuku, Ikebukuro, Ueno and Akihabara. They should all be on the list of places to see for any student of retailing.

Tokyo accounts for a quarter of the population, 27 per cent of the total number of households, around 60 per cent of wholesale sales and 27 per cent of retail sales (MITI, 1992b). Tokyo is even home to 9 per cent of the farming population. Metropolitan Tokyo now includes most of the Kanto region, with over 30 million people living within 50 kilometres of Tokyo station.

Only 1.3 million of these live in the eight most central Tokyo wards, but in addition to these, almost 3 million people commute into the centre to work every weekday (Asahi Shinbunsha, 1993a: 196). The average commuting time into a job in Tokyo is between one and two hours each way, and increasing (Bandō, 1991: 80). This commuting radius includes the cities of Yokohama and Kawasaki. Yokohama is the second largest city, with 3.25 million people, and Kawasaki is the ninth largest, with 1.2 million. Both have significant concentrations of retail facilities around their city-centre rail terminals. Yokohama station is particularly impressive, with three major department stores and four large shopping centres all within 100 metres of the station. Nevertheless, despite their size, large proportions of the populations from both cities commute into Tokyo to work every day.

The Tokyo area is the single most important consumer market, and the base to almost a quarter of all private business premises. It is the one market that no company can afford to ignore. Fashions, consumer fads and trends almost all begin in the capital. Daiei, the largest retailer in Japan, was founded in Osaka, but now has its headquarters in central Tokyo. Takashimaya, the third largest department store company, splits its headquarters into a Tokyo office and an Osaka office. Many young people move to Tokyo to find work. White-collar workers at large companies often find themselves temporarily posted there on assignment. One friend of mine posted to Tokyo by a large electrical manufacturer has been commuting back to his Kyoto home, 300 kilometres away, every weekend for the past ten years.

In terms of population, the Kansai region and the area around the city of Nagoya form the only other major markets that can truly rival Tokyo (see Figure 2.1). The centre of the Kansai market is Osaka, but, like Kanto, Kansai also encompasses two other large cities, Kyoto and Kobe, both with populations over 1 million. Nagoya has its own widespread commercial area of smaller cities, but none the size of those around Tokyo and Osaka.

While Tokyo people are confident and relaxed, people in and around Osaka are fiercely defensive of their own region, often looking to compete with the capital. Osaka, the third largest city according to the annual survey of registered households (Local Authorities Ministry, 1993), is the hub of the Kansai market. Up until the nineteenth century, Osaka was the national centre for trade and commerce and it still clings to its merchant roots. Retailing in Osaka city is more limited than in central Tokyo, with the Umeda and Namba districts being the only main shopping areas. A characteristic of Osaka's shopping facilities is some of the largest roofed shopping streets in Japan (see Chapter 5), each several kilometres long and having several hundred stores.

The total Osaka conurbation stretches south for over 120 kilometres. Kyoto to the east and Kobe to the west, with numerous smaller cities in between, make an area with a population of over 24 million people. The topography of the area, which is a relatively thin strip between the mountains and the sea, makes the transport system less complex and less extensive than the one around Tokyo. Consequently, Kyoto and Kobe are less dependent on Osaka.

Kyoto is the ancient capital of Japan, and maintains a traditional cultural atmosphere. The city has thousands of original wooden temples and shrines. It is famous in distribution terms as a bastion of the Large Store Law (see Chapter 4). It restricts the opening of large retail stores to protect both the skyline and the large numbers of small traditional retailers in the city.

Kobe, on the other hand, is the southern tip of the central Pacific coast market. The west and north of the city are semi-rural, while the east forms a high-income suburb of Osaka. It is an important fashion area and home to large textile companies. It is also Japan's third largest port and shipbuilding area.

Nagoya, in Aichi Prefecture, is an affluent, independent city and forms the core of the third largest urban area after Kanto and Kansai. For a city of 2 million, it is more provincial than Osaka or Tokyo, but people are affluent, and Nagoya resembles Kobe as a fashionable city. It is home to a number of large manufacturing companies, including the Toyota car manufacturing company. People in the city are exceptionally conscious of social hierarchy and this is reflected in their consumption behaviour. Nagoya is famous for hosting the most expensive wedding receptions in Japan, for example.

There are two main shopping areas in Nagoya, one in the city centre and the other around the main rail terminal. Unlike the Osaka and Tokyo areas, however, Nagoya has no large satellite cities, and the area forms the largest single-city market in the country.

Such regional differences present numerous marketing opportunities. People born in Kansai remain Kansai-loyal all their lives. Tokyo is a mixture of immigrants from the regions, most of whom seldom forget their birthplace or, in the second generation, their parents' home town.

In addition to those along the central Pacific coast, there are another four areas with populations over 1 million, around Fukuoka, Sapporo, Hiroshima and Sendai. None have the overriding consumer power of the three largest areas, but all form individual local markets. Each prefecture takes a strong pride in its own local history and culture, and especially in its local agricultural and marine produce.

There is also a wide climatical diversity. The northern prefectures have heavy snowfalls, with those between Hokkaido and northern Chubu being under snow for significant periods every year. Kyushu, the largest southern island, has a mild winter and a hot, humid summer, suitable for fruit and other warm-climate products. The southernmost islands of Okinawa are tropical, but too small to have great economic significance.

For the majority of companies, this diversity in other regions is less important than the three main urban markets, and then the other large regional cities. The following chapters also describe the concentration of wholesale and retail sales within these three conurbations. This is where most consumers live, and so where companies find their markets.

## THE POPULATION STRUCTURE OF JAPAN

There are currently three key population trends that have a significant influence on consumer marketing. First, the population will age rapidly over the coming decades, creating the so-called 'new silver market'. Second, within the present population, there are two narrow age ranges of significantly larger size than any other. The elder of these will become the same silver market. Third, the proportion of children under 15 is low, and will continue to decrease over the coming twenty years.

The following sections discuss these trends and the various interrelationships.

## The ageing population

Japan had a birth rate of only 9.8 per 1,000 people in 1992 (Asahi Shinbunsha, 1992). On the other hand, Japanese had one of the longest life expectancies in the world, 76 years for men and 82 for women (Asahi Shinbunsha, 1992: 201; Bandō, 1991: 13). Together these statistics mean an ageing population.

*Table 2.2* Projections of future population structure by age group, 1990–2030

|      | Total   | 0–14   | %    | 15–64  | %    | 65+    | %    |
|------|---------|--------|------|--------|------|--------|------|
| 1990 | 123,611 | 22,484 | 18.2 | 86,228 | 69.8 | 14,899 | 12.1 |
| 1995 | 125,263 | 19,993 | 16.0 | 87,116 | 69.6 | 18,154 | 14.5 |
| 2000 | 126,981 | 19,279 | 15.2 | 86,191 | 67.9 | 21,511 | 16.9 |
| 2005 | 128,662 | 20,120 | 15.6 | 84,166 | 65.4 | 24,376 | 19.0 |
| 2010 | 129,449 | 21,247 | 16.4 | 80,936 | 62.5 | 27,266 | 21.1 |
| 2015 | 128,852 | 21,076 | 16.4 | 77,002 | 59.8 | 30,774 | 23.9 |
| 2020 | 126,903 | 19,617 | 15.5 | 75,317 | 59.4 | 31,969 | 25.2 |
| 2025 | 124,226 | 18,065 | 14.6 | 74,563 | 60.1 | 31,598 | 25.4 |
| 2030 | 121,240 | 17,406 | 14.4 | 72,842 | 60.1 | 30,992 | 25.6 |

*Source*: Ministry of Health and Welfare (1991)

Table 2.2 further illustrates this ageing process. The population will peak in 2010 at around 129 million, and fall after this due to the low birth rate. The proportion of the population over 65 will continue to expand. The Ministry of Health and Welfare (1991: 32–6) predicts it will reach almost 28 per cent in 2045.

In social terms, this will make the population unbalanced, with only 56 per cent of the population in the potential labour force, aged between 15 and 64.

In the early 1990s there are only a few examples of companies that offer products and services for the new silver market, although public services for the elderly are becoming more common. Because the people who will make up this market are still in their forties, it is too early to see a significant marketing shift to target pensioner power, but the silver market will be an increasingly important factor over the next fifteen years.

### The baby-boom generations

Rapid ageing is a population trend, but the reason the population will become so unbalanced is because of a proportionally large baby-boom age group. Japan has two baby-boomer generations. One is now in its mid-forties and will become the new silver market when they retire in fifteen years' time. The other, their children, are in their early twenties. Both age groups form large population bulges.

In Japanese the baby-booms are called the *dankai sedai*, meaning the 'bulge generations'. Figure 2.2 clearly shows why. In 1990, these accounted for about 16 per cent of the population or 20.6 million people in two clear bumps in the pyramid, making them important consumer markets. In addition, the senior baby-boom generation were the vanguard of modern Japanese consumers, with succeeding generations learning and developing their behaviour accordingly.

Japanese writers make a clear distinction between the behaviour and attitudes of different generations (Fields, 1988a: 3–17; Maruyama, 1985; Ohashi, 1988; Tsujinaka, 1988; 1989). Grandparents the world over complain about the behaviour of the younger generations, but upheavals in the modern history of Japan since 1930 have brought sudden generational changes in attitudes and behaviour (see Larke, 1990).

The senior baby-boom are now concentrated between 42 and 47 years old, at the peak of their careers. Many are at the top of their earning potential with high incomes and falling expenses. Home making is completed, and their children are coming to the end of their university education, so releasing the burden of educational fees.

This generation were born soon after the Second World War. Many remember the food shortages and other hardships of the immediate postwar years, but have never experienced war itself. From their parents they learned the values of hard work, thrift and mutual co-operation. Such values helped to build a super-economy, with GNP growing by over 10 per cent a year from the early 1960s to the late 1970s, and exceeding 7 per cent a year for much of the late 1980s (EPA, 1992c). Japanese society also progressed and changed as a result.

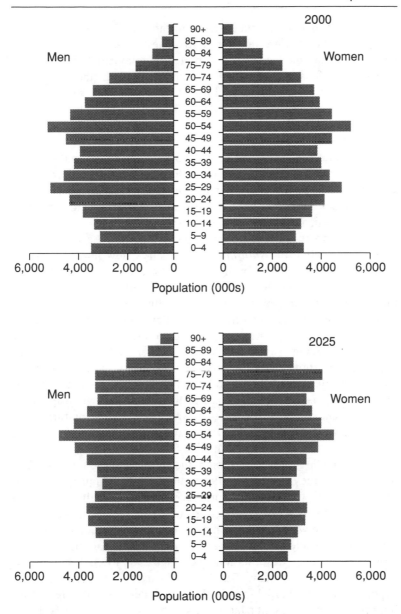

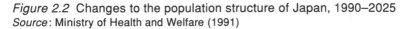

*Figure 2.2* Changes to the population structure of Japan, 1990–2025
*Source*: Ministry of Health and Welfare (1991)

The new consumer market arrived in Japan in the 1960s when the senior baby-boom were in their youth. They were the first Japanese teenagers to sample Coca Cola, commercial television, chain stores, Western music and McDonald's hamburgers. With these Western imports came marketing techniques and ideas.[1] The senior baby-boom generation also experienced the Tokyo Olympics first hand. In short, this generation was the first to experience the fun of free consumption and to enjoy a new mass consumer society.

Throughout the 1970s, as young workers and home makers, this same generation drove the economy. They set the pace both in the workplace and in the consumer market. They developed new consumer values and a greater ability and willingness to consume (Dentsu Sōken, 1989).

The successors to the senior baby-boom inherited the same values. These were called the *shinjinrui* or, literally, 'new human species' (Fields, 1988a: 7–19). Now in their thirties, the *shinjinrui* number some 15 million people, but spread over a wide age range. Rather than being another, separate generation, they represent a new type of behaviour (Adachi *et al.*, 1988). They work as hard as their forebears, and co-operate at work and in society as much as any stereotypical Japanese.[2] More than their elders, however, they have both the opportunity and the propensity to enjoy the fruits of their labours. While they still work relatively long hours, leisure, including shopping, is an important part of their lives. Growing up as the education and social infrastructure was just reaching maturity, the *shinjinrui* work hard for what they have, but they want to enjoy it too (see Sato and Tsuboi, 1993).

Then came the junior baby-boom, the children of the seniors. Born in the 1970s, they are now college students. Although young, and only just about to enter the workplace, the junior baby-boom is a very different generation. They grew up in the most successful economy in the world, and in a mature society. A tortuous education system, and a society that has come to judge ability on the results of university entrance examinations (see page 23 below), did not make their teenage years easy. But, other than that, this group have experienced few hardships in their two decades of life. More important, they represent a large market that is easy to identify. From conception to graduation, they have wanted for very little, and have co-operated enthusiastically as a test market (White, 1993).

A major part of the junior baby-boom's adolescent education was learning to be consumers. As children, companies offered them so-called 'character goods'. Character goods use cute, usually cartoon-based characters as their emblem, brand or sales point. Most are casual clothing, luggage, confectionary or stationery items. Companies produced these products in thousands of designs and variations, most priced within pocket-money range, and all designed to attract children's eyes. Companies such as Sega, the global giant of arcade games, Sanrio, the largest maker and distributor of character goods, and Tokyo Disneyland have all prospered as a result of the junior baby-boom. Of course, all this was paid for by their parents, but these parents are the same liberated consumers that make up the senior baby-boom. What better way for people to enjoy the economy they have built than to share it with their children?

The junior baby-boom was the motivation that built today's market for children. The value of this market will continue to grow with the increase in the number of grandparents, although the number of children will fall. Toy manufacturers are growing, and Japan will be a lucrative market for companies such as Toys'R'Us (*Nikkei Trendy*, 1992).

The recession of the early 1990s means that the junior baby-boom will be the first generation for years that has had to fight for jobs, although the situation is still nowhere as bad as in some European countries. This hardship aside, the junior baby-boom will continue to establish new patterns of consumption. Over coming decades, they will remain the group that companies watch to determine how consumers will change and develop. Below I describe how households are becoming smaller and spending more on discretionary items, how more women are entering and staying in the workplace, and how men are becoming more active consumers. The junior baby-boom will lead and expand these trends over the next twenty years.

**Household numbers and household size**

In 1992 there were almost 43 million households in Japan. The average household was 2.88 people (see Table 2.3), falling below 3 people for the first time in 1990. This is part of a long-term trend towards smaller households.

With the population ageing, many families still look after their elderly parents at home, but overall, the extended family is becoming less common. Linked to this, migration to the major cities is continuing, tempting young people away from rural regions, and, again, leading to fewer extended families. Elderly people are both

*Table 2.3* Population and households, 1982–93

|      | Population | Households | Persons per household |
|------|------------|------------|-----------------------|
| 1982 | 117,776,771 | 36,858,900 | 3.20 |
| 1983 | 118,601,534 | 37,425,866 | 3.17 |
| 1984 | 119,316,468 | 37,934,575 | 3.15 |
| 1985 | 120,007,812 | 38,457,479 | 3.12 |
| 1986 | 120,720,542 | 38,987,773 | 3.10 |
| 1987 | 121,371,798 | 39,536,307 | 3.07 |
| 1988 | 121,874,240 | 40,025,087 | 3.04 |
| 1989 | 122,335,313 | 40,561,404 | 3.02 |
| 1990 | 122,744,952 | 41,156,485 | 2.98 |
| 1991 | 123,156,678 | 41,797,445 | 2.95 |
| 1992 | 123,587,297 | 42,457,975 | 2.91 |
| 1993 | 123,957,458 | 43,077,126 | 2.88 |

*Source*: Local Authorities Ministry (1993)

healthier and more independent than was the case in the hierarchical extended families of the prewar years (see Nakane, 1973).

People move to the largest cities in order to take up jobs. The population of Tokyo will increase only slightly to 2000, but the population in the three surrounding prefectures of Chiba, Saitama and Kanagawa will grow faster than in any other region. This is partly due to the influx of people from other parts of Japan, but also due to people moving out of the capital to find cheaper house prices in the surrounding prefectures.

The family remains a strong institution, but younger people are becoming rapidly more independent. Most students still live at home during their university studies (Ministry of Education, 1992), but more and more are leaving home to attend better schools in the larger cities. Many, finding that the best jobs are in the same large cities, never return to their home town. Some even prefer to stay in the city after graduation simply because it is more exciting.[3]

In addition to the overall fall in household size, the number of single-person households is growing. In 1992, some 9.4 million people lived alone. Of these, over half were in their twenties (Asahi Shinbunsha, 1993a), and 34 per cent lived in the Tokyo area.

Households in Tokyo are relatively smaller than in the rest of the country, averaging only 2.36 people (Local Authorities Ministry, 1993). Many retail facilities have developed to supply this market. Tokyo has a greater density of convenience stores and fast-food restaurants, for example, and the number will grow steadily in the 1990s.

Overall, there are roughly 2 million more men of marrying age than there are women. Many of these will live alone for a long period, and many will live in Tokyo. In addition, men posted on assignment away from their homes often make the move without their families, becoming pseudo-singles who, after years of being looked after, need the services of restaurants and fast food more than most.

The size of households will continue to fall, especially in the larger urban areas. This will have a significant effect on the retail market, and encourage the continuing growth of convenience shopping and leisure services.

## DEMOGRAPHIC CONSUMER GROUPS

Generally speaking, the Japanese are a single homogenous race and immensely proud and defensive about their racial purity. Only 1.1 million, less than 1 per cent, of the population are non-Japanese. Of these 80 per cent are of Korean or Chinese descent, and have lived in Japan all their lives, speaking only Japanese and taking Japanese names (Ministry of Justice, 1991).

Most were forcibly brought to the country before the Second World War, but Japan has granted citizenship to very few because they are not Japanese by blood. On the other hand, immigration laws look favourably on third-generation children of Japanese emigrants who return from Brazil and the USA, and who often understand the language and culture less than resident Koreans and Chinese.

The Japanese consumer market is racially homogenous compared to most Western nations. The Japanese also like to consider themselves as all being equal. Opinion surveys suggest that up to 90 per cent consider themselves 'middle class' (RICE, 1988). Income differentials exist, and Japan has its own wealthy and poor, but not to the degree found in many Western nations. In the broadest sense, similarity between consumers, whether real or implied by consumers themselves, makes target groups easy to identify.

Within different age groups, sex groups and geographical regions, consumer behaviour and opinions are surprisingly uniform. It is worthwhile to consider a broad, macro categorisation of consumer types. As natives, all Japanese companies have this knowledge, but it is surprising how often it is overlooked by Western businesses.

Table 2.4 Characteristics of main consumer types in Japan[a]

| | Education years 0–17 29.8 million | Adult males 18+ 45.6 million | Young adult women 18–27 9 million | Housewives 28+ 39.4 million |
|---|---|---|---|---|
| Age range: Population (1992): | | | | |
| Income characteristics | Low income, growing as enter teenager years; often do little paid work until high school | Main income earners, income growing by age and occupation; main breadwinners in any family | Individual income below average, but almost all is disposable income; most living at home | Low personal income, but most return to work once youngest child is in school, for pocket money |
| Shopping characteristics | Shopping increases with age, but very busy in late teens; then as college students shop a great deal | Shop very little; younger men shop for own interests, but mainly too busy with work | Shop to use their income after work; lots of time and highly motivated to shop | Shop daily for family needs and also have time to shop for own pleasure, including trips into city centre |
| Spending characteristics | Buy small toys when very young, then mainly hobbies, mainly car stationery and some clothes | Shop for own hobbies, mainly car related, sports and entertainment | Shop to spend money on clothing, dining out, various leisure, travel | Basic household goods, also for own leisure, dining out, hobbies |

[a] These types are generalisations only. The population figures include widows, widowers, divorcees etc. Married women overlap the Young adult women and Housewives categories.

Table 2.4 provides a stylised interpretation of the main consumer types. The table may seem oversimplified, but it provides the basis for general description. More detailed information is necessary when looking at consumer reaction to individual stores or products, but even such analysis requires the basis that the table provides. Such generalisations could not be drawn in Europe or the USA because of greater macro diversity. In Japan, differences occur between Tokyo and the rest of the country, between men and women and between age groups, but most other factors are surprisingly uniform.

## The education years

Education has a profound effect on social position in Japan. More than any other factor after age and sex, educational record determines the way people live, where they work, who they marry and, consequently, their consumption behaviour. Education routes are varied, but the basic pattern is set. The basic process is as follows.

Education starts early, with kindergarten beginning at the age of 3. At this early stage, some parents might try to get their child into a school that offers kindergarten to university education. The advantage is that the child can avoid years of preparation for university entrance at age 18. The disadvantage is that candidate toddlers have to take an entrance exam to enter the kindergarten. Such schools are popular and expensive, and the exams are not easy.

Whether the child takes a private or public route, elementary school begins at 6, progressing on to junior high school at 12. Everyone must learn the Chinese characters that make up the Japanese writing system, and this takes time. No one jumps grades.

Compulsory education ends at 15, but about 95 per cent of Japanese go to high school for another three years, and around 70 per cent graduate (Asahi Shinbunsha, 1992: 224). Usually, those that drop out of education before 20 are destined for low-level jobs.

After graduating from high school, 37 per cent of women and 35 per cent of men continue into some form of higher education (Ministry of Education, 1992). Most women go to two-year junior colleges where they study languages, bookkeeping or technical skills like computing or dressmaking. Most boys, and an increasing proportion of girls, go to four-year universities.

There are over 500 universities, three quarters of them privately run (Asahi Shinbunsha, 1992: 223). Every faculty in every university conducts its own entrance examinations, and every university faculty is ranked by cram schools according to the difficulty of its entrance examination. The best medical, engineering and pure science faculties in the top national universities are the most difficult, followed by similar departments in private universities (Senno, 1993). Entrance exams are multiple choice only. They test the volume of hard facts that each student has memorised over the preceding years. Interviews or applied creative thinking are required only in rare cases (*Economist*, 1990a).

The education system influences society in two profound ways. First, because of the emphasis on men as opposed to women in society as a whole, women are not as strongly motivated to enter the better schools (see Bandō, 1992: 26–7). Sex discrimination is traditional and an enduring part of Japanese society. Improvement has been much slower than in other advanced nations. Many girls do go on to higher education now, but still fewer girls than boys apply to four-year colleges. As girls are not expected to pursue a career, many parents and schools think they have less need to study.

Second, but more important, the school from which a person graduates determines their social position and prospects for the rest of their lives. Students from the most prestigious universities have an advantage in the job market regardless of true ability, making university entrance the overriding priority. If they fail to enter a good university at their first attempt, rather than go to a low-level college, many people, but mostly men, study for an extra year or more after high school. Some retake exams year after year.

Companies and universities perpetuate this situation. In many subject areas universities do little to make graduation competitive, and few students fail. Consequently, college students are renowned for having no motivation and for not studying. Companies understand that the value of most university education is limited, and select applicants by school name alone. Companies rely on in-house training to teach their new labour force, expecting them to know very little to begin with.[4]

The education system is a great equaliser. The only differentiating factor is the volume of study any student does, and how much time they spend doing other things like watching TV and playing in sports teams. As school pupils approach university entrance exams at 18, they have less and less time for other things. As consumers, while their pocket money increases, their opportunity to shop is reduced. As child consumers, Japanese pass through three stages that correspond closely with the three main stages of general education.

Even at elementary school, children soon learn the importance of brand image as an indication of quality (Cendron, 1984; Johanssen, 1984; Wada, 1992). Expensive, branded clothing for children, such as Miki House, is highly popular. Children themselves buy cute, character design stationery goods and toys from as young as 3 years old (Across, 1988; Larke, 1990).

The first real consumer market, however, emerges as children enter junior high school. As with teenagers the world over, self-consciousness and self-image become more important, and school pupils begin to exercise their choice behaviour over a wider range of merchandise. While the pressure of study increases, strolling around shops is a favourite pastime for young people at this age.

High-school students, especially girls, who are under relatively less pressure, are often seen as trend leaders and are commonly used for market research focus groups. But for most 15- to 18-year-old children, high school is three years of preparation for the 'entrance exam hell' – *nyūgaku shiken jigoku*. Leisure time is at its lowest. Only those who do not intend to enter college are free to develop their instincts as consumers.

Then comes college, and college life is quite the opposite. Sports and social activity are the two main student occupations. In addition, some 58 per cent of all students live at home (Ministry of Education, 1991), and most work in 'part-time' jobs. The average student made around ¥386,000 a year from part-time work alone in 1990 (Ministry of Education, 1992), although many have time to earn over ¥100,000 a month if they need to (Tsujinaka, 1989). This money is for one thing only: spending. College is the first chance for young people to date, drive, drink and buy clothes.

For the girls, this is just the beginning of their lives as adult consumers, but, for many boys, this is the lifelong peak of their personal shopping activity.

After college, almost 100 per cent of graduates find employment. They become, in Japanese, *shakaijin* or 'social beings'. Both young men and young women still live at home or in a company dormitory and most of their new salary is disposable. Parents rarely expect to receive housekeeping money even after their children have started full-time work.

On the other hand, major differences again appear between men and women. There are three adult consumer types. One is male – the salarymen – and two are female, 'OLs' and housewives.

## Adult males: salarymen all

The majority of males enter white-collar work. They become a 'salaryman' (*sarariman*). The term often indicates any man on a regular income, but, as over 60 per cent of the labour force is employed in the tertiary sector, most are white collar workers.

Gradually, from the day they begin work, the average male shops less and less. Having spent four relatively relaxed and carefree years at college, companies expect their new male employees to study and prepare for a long career. Lifetime employment is an aspect of Japanese business, and although only the largest companies can guarantee such security, even the smallest firm tries to avoid firing employees.[5] In return, new employees are expected to be loyal and very hard-working. Daily overtime is normal, and men who do not work as long as others stand out from the crowd.

In recent years, Japanese have been concerned with '*karoshi*' – death from overwork. Japanese work long hours, but it is more than this. Many workers are put under tremendous social pressure to conform and support the company and colleagues, even when detrimental to their health and their family and social lives. Even when they know they are exhausted, many find it impossible to say 'no.'

Including overtime, the average Japanese works 2,016 hours a year (Ministry of Labour, 1992). Even if overtime, accounting for about 8 per cent of the total, is omitted, standard working hours still exceed total working hours in America, Germany, Britain or France (Asahi Shinbunsha, 1992). The government is concerned that Japanese work too hard, and makes periodic attempts to reduce annual working hours (EPA, 1992a). Leisure time is increasing slowly, but most men hardly ever shop, relying totally on the women of the family to supply their needs. Younger men want to buy clothes and cars, but over the years, many even lose interest in such discretionary items (Nikkei Ryūtsū Shinbun, 1993c).

The main form of consumption for salarymen is food and drink. Drinking is a social norm, and most men drink socially on a regular basis, often every day. Entertainment expenses at Japanese companies are high. In 1990, firms spent over ¥5.6 billion on entertainment (Asahi Shinbunsha, 1992: 70).

Other than this men are not heavily involved in purchase decisions. They may be allowed to choose the type of beer drunk at home, and the kind of car the family drives, but even then the final purchase decision is made by the housewife (see page 28).

## Young women: the 'OLs'

'OL' (in Japanese ō-eru) is standard Japanese for 'office lady': a female office worker. The actual work they do varies, from operating computers and switchboards and keeping books and accounts, to photocopying and making tea for their male colleagues. Most companies do not allow women to pursue careers. They expect female employees to quit on marriage or, at the latest, on pregnancy. If employee redundancies become unavoidable, women part-time employees are the first to lose their jobs.[6]

More and more female students, having gone through the nightmare of entrance exams and then the monetary expense of four years at university, now dream of proper careers. Indeed, being less sheltered by society than males, and having to compete in a male-oriented world, most female university graduates are at least as capable as their male counterparts. However, through Western eyes, many women seem incredibly pragmatic about their career prospects, and few feel really cheated by their lack of recognition.[7]

Women face other prejudices. Many companies view women as potential scandals. If a job is away from home, both men and women live in company dormitories. For men, dormitories are easy, cooking-free clubs for boys. Similarly too for women, except that, if they cannot live in their family home, living in a dormitory becomes a condition of employment. Most companies will not employ women who cannot or will not live at home or in a company-controlled dormitory, simply because they are seen as a risk (Yoshida, 1993b).

For an advanced economy, the social position of women in Japan is unforgivably low, but they do benefit in other ways. Prior to marriage, not having the chance to train for a career, but earning a steady living, an OL is free to enjoy her earnings. Unless they are lucky enough to have a career, women face few of the work pressures that confront men. Most OLs work strictly nine to five, and the rest of the time they are consumers.

For many OLs, their pay is all disposable income. Living free at home or cheaply in a dormitory, the money they earn is for clothes, eating out, travel, discos and drinking. Later in their twenties, some money may be set aside for marriage. OLs are an important consumer type, numbering some 9 million young women (Sōmuchō, 1991a). They lead both the fashion and the travel industries, as they have both the money and the time to spend it. For many service industries they represent the main target consumers. As most young men take advantage of their limited free time by dating, they even directly influence consumption patterns of young males.

## Wives: the seat of power

Even more than in other nations, the single most powerful group of consumers are wives. In their desire to be equal, all Japanese want to marry and have children. Society puts considerable pressure on both women and men if they do not marry by an appropriate age. Almost a quarter of all marriages are still by *o-miai* – formally arranged through go-betweens (Bandō, 1992: 11).

People are now marrying later and having fewer children. The average age at marriage in 1990 was 25.8 years old for women and 28.4 years old for men (Bandō, 1992: 5), both about two years later than in 1980. Once married, men remain breadwinners, and women, perhaps after a short period when they continue to work, become full-time housewives.

Invariably wives take complete control over family expenses. Before the age of electronic banking, husbands would bring home their pay packets every month, and, as their children looked on, solemnly present it to their wives over the dinner table (Fields, 1983: 48–9). There are no joint bank accounts in Japan. The husband's salary is paid into the family account, which has only one cash-withdrawal card, one account book and one controller: the wife.

Some wives still keep a daily register of household cash flows, keeping a tight family budget, and supermarkets sell special account books for that purpose. Husbands receive a monthly allowance to cover commuting, lunch, cigarettes and beer. Some men negotiate this sum, but many have it dictated to them, and, although few would admit it, most men have little real control (Nagura, 1993). Most wives give a fixed sum, and husbands are expected to live within those limits, begging a little extra if they overspend.[8]

This system has many practical attributes. The woman is free to pay bills,[9] control family shopping and plan carefully for major expenses such as buying a car, buying a house and paying for the children's education. Most women take this responsibility very seriously. The children's education is the most important part of the budget, followed by basic household needs. Husbands may suggest buying a new car or a new stereo, and they often decide the model, but the housewife decides whether or not to purchase. On the other hand, many housewives have the time and financial flexibility also to budget for their own entertainment. This may be anything from coffee mornings or tennis lessons to the occasional tourist trip.

Not all women remain housewives. Over 50 per cent of the 31 million currently married women had some form of employment in 1990 (Ministry of Labour, 1991). This proportion increased consistently during the 1980s. Most wives stop work until their children reach elementary school age, but more and more are returning later on in part-time [10] positions. They do these jobs to fill their time and to top up the family budget. Some use this work as a source of pocket money.

One direct effect of the increase in the number of working women has been the success of convenience shopping systems. These include mail order (Chapter 3) and convenience stores (Chapter 5), both of which allow housewives to maintain their family roles outside office hours. Larger department stores also offer a wide selection of prepared and semi-prepared foods in their basement food halls (Chapter 6). Working housewives flock to these basements after work to buy items for the evening meal (Fukunaga, 1993b; Yoshida, 1993c).

Married women are the most important consumer decision makers in Japan. They do almost all of the shopping and, within the tight sex roles defined by society, they learn to enjoy shopping early. Men have neither the time nor the inclination to shop. It is the female consumer, then, that retailers and other marketers must cater for primarily.

## HOUSEHOLD INCOME AND EXPENDITURE PATTERNS

### Some notes on income levels

Incomes are relatively evenly spread in Japan. Some of the richest men in the world are Japanese (*Fortune*, 1993), but few executives receive incomes that are significantly inflated relative to workers on the shop floor. Senior Japanese executives receive half the pay of counterparts in the UK, and one sixth of those in the US (Byrne and Hawkins, 1993).

There are a number of explanations for this, but the main reason is the proportion of family-owned and family-operated businesses. Of the 47 million people in the labour force in 1990, over 15 million (31.9 per cent) were self-employed or family workers (Eurostat, 1992: 127). This figure is far higher than that for any other advanced nation, including the USA, and indicates the Japanese desire to be entrepreneurs. Family owners profit from the success of the business, but, because executives are rarely appointed as professional managers, cases of head-hunting, performance-related pay systems and inflated incomes are rare.

In addition, as in education, the chief determinant of income in most industries is not ability, but age. Companies maintain strict guidelines for determining employees' income that depend on the position and age of each individual, but as position is determined according to when a person entered the company, age becomes the sole criterion. Companies have many management ranks, and there is some internal competition between employees of similar age, but little between people of different ages.[11]

There is one way in which incomes are not spread evenly: between men and women. For similar occupations, women earn only 57.2 per cent as much as men in jobs that pay hourly wages, and, in jobs paying monthly salaries, only 50.7 per cent. This compares with ratios of almost 70 per cent in Britain and the USA, and over 90 per cent in Australia (Bandō, 1991: 86–7). The Japanese constitution supposedly guarantees women's rights, but this is rarely backed up in the courts. In the early 1990s, the recession hit young female job seekers hardest. Companies do not want female university graduates. Expecting women to retire at marriage or at childbirth, companies see them as expensive temporary employees. As noted above, well educated women still find themselves making tea and photocopies for their male colleagues (Kashima, 1993).

The following sections look at how consumers spend this income as household units. Table 2.5 gives overall figures for the main categories of household expenditure from 1980 to 1992 and the discussion refers back to these general data while looking at more detailed expenditure patterns. During this period, average monthly expenditure per household increased from ¥230,568 to ¥333,661. Within the table, some categories of expenditure suggest long-term changes.

## Expenditure on food

The largest single item within the family budget is food, accounting for just under a quarter of total expenditure in 1992. This was a 4 per cent fall on the 1980 figure, indicating, as in other advanced nations, a clear, long-term decrease in the importance of food within household spending (see Table 2.5).

Table 2.5 Major categories of monthly household expenditure, 1980–92

|  | 1980 | | 1985 | | | 1992 | | |
|---|---|---|---|---|---|---|---|---|
|  | ¥ | % share | ¥ | % share | % change 85/80 | ¥ | % share | % change 92/85 |
| Total monthly income | 349,686 | 100.0 | 444,946 | 100.0 | 27.2 | 563,855 | 100.0 | 26.7 |
| Disposable monthly Income | 305,549 | 87.4 | 373,693 | 84.0 | 22.3 | 473,738 | 84.0 | 26.8 |
| Total monthly living expenditure | 230,568 | 100.0 | 273,114 | 100.0 | 0.0 | 333,661 | 100.0 | 0.0 |
| Food | 66,923 | 29.0 | 73,735 | 27.0 | -2.0 | 82,381 | 24.7 | -2.3 |
| Housing | 10,682 | 4.6 | 12,686 | 4.6 | 0.0 | 18,251 | 5.5 | 0.8 |
| Fuel and light | 13,225 | 5.7 | 17,724 | 6.5 | 0.8 | 18,516 | 5.5 | -0.9 |
| Household goods | 9,875 | 4.3 | 11,665 | 4.3 | 0.0 | 13,092 | 3.9 | -0.3 |
| Clothing | 18,163 | 7.9 | 19,606 | 7.2 | -0.7 | 22,344 | 6.7 | -0.5 |
| Medical insurance | 5,865 | 2.5 | 6,931 | 2.5 | 0.0 | 9,299 | 2.8 | 0.2 |
| Transport and communications | 18,416 | 8.0 | 24,754 | 9.1 | 1.1 | 31,090 | 9.3 | 0.3 |
| Education | 8,325 | 3.6 | 10,853 | 4.0 | 0.4 | 15,394 | 4.6 | 0.6 |
| Reading and recreation | 19,620 | 8.5 | 24,191 | 8.9 | 0.3 | 32,815 | 9.8 | 1.0 |
| Other expenditure | 59,474 | 25.8 | 70,970 | 26.0 | 0.2 | 89,480 | 26.8 | 0.8 |

Source: Sōmuchō (1993b)

*Table 2.6* Percentage of monthly food expenditure by category, 1965–91

| Food category | 1965 | 1991 | Change |
|---|---|---|---|
| Rice | 18.2 | 5.9 | −12.3 |
| Bread | 2.1 | 2.9 | 0.8 |
| Noodles | 2.0 | 2.0 | 0.0 |
| Other cereals | 0.6 | 0.4 | −0.2 |
| Fish and shellfish | 11.7 | 12.4 | 0.7 |
| Meat | 8.5 | 9.7 | 1.2 |
| Milk, dairy products, eggs | 8.6 | 4.9 | −3.7 |
| Vegetables, seaweeds | 12.5 | 12.7 | 0.2 |
| Fruit | 5.7 | 4.4 | −1.3 |
| Oils, fats and seasonings | 5.9 | 3.9 | −2.0 |
| Confectionery | 6.5 | 7.1 | 0.6 |
| Prepared foods | 2.9 | 8.5 | 5.6 |
| Beverages | 2.7 | 3.7 | 1.0 |
| Alcoholic beverages | 4.7 | 4.8 | 0.1 |
| General dining out | 6.0 | 15.0 | 9.0 |
| School lunches | 1.3 | 1.8 | 0.5 |
| | 100.0 | 100.0 | |
| Total food expenditure (¥) | 17,858 | 83,051 | |

*Source*: Asahi Shinbunsha (1992: 178)

Consumers have changed their diet quite considerably since the 1960s. In terms of overall expenditure on food (Table 2.6), the percentage expenditure on rice fell from 18.2 per cent to under 6 per cent between 1965 and 1991. The only food categories to increase their share of expenditure by more than one percentage point were meat, prepared foods and dining out.

These changes are significant. Japanese are eating less rice and more bread (Maruetsu and Misawa, 1992). Table 2.7 shows a fall in the daily consumption of rice per person of almost 50 per cent. This is due partly to the relatively high price of rice, roughly six times the world market price (Asahi Shinbunsha, 1993b: 133), and partly to the so called Westernisation of Japanese eating habits (Hirose *et al.*, 1993; Makihara, 1992; Osahi and Fujiyasu, 1993). Table 2.7 also shows the increase in consumption of bread (wheat), vegetables and, especially, foods from animals. Traditionally, Japanese ate a lot of fish, but meat was not a major part of their diet until recently. Imported meat has reduced prices and made it more widely available. Consumption of oils and fats also increased markedly in the 1980s as the Japanese diet took on a more Western form.

*Table 2.7* Daily intake per person of main food types, 1960–90 (grams/%)

| Food type | 1960 | % | 1970 | % | 1980 | % | 1990 | % | % change 90/60 |
|---|---|---|---|---|---|---|---|---|---|
| Rice | 358.4 | 32.6 | 306.1 | 24.2 | 225.8 | 16.9 | 197.9 | 15.0 | −44.8 |
| Wheat | 65.1 | 5.9 | 64.8 | 5.1 | 91.8 | 6.9 | 84.8 | 6.4 | 30.3 |
| Potatoes | 64.4 | 5.9 | 37.8 | 3.0 | 63.4 | 4.7 | 65.3 | 4.9 | 1.4 |
| Sugar | 12.3 | 1.1 | 19.7 | 1.6 | 12.0 | 0.9 | 10.6 | 0.8 | −13.8 |
| Oils and fats | 6.1 | 0.6 | 15.6 | 1.2 | 16.9 | 1.3 | 17.6 | 1.3 | 188.5 |
| Beans | 71.2 | 6.5 | 71.2 | 5.6 | 65.4 | 4.9 | 68.5 | 5.2 | −3.8 |
| Foods of animal origin | 147.4 | 13.4 | 250.0 | 19.8 | 313.3 | 23.5 | 338.9 | 25.6 | 129.9 |
| Vegetables | 214.1 | 19.5 | 249.3 | 19.7 | 251.4 | 18.8 | 250.3 | 18.9 | 16.9 |
| Fruit | 79.6 | 7.2 | 81.0 | 6.4 | 155.4 | 11.6 | 124.8 | 9.4 | 56.8 |
| Seaweed | 4.7 | 0.4 | 6.9 | 0.5 | 5.1 | 0.4 | 6.1 | 0.5 | 29.8 |
| Seasonings, beverages | 75.6 | 6.9 | 163.4 | 12.9 | 134.4 | 10.1 | 157.7 | 11.9 | 108.6 |
| Totals | 1,098.9 | 100.0 | 1,265.8 | 100.0 | 1,334.9 | 100.0 | 1,322.5 | 100.0 | 20.3 |

*Source*: Ministry of Health and Welfare, in Asahi Shinbunsha (1992: 179)

The other significant change in eating habits is the increase in expenditure on prepared foods and dining out. Restaurants and coffee shops are a major part of the retail landscape. Most of the major retail groups also operate restaurant chains (see Chapter 7). These vary from cheap fast-food chains selling noodles, Japanese lunch boxes (*o-bentō*) or Western hamburgers, to high-quality, high-price family restaurants that aim to take ¥2,000 to ¥3,000 per customer.

The increase in spending on prepared foods is also part of a general and increasing demand for convenience. As both the number of single-person households and the proportion of working wives increase, there is more demand for speed and convenience in food shopping. Prepared and semi-prepared food includes expensive, high-quality dishes sold in department store food halls, and cheap packed lunches and delicatessen items available at convenience stores. Both are increasingly popular. A wide selection of new 'fast-lunch' services are now becoming available in Tokyo (Fields, 1993b). Similar to sandwich shops in the UK or the USA, other services also offer a varied combination of mix-and-match items to include in boxed lunches.

In response to this, supermarkets offer a larger range of frozen products, but most have not copied the department stores and convenience stores in offering delicatessen items. The only exceptions are for items such as sushi, tempura or mayonnaise salads[12] that are difficult or time-consuming to prepare at home. Instead, supermarkets offer fresh food in a greater variety and in more convenient forms, including vegetables in half-cuts, cuts with leaves and without leaves, and non-organic and organic variations. This again offers the customer greater convenience. Smaller food retailers cannot provide the same level of variety, and this is one reason they struggled in the 1980s (see Chapter 3).

The proportion of expenditure on food will continue to fall as Japanese consumers become more affluent. While the high demand for fresh produce, notably vegetables and fish, will remain, increased imports of cheap meat, and future imports of cheap rice,[13] will continue to change eating habits. Japanese cuisine is notoriously time-consuming to prepare, and prepared food and eating out will remain popular for these reasons alone.

## Housing and other basic household items

Household goods, clothing, fuel and light all took a smaller proportion of household expenses in 1992 than in 1980. People spend proportionally less on these items as they increase in affluence (see Table 2.5).

Housing costs, however, are another matter (Sanwa Bank, 1990). Housing expenses grew faster than any other major category between 1980 and 1992. Land prices in Japan are some of the most expensive in the world. Between 1960 and 1991 the cost of housing increased by over 700 per cent, second only to the increase in the cost of education. Figure 2.3 shows that the price of residential land increased by about four times the rate of consumer price increase between 1980 and 1991, and the price in the largest cities by over ten times (Asahi Shinbunsha, 1992: 184; 1993b).

The high cost of land and rents is a major problem for consumers. In the late 1970s, a report referred to housing in Japan as being like 'rabbit hutches' (Wilkinson, 1983: 208–9). While many Japanese found this insulting, most are well aware that the poor standard of housing is the single most important restraint on their standard of living. Dwelling space per capita is only 25.2 square metres in Japan, compared to 61 in the USA and 35.2 in the UK.

While 61 per cent of households own their own homes (Sōmuchō, 1988b), those that do not face paying some 8.7 times the average annual salary for a home in Tokyo, and almost six times elsewhere. This is much higher than in other advanced countries (see *Economist* 1992; Ministry of Labour, 1991). All the same, families dream of having their own houses, moving further and further away from large cities in order to make the dream true.

Japan has a land area of 378,000 square kilometres, more than the UK, Germany or Italy, but some 60 per cent of this land is uninhabitable at present. When uninhabitable land is omitted from the total, the average population density is over 820 people per square kilometre. Until building land can be made easily available, housing costs will continue to be a major factor within the household budget.

## Expenditure related to education

Educational expenses accounted for only 4.6 per cent of total household expenditure in 1992, but, after housing, this category increased more than any other after 1980 (see Table 2.5). Between 1960 and 1991 the cost of education rose by some 1,148 per cent (Asahi Shinbunsha, 1992). As I described on pages 23–5, education is vital within Japanese society. Every parent knows this and is

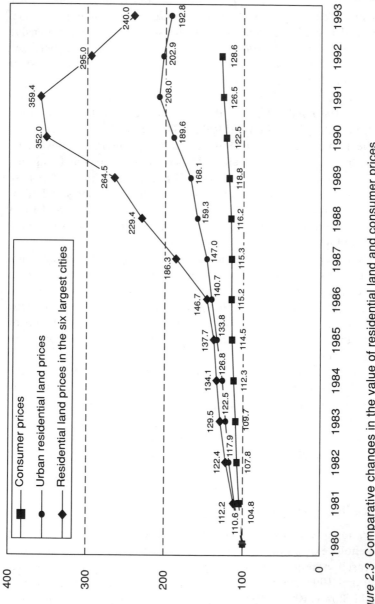

*Figure 2.3* Comparative changes in the value of residential land and consumer prices
*Source*: Compiled from Asahi Shinbunsha (1992; 1993b: 200)

willing to spend a lot of money helping their child along the road of life. Adult education, especially popular among adult women, also increased in this period (Nikkei Trendy, 1993a).

Children must memorise a vast array of historical and technical facts for entrance examinations, and the most common method is to expose them to as much study as possible over as long a period as possible.[14] From an early age, children attend cram schools in addition to compulsory education, sometimes starting as early as 3 or 4. As they become older, and the university entrance exam looms, out-of-school study time increases, and home teachers are employed to visit the children several times a week. Consequently, expenditure on children's education increases. While overall education-related expenses increased by a nominal 85 per cent between 1980 and 1992, fees for private tutors increased by twice this figure, the highest increase for any single subcategory of household spending (Sōmuchō, 1992b).

A number of factors will affect this category in years to come. The birth rate is low and there will be fewer children to educate in the future. In order to maintain their incomes from fees, universities will make entrance easier, and there will be few moves towards more applied examinations. This will mean that the name of the university rather than the subject of study will remain the key to successful job applications. In turn, this will continue to push up the volume of necessary preparatory education, and so increase household spending on education.

Children will also have access to increasingly sophisticated and expensive methods of study, especially computer-aided instruction. On the whole, therefore, education expenses are likely to increase at a rapid rate in the near future. The increase in educational spending will slow into the twenty-first century as the number of children falls.

## Transport and communications expenditure

Transport expenses grew in the 1980s mainly due to an increase in the ownership of private cars. The number of registered private cars increased from 23.6 million in 1980 to over 35 million in 1990 (Ministry of Transport, 1991). Japan relies almost totally on imported fuel, and with automobile costs taking the largest proportion of transport expenditure, this becomes a significant part of many household budgets. Economic prosperity and aggressive marketing of cars also brought larger and/or faster cars onto the market in the 1980s, and a greater consumption of gasoline to run them.

Commuter transport in the larger cities is excellent. The Tokyo system is especially good. While crowded, the train, subway and bus systems are fast and regular, cover most of the city and are cheap. Nagoya and Osaka also have extensive commuting systems. Other cities do not have quite the same density of routes and are not as cheap, but they are as efficient. Public transport costs remained stable in the 1980s, with the largest increase coming in 1989 with the introduction of a 3 per cent Consumption Tax.

The use of public transport is growing, however. The road system is poor, and while more people are buying cars, most are for leisure, not for commuting purposes. People are travelling to work over greater distances, moving out of the centre of cities in order to be able to afford their own homes. By 1992, transport was the fourth largest item of expenditure.

Due to pollution and road congestion, local governments occasionally make some minor attempts to encourage the use of public transport. In Tokyo, public transport is cheap and convenient, but in other areas people are less willing to live without a car. Most men like cars, and young men often want to buy nothing else. The crowded land area of Japan makes road transport difficult, however, and, in the long run, public transport is likely to become increasingly important.

### Recreational expenses

Recreational expenses were the third largest item in the household budget in 1992 (see Table 2.5), but were also one of the fastest growing categories. Consumers have more money to spend on leisure-related merchandise and activities. About 80 per cent of recreational spending is used for basic leisure goods such as games, sports goods and recreational services, including entrance fees to various sporting and cultural events and tourist trips.

In mid-1992, the government announced a five-year plan to improve the standard of living in Japan. The plan promises to create world-class standards of living or a lifestyle superpower (*seikatsu ōkoku*). One of the major points within this plan is to reduce the average number of working hours per year from more than 2,000 in 1992 to under 1,500 by 1995 (EPA, 1992a). The economic recession, which has reduced the amount of work available to companies, is also helping to increase the amount of time spent on leisure.

When applying for jobs at age 22, young people are as interested in the number of holidays a year as they are in career prospects and salary. Young people demand more free time and more money, and have more willingness to use both.

Leisure is expensive, but as new, cheaper pursuits become more common, spending on recreational facilities will continue to grow. The travel industry grew strongly during the 1980s, encouraged by the high yen. Between 1980 and 1991, the number of overseas travellers doubled from 4 million to 10.6 million per year. Almost 82 per cent of these travellers were tourists. Young women can take longer holidays than their male counterparts, but the number of men travelling abroad for reasons other than business is also growing slowly (Sōrifu, 1992).

In some ways the standard of living in Japan does not reflect the country's high gross national product. Lack of space keeps housing small and expensive and people work long hours. Younger people especially are dissatisfied with this situation. They ski, go to discos, attend the new J-League professional soccer league and take full advantage of their allocated holidays. More importantly, they are more willing to do all this than were any of their elders. Leisure spending will continue to grow, driven by the younger generation.

### Social expenses

The final category within Table 2.5 is 'Other expenditure'. Within this category, the subcategory of social expenses is the second largest single part of the family budget. In 1992 social expenses accounted for 9.9 per cent of the monthly budget. These include entertaining guests, gift items and monetary gifts at weddings and funerals. Gift-giving is a social norm, and one that is directly connected to shopping and consumption. The nature of gift-giving in Japan is different from in the West. Gift purchases account for a large percentage of the retail market, and are an unusual and important part of consumption, shopping patterns and retailing in Japan. Gift shopping and gift-giving are important enough to consider separately below (pages 50–4).

### Purchase and ownership of consumer durables

In the 1980s household items and clothing took a steadily smaller percentage of family expenditure as the markets for such items became saturated. Japan is home to some of the largest consumer electrical and automobile manufacturers in the world. Consequently, consumers have access to almost any kind of consumer durable, including some unavailable anywhere else. In many ways, Japan is a test market for goods using the latest technology. The lack and cost of space within the home, however, reduce the number of items a household can actually own.

In 1992, almost 100 per cent of households owned colour TVs, refrigerators and washing machines, and around 80 per cent owned cars. Moreover, for every 100 households there were 203.6 colour TVs – more than two per home (EPA, 1992b). In addition to the lack of space to keep electrical and other household items, most homes have all they need already.

Table 2.8 summarises the ownership rate and purchasing patterns for selected durables in 1991. The average interval between purchases for this sample of durables was seven and a half years. TVs, refrigerators, washing machines and vacuum cleaners are purchased only when the old item breaks. Newer-technology items, such as video cameras and word processors, are bought more frequently, to keep up with rapid improvements in the level of technology which add new functions and greater utility to newer models.

Cars are bought frequently, on average once every five or six years. This is due to marketing strategies that emphasise rapid model changes, as well as tough laws on car maintenance. Most car models are out of date after four years, and the cost of repair or replacing even fairly minor parts is high (see *The Economist*, 1991b). The main reason given for buying a new car was the opportunity to trade in the old one, as second-hand car values are low (see *The Economist*, 1991b). This short-term use of cars at home contrasts with the image of long-term durability that Japanese car manufacturers have tried to build in overseas markets.

**Future household expenditure patterns**

Many of the current household expenditure trends will continue to strengthen. With the exception of dining out and prepared foods, the food market will only expand with natural increases in population, and, as a proportion of total expenditure, it will continue to decline. Retailers who can add interest and new ideas and services, such as convenience stores and large superstore

Table 2.8 Purchase patterns for major consumer durables, 1991

| Durables | Percentage ownership | Units/100 households | Purchase rate (years) | Reason for new purchases | | |
|---|---|---|---|---|---|---|
| | | | | Improved model | Old unit broken | Other |
| Refrigerators | 98.1 | 117.2 | 10.4 | 18.2 | 65.4 | 16.4 |
| Washing machines | 99.2 | 107.9 | 8.4 | 12.0 | 79.1 | 8.9 |
| Vacuum cleaners | 98.1 | 131.7 | 8.3 | 13.6 | 74.6 | 11.8 |
| Air conditioners | 69.8 | 131.2 | 10.6 | 19.6 | 57.5 | 22.9 |
| Colour TVs | 99.0 | 203.6 | 9.0 | 17.9 | 72.1 | 10.0 |
| VTRs | 63.8 | 83.5 | 6.6 | 18.4 | 72.6 | 9.0 |
| Video cameras | 26.0 | 27.3 | 4.9 | 57.2 | 33.4 | 9.4 |
| Word processors | 32.6 | 35.8 | 4.1 | 70.1 | 15.0 | 14.9 |
| New cars | 46.8 | 59.7 | 6.0 | 28.5 | 26.8 | 44.7 |
| Second-hand cars | 41.7 | 54.4 | 5.1 | 20.8 | 42.5 | 36.7 |

Source: Compiled from EPA (1992b).

retailers, will do well. The same will be true in the clothing and household goods sectors.

The growth in housing expenses also appears to have reached its peak. Land speculation, which fuelled the rise in land prices in the mid-1980s, has now almost disappeared. Land prices are falling, and the Ministry of Finance will probably try to prevent another rapid increase occurring again. Housing expenses are likely, therefore, to remain high, but stable.

Educational expenses will continue to grow, but the rate of increase will slow into the next century. The number of children has reached a peak with the junior baby-boom. New educational services will continue to appear, and parents will still demand the best for their offspring. Adult education will also remain a popular alternative leisure activity.

Where expenditure growth will occur is in leisure, social spending and spending on health. Up to 1992, medical expenses accounted for less than 3 per cent of the family budget, but this is increasing rapidly. Hospital stays in Japan are longer than anywhere in the world, and, according to *The Economist* (1991a), Japanese also have the worst rates of illnesses due to over-medication in the world. The medical system encourages some physicians to prescribe drugs in order to make a living. Most men smoke and drink (Sōrifu, 1989), and the population is ageing. All three factors mean medical expenses are likely to increase dramatically over coming years.

Finally, leisure will increase. Many Japanese consumers still believe in hard work and little play, but there is now less work for them to do, and their children certainly do not want to work so hard. Social spending, especially on gifts and entertaining, will remain high because of an interesting aspect of Japanese society. I look at this below.

## SHOPPING IN A HOMOGENOUS SOCIETY

The preceding sections showed just how homogenous Japanese society is. Compared to the West, income, education, spending and individual social awareness are surprisingly uniform.

This does not mean that changes do not occur. New generations are more amenable to leisure and discretionary consumption, and Japanese are highly materialistic. Some factors, such as size of homes and the volume of leisure time, that define standard of living in many Western nations, cannot be judged in the same light in

Japan. Lack of space is the chief limiting factor. For example, homes are small and expensive and traffic congestion is severe. Long hours of work are almost traditional, and some husbands have little else to look forward to.

To make up for these problems, in the 1970s and 1980s consumers bought durable goods and discretionary items such as clothes to the point of saturation (see pages 39–40). Clothing takes little space, but can display a person's wealth effectively. Many people carrying Louis Vuitton bags or wearing Rolex watches live in a single cramped room.

More recently, owning all the durables they require, consumers are moving discretionary consumption into new directions. Large retail organisations play a major part in encouraging this behaviour. The variety of retail formats is still expanding, with new variations appearing all the time. Consumers take retail variety for granted, and their behaviour is deeply affected by it. Shops offer consumers variety and convenience. Retailers are found everywhere, carry a wide range of merchandise and open at convenient times. Increasingly retailers also offer a wide range of service facilities, and attempt to make shopping as much a leisure activity as skiing or watching TV.

According to the annual survey of time use, Japanese people spend only twenty-eight minutes a day shopping (Sōmuchō, 1993a), but shopping is an important part of life, especially for women (see below). It has become part of the Japanese culture, and is very much part of leisure time (Sato, 1985).

Mukoyama (1990: 12–13) notes that convenience and product quality are the two main factors when consumers choose a store. The data in Table 2.9 support this view, with closeness to home being an indication of convenience. The table also ranks merchandise assortment and low prices highly, with product quality ranking fourth. The convenience of one-stop shopping is increasingly popular, with consumers looking for stores with a wide range of merchandise. Both location and assortment are convenience-related factors.

According to Table 2.10, price is the most important factor when choosing products.[15] Table 2.9 indicates low prices, but some consumers deliberately seek expensive items (see Nikkei Ryūtsū Shinbun, 1989c). In such cases, consumers are not shopping just for basic utility such as buying groceries. They shop for leisure or for other social reasons.

After price, the second most important factor in product choice

Table 2.9 Japanese consumers' choice factors for stores (%)

| | Foods | | Clothing | | Household items | |
|---|---|---|---|---|---|---|
| | 1988 | Change 88/78 | 1988 | Change 88/78 | 1988 | Change 88/78 |
| Closeness to home | 49.5 | -15.9 | 27.6 | -10.9 | 41.5 | -14.1 |
| Merchandise assortment | 39.1 | 21.2 | 31.0 | 5.1 | 41.4 | 14.1 |
| Low prices | 29.0 | 15.2 | 31.0 | 11.9 | 40.4 | 17.5 |
| Good-quality merchandise | 16.6 | 6.2 | 31.9 | 4.9 | 10.4 | 1.9 |
| Self-service | 15.5 | 9.7 | 13.1 | 5.0 | 16.8 | 7.7 |
| Convenient opening hours | 13.9 | 5.4 | 8.4 | 2.3 | 11.5 | 3.1 |
| Familiar, well-known store | 13.1 | -17.8 | 8.7 | -6.4 | 8.0 | -7.5 |
| Trustworthy store | 4.3 | -1.1 | 7.0 | 0.7 | 2.7 | 0.4 |
| Good service | 3.1 | 1.0 | 3.3 | 0.3 | 2.6 | 0.0 |
| Good atmosphere | 3.1 | 1.7 | 7.5 | 0.7 | 4.0 | 2.2 |
| High-class goods | 1.0 | 0.4 | 6.0 | 0.7 | 0.3 | -0.1 |
| Credit cards can be used | 0.6 | 0.5 | 5.3 | 3.9 | 1.1 | 1.0 |

Source: Adapted from MITI (1989a: 71)

Table 2.10 Japanese consumers' choice factors for products

|  | Women | Men | Overall |
|---|---|---|---|
| Price | 78.9 | 67.3 | 73.1 |
| Store | 35.9 | 30.1 | 33.4 |
| Opinions of peers | 21.1 | 21.7 | 21.4 |
| Brand | 19.5 | 20.8 | 20.1 |
| Advertising | 16.1 | 16.5 | 16.3 |
| Other factors | 5.5 | 6.6 | 6.0 |
| Don't know | 2.1 | 5.9 | 3.7 |

Survey of 2,353 consumers (1,341 women, 1,012 men), multiple answers.

Source: Sōrifu (1987)

was the store. The choice of store is at least as important as choice of product or brand. Nakanishi and Aoki (1985: 43) suggest that, for discretionary shopping trips, consumers go to a certain shopping area and then move around between stores, choosing first the shopping area, then the store and finally the product. More recently however, consumers are becoming more concerned with the price–quality relationship (Hoshino 1990). They are no longer willing to pay exorbitantly high prices for goods that are not clearly distinguished by higher quality, which was not always the case during the so called bubble economy of the late 1980s. In the following chapters I describe how this has encouraged the emergance of discount retailing and has harmed the sales of department stores.

Japanese consumers know their stores well and hold different expectations for different store types (see Table 2.11). For example, consumers expect low prices at large and small supermarkets and superstores, but not at speciality stores which are noted for product quality. Consumers require product assortment from department stores, and familiarity and ease of use from independent retailers. At the time of the survey in Table 2.11, consumers were still unclear about the role of convenience stores. A similar survey today would include a 'convenience' factor to describe this category. Other retail formats, especially independent stores, are also likely to score well on such a category.

The traits presented in these surveys do not suggest anything truly unique to Japan, but it is clear that choice of store is important to the consumer. Shoppers, particularly women, use stores frequently, and know their favourites well. They are well aware of

Table 2.11 Consumer expectations of the main retail formats

| | Department stores | Large superstores | Small superstores | Convenience stores | Speciality stores | Independent stores |
|---|---|---|---|---|---|---|
| Wide merchandise range | **60.9** | 44.0 | 18.4 | 16.8 | 22.5 | 7.7 |
| Good merchandise quality | 49.7 | 22.9 | 19.6 | 13.0 | **54.3** | 22.2 |
| Good service | 18.0 | 13.8 | 22.4 | 14.9 | 25.3 | 39.7 |
| Low prices | 16.8 | **59.2** | **49.5** | 21.8 | 13.6 | 22.7 |
| Friendly atmosphere | 8.3 | 12.8 | 30.6 | 15.3 | 14.5 | **46.8** |
| Other factors | 0.5 | 0.3 | 0.6 | 1.7 | 0.4 | 0.5 |
| Don't know | 11.3 | 10.5 | 14.3 | **45.3** | 17.5 | 13.0 |

Main category for each format is picked out in bold; multiple answers in survey.

Source: Sōrifu (1987: 20) survey of 1,012 men and 1,341 women.

shopping facilities in their area, and can discuss minute attributes of stores, choosing stores on the basis of clearly defined attributes. Most store choice behaviour is similar to that of consumers in the West, with stores being chosen on the basis of location, pricing and merchandise range, but Japanese consumers are more aware of less tangible factors such as store atmosphere (see Larke, 1991). This is especially true for discretionary shopping.

Large stores have a constant flow of customers throughout the week. Tokyo department stores have a daily customer flow of some 40,000 to 50,000 people during mid-week, with numbers peaking in late afternoon and early evening. At weekends, these figures may triple. Stores located at major rail terminals in Tokyo have up to 300,000 people passing through their doors in a single day (Creighton, 1988: 75) although only a proportion of these will be customers.

Shopping is a significant part of Japanese lifestyles, but actual shopping activity varies between consumer types.

## Shopping and sex roles

Japanese women shop very frequently.[16] In a large sample of consumers (Figure 2.4), a quarter shopped every day, and almost three quarters shopped at least three or four times a week. Women shop almost every day for food because of the Japanese preference for fresh produce. Younger, unmarried women also spend a great deal of their leisure time shopping and browsing.

Other surveys confirm these results. Aoki (1983a; 1983b) found that 66.1 per cent of consumers shopped daily for foodstuffs. Compared to those in New York, London, Paris, Stockholm and Bonn, Tokyo consumers shopped more frequently for salad vegetables, fish, eggs, spoons, vacuum cleaners and men's briefs (Shōhin Kagaku Kenkyūjo, 1981: 74).

Shopping is clearly differentiated by sex. Around 35 per cent of men almost never shop (see Figure 2.4). Women, be they mothers, girlfriends, sisters or even daughters, supply every material need of male consumers, from food to underpants. Male shopping is usually limited to sports goods, car accessories, audiovisual equipment for the home, and books and magazines.

When a man shops for himself, he is often accompanied by his wife – similarly in the West, but in Japan, without his wife, the man has no money to spend. The man is the breadwinner, and the woman is the home builder, accountant and shopper. A recent

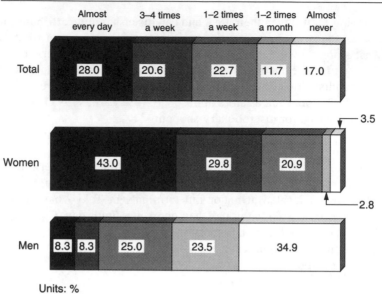

Units: %
Sample size: 1,341 women  1,012 men

*Figure 2.4* Shopping frequency among Japanese consumers
*Source*: Sōrifu (1988: 2)

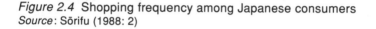

advert for fitted kitchens describes how purchasing a kitchen will improve not only the wife's cooking, but also the husband's desire to work hard – presumably because of the better meals his wife cooks!

Women have unnecessarily low status in thc workplace, but they rule the home. They are the decision-making consumers. They do almost all of the shopping and, within the tightly defined sex roles, many learn to enjoy shopping as a leisure activity and a chance to get out and meet people. Again, female consumers are the most important of all.

## Shopping and the seasons

Japan has four distinct seasons, and these have a significant effect on consumer and shopping behaviour. With both climatic changes and religious festivals, this is true in the West too, but Japanese retailers exploit these seasonal differences to the full.

Because the housewife demands fresh fish, vegetables and fruit, seasonal changes in fresh food products are especially important. Japan can grow most kinds of fruits and vegetables, but production volume is too small to meet demand, and most are imported. For example, plums, cherries and melons are available only in early summer. There are a range of vegetables that are available all year round such as giant radish and burdock root.

Many fish are also available by season, although tuna and most shellfish are eaten all year round. Next to rice, fish is the most important part of the Japanese diet and still the most common protein.

Supermarket shelves reflect this diet and its seasonal changes. Fresh vegetable and fruit sections and the fresh and frozen fish cabinets are larger than in most Western supermarkets, for example. The selection of fish products is particularly large, perhaps with several dozen types of both coastal and deep-sea fish, and a number of shellfish. Most supermarkets carry several different types of squid, each semi-prepared in several different ways. Of course, the range varies by store, with the big suburban Tokyo supermarkets carrying the largest selection.

Other clear seasonal variations occur in the clothing market. Seasonal variations in both temperature and humidity mean that people maintain at least two wardrobes. As in most of Asia, businessmen wear suits even in the hottest weather. Many companies have dress rules of some kind that indicate when people should change from winter to summer attire – usually 1 June. Companies provide their OLs with summer and winter uniforms, but men wear their own suits. All but the northernmost parts of Japan also have a rainy season in July which calls for different clothing and accessories again.

Climatical changes vary across the country because Japan stretches across fifteen degrees of latitude, from Hokkaido in the north – snowbound in winter, warm but dry in the summer – to Okinawa in the south – temperate in winter, hot and humid in summer. As in the West, apparel ranges change with the seasons, but in Japan there are also wide regional differences in the types of clothes because of differing local climates. Department stores lead seasonal fashion changes, displaying ranges of swimsuits, lightweight men's suits, ski wear and heavy-duty woollens as appropriate.

Seasonal shopping and merchandise are not limited to food and clothing. Festivals and celebrations are also a major part of Japanese life. Each town, village or, in some cases, shopping street has at least one annual festival. Local stores are always quick to promote these and take advantage of the increase in customer traffic.

Of course there are also annual nationwide festivals and celebrations, all of which retailers support to the full. Most are gift-giving occasions. While this is a seasonal aspect of shopping and consumer behaviour, gift-buying and gift-giving are so different from in the West, and the gift markets are so large, that this topic deserves special discussion.

### The influence of social hierarchy on store choice: gift shopping

There are two gift markets in Japan. On the one hand, as in the West, there is a discretionary market for birthdays, Christmas and gifts among friends and family. On the other, there is a far larger market for obligatory, socially required gifts.

Table 2.12 summarises the major gift markets. Yasumori *et al.* (1993) estimate the gift market for 1992 as some ¥10.2 trillion, or almost 7 per cent of total retail sales. The table also shows that individual gifts account for about two thirds of the market, with corporate gifts accounting for the remainder.

Many or most of the occasions listed in the table are familiar in the West, but it would be wrong to say they represent similar markets with similar motives. Young people commonly exchange gifts for fun and affection, but the gift markets with the highest value are for obligatory gifts.

The non-obligatory gift market is still relatively new and under-developed. The largest is Christmas. Japan is not a Christian country,[17] but both retailers and children prefer people to forget that, and the Christmas market grew steadily in the 1980s. Children may feel pressure to study, but few want for toys and other goodies. As Table 2.12 shows, however, the economic recession of 1992 hit the Christmas market much harder than the obligatory gift markets, reducing Christmas gift sales by 13 per cent (see Kurosumi and Omuko, 1993).

In addition to the Christmas market, there is a smaller, but growing market for gifts exchanged between young people, including birthday gifts. Again, the junior baby-boomers drive this market. Both girls and boys buy and give presents, although recipients are largely female (see *JEJ*, 1990).

This discretionary gift market is less important than the non-discretionary market, and in this way gift-giving is different from in

*Table 2.12* Personal gift occasions and market sizes

| Occasion | Date/season | Estimates of gift market values (¥ million) | | |
| --- | --- | --- | --- | --- |
| | | 1989[b] | 1991[c] | 1992[c] |
| **Personal gifts** | | | | |
| Adult's Day | 15 January | 23,000 | n.a | n.a |
| Valentine's Day[a] | 14 February | 100,000 | 145,455 | 144,000 |
| White Day | 14 March | 23,000 | 47,982 | 52,300 |
| School/company entrance | April (1st week) | 200,000 | n.a | n.a |
| Mother's Day | May (2nd Sunday) | 170,000 | 311,111 | 308,000 |
| Father's Day | June (3rd Sunday) | 150,000 | 268,687 | 266,000 |
| O-chūgen[a] | June–July | 740,000 | 724,220 | 739,000 |
| Halloween | 31 October | 5,000 | n.a | n.a |
| 7–5–3 Festival | 15 November | 22,000 | n.a | n.a |
| Christmas | 25 December | 300,000 | 708,736 | 616,600 |
| O-seibo[a] | Dec.–Jan. | 960,000 | 957,959 | 938,800 |
| Engagement ceremony[a] | Perennial | 230,000 | n.a | n.a |
| Marriage ceremony[a] | Perennial | 240,000 | n.a | n.a |
| Births | Perennial | 320,000 | n.a | n.a |
| Buddhist ceremonies | Perennial | 300,000 | n.a | n.a |
| Others | | – | 3,581,979 | 3,438,700 |
| **Company gifts** | | | | |
| O-chugen[a] | Jun.–Jul. | 430,000 | 356,979 | 342,700 |
| O-seibo[a] | Dec.–Jan. | 460,000 | 480,000 | 427,200 |
| Commemorative days | Perennial | 300,000 | 2,090,000 | 1,672,000 |
| Novelties and premiums | Perennial | 1,200,000 | 1,260,000 | 1,071,000 |
| Others | | – | 166,938 | 167,600 |
| Total | | 6,173,000 | 11,100,046 | 10,183,900 |

[a] Indicates substantial obligatory gift-giving as a norm.
[b] 1989 estimates from K. Sawada, Robinsons Japan.
[c] Author's calculations.

*Source*: Yasumori *et al.* (1993)

the West (see Befu, 1986; Green and Alden, 1988). In the obligatory gift market, the phrase 'it's the thought that counts' rarely applies. The motive and the physical gift, including type of product, presentation, packaging and, not least, monetary value, are far more important. This is always true for obligatory gifts, and means that consumers choose gifts with care, having them wrapped according to recipient and motive.

Most gifts are given to one's social superiors (Age of Tomorrow, 1990). They are given in appreciation for a favour done or one anticipated.[18] As the substance of the gift is so important, large, prestigious department stores dominate the formal gift market. Table 2.12 lists fifteen personal gift occasions, but only six of these, Christmas, Halloween, starting a new school or job (both in April only), Adult's Day,[19] 7–5–3 Day[20] and childbirths, are totally discretionary. White Day (Ato, 1990; and see below) and Mother's and Father's Days are largely discretionary, but even these sometimes carry a degree of obligation. The remaining six personal gift occasions and all five corporate gift occasions are obligatory gift-giving markets.

Valentine's Day is a classic case. Retailers and confectionary manufacturers imported this Western concept to Japan in the 1960s. They successfully marketed 14 February as a day for women to give chocolate to their chosen male suitors, with the Valentine's Day market in 1992 exceeding ¥144,000 million.

Unfortunately, while the chance for women to give presents to men worked as a new, unusual idea, in the male-dominated Japanese society, it produced a one-way flow. No Japanese man gives gifts for Valentine's. To balance this oversight the same confectionary companies invented 'White Day' for 14 March. This is the day for men to return the favour of the Valentine's Day chocolates they received a month earlier.

Men were originally expected to give white chocolate, hence the name of the day. More recently, the range of gifts has expanded to include flowers and liquor. On Valentine's Day women often go to the trouble of making chocolates by hand to give to their favourite suitors. Lingerie is also a popular gift on White Day, and there are even vending machines selling ladies' panties packaged in drink-like cans, allowing embarrassed males to buy with ease.

Valentine's Day has now taken one step further. Not wanting to favour any particular man in the office, OLs often make sure they give each male colleague at least one small chocolate. This has become known as *giri-choko*, literally 'duty chocolates'. In a survey by Keio department store in 1987, 23.2 per cent of respondents gave Valentine's gifts out of duty or obligation (JMA, 1989).

Valentine's Day well illustrates how Japanese give gifts out of obligation. Valentine's is, however, well behind the two main obligatory gift markets. These are the mid-year *o-chūgen* season and the year-end *o-seibo* season. These coincide with twice yearly bonuses that are paid to almost all full-time employees.

The sales of most retailers peak in December and July. Department store sales rise more sharply than superstore sales in these months, because there is more prestige value in purchasing from a famous, expensive department store than there is from the neighbourhood supermarket. In 1992, however, the first economic downturn for almost fifteen years led many consumers to actually look for cheaper gifts. This was one of the most important factors in the slump in department store sales and the superstore chains benefited accordingly (see Chapters 6 and 7 for detailed discussion).

Individuals and companies feel obliged to give gifts to 'patrons, benefactors, bosses, and sundry superiors' (Woronoff, 1981: 286). Fields (1988a: 84) notes a 1985 survey where the average married salaryman had non-routine expenses amounting to 2 per cent of his annual income at New Year, and some 22 per cent of this expenditure was used on *o-seibo* gifts, excluding gifts for family members.

Companies buy gifts en masse from department stores to give to their customers. Many people now believe this is a wasteful and corrupt tradition, but the practice is too widespread to disappear (Fields, 1990a; Nikkei Ryūtsū Shinbun, 1993b).[21] *O-seibo* and *o-chūgen* gifts are tied to social status and obligation, and society maintains and encourages both. The simple act of giving a gift is not enough. The gift must be correct in every way – what is given, its value, its presentation and where it was purchased. Creighton (1988: 283) sums this up well:

> In theory gifts are voluntary, but everyone knows they are given under obligation . . . personal sentiment – affection, intimacy, friendship – [has] no place in choosing gifts or who is to receive them . . . the price of the gift should be clearly discernible . . . [and the custom is] against mutual exchanges: the flow is from inferiors to superiors.

In this way, gift purchases link social hierarchy with shopping behaviour. Most large stores dedicate a whole floor to displaying gift items during these seasons. Most gifts are special boxed sets of foods or household goods. Popular items in 1992 were canned beer, soap, salad oil and roast ham (Sakamoto *et al.*, 1993). Even some Western companies produce specially packaged items aimed at this market.

Department stores not only take orders, but also advise on the suitability of a gift in relation to the potential recipient. Consumers must weigh the relative status of the giver and receiver before choosing the gift, higher-status people receiving more expensive gifts. With such a complex social hierarchy in Japan, choosing the right gift is a difficult task. For a fee, department stores will take over the whole business of choosing, wrapping and sending out a customer's required gifts (Creighton, 1988: 293–4). Large stores also send sales representatives to overseas companies in Japan to advise them, first that such gift-giving is appropriate, and secondly on suitable gift items.

Largely as a result of gift shopping experiences, Japanese consumers are very sensitive to the brand image of a store. Department stores wrap all purchases, not only gifts, meticulously in their own distinctive paper, making it clear where the purchase was made (Fields, 1983: 164; 1988a: 102). Mitsukoshi, arguably the most prestigious department store, suffered a marked decline in sales after a boardroom scandal in the early 1980s. Many customers boycotted the store for gift purchases, because the Mitsukoshi wrapping paper was besmirched (Fields, 1983: 164). It took until the late 1980s for Mitsukoshi to recover its prestige, and regain its position in the obligatory gift market.

An understanding of the importance of gift-giving in Japan helps a great deal when looking at shopping behaviour, store choice and product choice in general. Consumers in different regions are sensitive to the merits and demerits of large stores in their own areas (Larke, 1991). Different generations seek out different store types and expect different levels of service. All are equally aware of the social importance of using a store. Again, this relates to shopping as being a leisure activity – deciding where best to shop, on occasion where best to be seen shopping, and, additionally, where best to buy.

Japanese consumers are said to be choosy about quality. This has a lot to do with gift-giving and gift-shopping. In this way at least, consumers in Japan have quite different experiences and expectations to those in the West.

## EVERYTHING YOU NEED TO KNOW ABOUT JAPANESE CONSUMERS

This chapter provides basic general information on the consumer environment in Japan. Some aspects of this environment are distinctive, for example the age structure of the population or gift-giving behaviour, but it would be wrong to conclude that consumers are any different from those in the West or elsewhere. It is more important to understand consumers as they are, and the environment that surrounds them. Retailing, which is the topic of the rest of the book, is a major part of that environment, but it is impossible to understand retail developments without first knowing something about the consumers that they aim to serve.

What this chapter does is to provide the background to any discussion of retailing in Japan. In addition, however, it shows that Japanese consumers are open for research. Inevitably, Japanese materials are the main sources for this research, and, due to the language, this is often the largest single barrier to understanding. The question then is not, 'Are Japanese consumers different?' but more, 'Can we understand Japanese consumers?' Through proper application of the wide array of Japanese statistics and data sources available, this chapter shows that it is possible to understand. The remainder of the book, in looking at the retail environment, shows how retailers have applied this knowledge and understanding.

# Chapter 3

# Japanese distribution
## Criticism, problems and change

In many Western countries, retailers now dominate distribution channels. They undertake functions such as product design, physical distribution and sometimes even production. The growth and expansion of large retailers in Japan is one of the main themes in this book, but even the largest still lag behind their Western counterparts in terms of such vertical integration and in their influence over distribution channels. Whereas backward integration was a major phenomenon in distribution channels in the 1970s in the West, in Japan it is only just beginning on a significant scale.

The overriding reason for this is that the retail industry is highly fragmented. There are hundreds of thousands of small retail stores and businesses. Compared to other advanced nations, many Japanese have a strong desire to operate their own small businesses, and both society and formal legislation work to encourage and protect them. The historical development of the distribution system caused this fragmentation to develop. Large manufacturers are still the most powerful actors within distribution channels. The wholesale sector is also large and highly fragmented, because it continues to provide functions which both manufacturers and retailers require in order to operate well. The situation was similar in Western systems until recently, but has now been superseded by developments in large-scale retailing.

Simply put, the distribution industry in Japan is quite different from distribution systems in many equally advanced Western countries. For example, the role of independent wholesaling has become almost obsolete in some Western nations, but wholesalers are still an important part of distribution channels in Japan. Not only is the system unusual, but, along with Japanese trade surpluses, some Western countries have made it a political issue, suggesting that the distribution system excludes imported goods.

This chapter provides an overview of the distribution system. It shows how the wholesale sector continues to play a major role within the system and describes how major manufacturers attempt to control distribution channels. Finally, it considers the most recent developments in the distribution system, and notes how the larger retailers are playing an increasingly active role.

This is also a convenient place to introduce more general aspects and trends. The following section provides a review of Western criticism of Japanese distribution. Later, the chapter introduces the topics of information technology in distribution and other sectors on the fringes of the retail industry, namely direct mail and vending machines.

## THE WESTERN VIEW OF DISTRIBUTION IN JAPAN: A REVIEW

As early as the 1960s, distribution in Japan was a topic of international study (see Murata, 1961; Weigand, 1963). Then, as today, the main points of interest were numerous business customs and practices, most of which were either unknown or even illegal in the West. Much of the literature in English focuses on the problems of the system as seen in Western eyes.[1] Other authors have covered these aspects of distribution in Japan in detail, so this section provides a brief review and update.

### Entering the Japanese market

By the beginning of the 1960s Japan was finally shaking off its postwar hardships. The Tokyo Olympics in 1964 were a watershed for both the Japanese economy and society (see Fields, 1983; 1988a). Western marketing ideas flowed into Japan at the time. Western companies were soon attracted by the large consumer market (Lazer et al., 1985). In the 1960s, imports from the USA were common, and consumers showed a positive preference for the then superior quality of overseas goods (Fields, 1983: 6–13; Glazer, 1970; Gröke, 1972).

As the export economy grew, Japan required fewer imported manufactured goods, while at the same time maintaining a strong demand for raw materials. After achieving a trade surplus in the 1960s, the oil shocks of 1974 and 1979 brought Japan trade deficits, but by the mid-1980s the trade surplus was very strong indeed (see Table 3.1). In 1992 Japan exported goods and services to the value of ¥13.5 billion over and above the value of imports. The surplus of trade to the USA alone was equivalent to some 41 per cent of this total. Arguably, Japan achieves this surplus by providing American and European consumers with the products they want (Economist, 1989a; 1989b), but the surplus is now so large and so unbalanced with some countries, that it draws ever increasing criticism.

*Table 3.1* Selected trade and economic statistics, 1965–92 (in ¥000 million)

|  | Total exports | Total imports | Trade surplus | GDP | Per capita GNP |
|---|---|---|---|---|---|
| 1965 | 304.3 | 294.1 | 10.2 | 101,109.2 | 266.0 |
| 1970 | 695.4 | 679.7 | 15.7 | 171,661.4 | 571.0 |
| 1975 | 1,654.5 | 1,717.0 | −62.5 | 213,107.8 | 1,085.0 |
| 1980 | 2,938.2 | 3,199.5 | −261.3 | 266,722.1 | 1,671.0 |
| 1985 | 4,195.6 | 3,108.5 | 1,087.1 | 320,397.2 | 2,124.0 |
| 1990 | 4,145.7 | 3,385.5 | 760.2 | 399,043.1 | 2,723.0 |
| 1992[a] | 4,301.0 | 2,950.9 | 1,350.1 | 420,454.2 | 3,404.5 |

[a] 1992 figures are estimates.
*Source*: Asahi Shinbunsha (1993b)

In the late 1970s and early 1980s Western trade negotiators successfully fought to remove almost all visible barriers to trade with Japan such as tariffs and excessive product standards (MITI, 1983). By the mid-1980s, many less tangible barriers, such as overly stringent testing standards for imported goods, were also removed.

By the 1990s, many overseas companies had achieved success in the Japanese market. Most are global-scale firms such as Coca Cola, McDonald's, Procter & Gamble and Unilever (see JETRO, 1982; 1983a; Ozaki, 1989), but some smaller companies, those offering suitable products, have also prospered.[2]

The market place does not discriminate against foreign companies or foreign products, but, to achieve success, any overseas firm faces a steep learning curve (Fields, 1989a; JETRO, 1987; MIPRO, 1980). In 1993 only a few industries, notably agriculture, enjoyed a significant level of government protection. Even the food market, despite huge political and popular opposition, will be opened in the very near future.[3]

Japanese companies compete on basically the same terms, with the same problems and difficulties, as firms from overseas. The government promotes imports through organisations such as the Japan

External Trade Organisation (JETRO) and the Manufactured Import Promotion Organisation (MIPRO). The advice given is always the same – make sure the product is suitable, have a long-term strategy and do not expect favouritism. Fields (1988a: 120–3) argues that entering the market is as problematic for a Japanese company as it is for one from overseas.

While many commentators have noted the trend towards marketing globalisation, others insist that it is unreasonable for overseas companies to expect significant short-term success simply on the basis of results in other nations. Experts point out that Japan is not a small part of a single global or advanced 'Western' market, rather it is very different from most markets in North America and Europe (Fields, 1988a: 189–230; Morita et al., 1987: 250–79; Ohmae, 1989). The exceptions, that is companies succeeding in Japan with the same business formulae they use elsewhere, are rare, and even they realise the need to adapt to local conditions (Fields, 1992).

Companies can reduce the problems and difficulties of entering any overseas market through sufficient preparation. Such preparation, especially the effort to gain understanding of differences and anomalies, is vital for Japan. Assuming the company has the right product, presented in the appropriate manner with the correct intensity and attitude, there is no reason why it should not be a success in Japan as much as in any country.

## Structural impediments and the distribution system as a non-tariff barrier

Even in the 1970s, some Western politicians were suggesting that the distribution system was a non-tariff trade barrier (see Wilkinson, 1983: 201). In 1989, the Structural Impediments Initiative (SII) trade negotiations between Japan and the USA were the first to make the system a key issue. During the SII, the American side criticised many aspects of Japanese business, including agriculture and anti-trust laws, but, taking Japanese press coverage as a measure, American demands for changes in the distribution system were by far the main point of public concern.[4]

The final report listed six aspects of business and society in Japan that may hinder trade (MITI, 1990b). Four of these – inefficient distribution procedures and facilities, anti-competitive business practices, *keiretsu* business groupings and controlled price mechanisms – all relate directly to the distribution system, and the other two, savings and investment patterns and inefficient land use, are indirectly related.

So what is wrong with the distribution system? Differences in the system became a talking point in the early 1970s (Murata, 1973; Tajima, 1971; Yoshino, 1971). Shimaguchi (Shimaguchi, 1977; Shimaguchi and Lazer, 1979; Shimaguchi and Rosenberg, 1979) consolidated this work and provided a framework for the study of the precise problems involved. Later, Western studies, especially those produced in the USA, became more critical. The ACTPN (1989: 72–3) describes the system as complicated, archaic and a barrier to foreign goods, while the USITC (1990: vii) states that some aspects of the system impede access to existing channels by new entrants, including new Japanese companies.

The issues that the SII raised can be summarised in five main problem areas. They note that the distribution system in Japan:

- is highly fragmented
- employs multi-layered distribution channels
- tolerates tight control of channels by larger manufacturers
- employs inconsistent and anti-competitive business practices
- is controlled by unnecessary government legislation.

All five aspects have existed for a long time and are integral factors within the distribution system, affecting all companies operating within the Japanese market. This chapter reviews each of these first four points, and Chapter 4 looks at the Large Store Law, the most criticised point of all.

Many of the criticisms are at least partly valid. In general, Japanese observers and academics take a defensive stance, often attempting to explain the system from a subjective, cultural perspective. Unfortunately, there are few examples of work that provide a positive point of view. A negative approach does little to silence the original critics. Japanese work goes into greater depth, but that written in the West is often more forthright.

The distribution system in the 1990s is now evolving rapidly. Companies operating within the system are addressing problems and working to improve the system overall. The trade issue means that political pressure to change also comes from outside Japan. In the end, however, companies in Japan will decide how best to develop their distribution system for their own goods and services. Where companies can make changes, they will do so if it benefits themselves and their customers, be they Western or Japanese. This is exactly how it should be. It may seem as though years of overseas criticism are at last having an effect. In truth, companies now feel it is the time to change.

## A FRAGMENTED DISTRIBUTION STRUCTURE: SO MANY SHOPS

The wholesale and retail sectors of Japanese distribution are both highly fragmented. According to the 1991 Census of Commerce[5] there were 436,000 wholesale outlets, and almost 1.6 million retail outlets. Both figures are higher than in the USA, a country which has twice the population and twenty-five times the land area.

In the early 1980s the number of retail outlets peaked and it is now in decline. The number of wholesale outlets continues to grow, as companies attempt to improve distribution efficiency to small retailers (see below). There were more wholesale outlets in 1991 than at any time on record (see DEIJ, 1988: 1, for historical figures).

In both sectors there is a continuing trend towards larger, more efficient companies. Currently, the level of concentration within distribution is low, with no really dominant companies outside the manufacturing sector, but this is changing slowly. At present, the overriding characteristic of both the wholesaling and retailing industries is the large number of very small outlets.

Manufacturers and wholesalers support and promote a fragmented retail structure. Since the 1950s, manufacturers have dominated distribution channels, preferring to deal with small, easily influenced retail companies. Japanese law, while seeking to protect small retailers as a whole, avoids confrontation with big business and does little to curb their power. Anti-monopoly legislation and consumer protection exist, but are applied only where absolutely necessary.

The following sections consider this situation in detail.

### The physical structure of wholesaling

Table 3.2 summarises the structure of the wholesale industry using data from the Census of Commerce (MITI, 1992a; 1992b). While there was a decline both in numbers of businesses and in numbers of outlets in 1985, both have since recovered to reach new highs in 1991. The number of people employed also grew over the decade, increasing by 6 per cent. Wholesale sales rose throughout the decade, with highest increases in 1982 and 1991, in accordance with high sales growth in the retail sector (see pages 69–78).

Table 3.2 Summary statistics for the wholesale industry, 1982–91

| | 1982 | % Change 82/79 | 1985 | % Change 85/82 | 1988 | % Change 88/85 | 1991 | % Change 91/88 |
|---|---|---|---|---|---|---|---|---|
| Businesses | 314,835 | 11.7 | 302,439 | -3.9 | 313,009 | 3.5 | 333,808 | 6.6 |
| Outlets | 428,858 | 16.3 | 413,016 | -3.7 | 436,421 | 5.7 | 475,983 | 9.1 |
| Employees[a] | 4,090,919 | 11.4 | 3,998,437 | -2.3 | 4,331,727 | 8.3 | 4,772,709 | 10.2 |
| Sales (¥ million) | 398,536,234 | 45.2 | 427,750,891 | 7.3 | 446,483,972 | 4.4 | 573,164,698 | 28.4 |
| Average per business: | | | | | | | | |
| Outlets | 1.36 | 4.2 | 1.37 | 0.3 | 1.39 | 2.1 | 1.43 | 2.3 |
| Employees | 12.99 | -0.3 | 13.22 | 1.7 | 13.84 | 4.7 | 14.30 | 3.3 |
| Sales (¥ million) | 1,265.86 | 29.9 | 1,414.34 | 11.7 | 1,426.43 | 0.9 | 1,717.05 | 20.4 |

[a] Full-time only

Source: Calculated from MITI (1984; 1986; 1989a; 1992b)

Table 3.3 Wholesale outlets by number of full-time employees, 1982–91

| No of full-time employees | 1982 | | 1985 | | 1988 | | 1991 | |
|---|---|---|---|---|---|---|---|---|
| | Outlets | % change 82/79 | Outlets | % change 85/82 | Outlets | % change 88/85 | Outlets | % change 91/88 |
| 1–2 | 99,857 | 25.5 | 93,007 | −6.9 | 95,315 | 2.5 | 101,786 | 6.8 |
| 3–4 | 108,129 | 17.4 | 105,122 | −2.8 | 110,085 | 4.7 | 123,309 | 12.0 |
| 5–9 | 119,599 | 13.8 | 115,089 | −3.8 | 121,612 | 5.7 | 132,089 | 8.6 |
| 10–19 | 60,507 | 11.2 | 59,348 | −1.9 | 64,686 | 9.0 | 70,474 | 8.9 |
| 20–29 | 18,343 | 9.9 | 18,379 | 0.2 | 20,079 | 9.2 | 21,424 | 6.7 |
| 30–49 | 12,558 | 8.3 | 12,478 | −0.6 | 13,896 | 11.4 | 14,931 | 7.4 |
| 50–99 | 7,043 | 6.7 | 6,916 | −1.8 | 7,789 | 12.6 | 8,441 | 8.4 |
| 100 or more | 2,822 | 10.9 | 2,677 | −5.1 | 2,959 | 10.5 | 3,529 | 19.3 |
| Total | 428,858 | 16.3 | 413,016 | −3.7 | 436,421 | 5.7 | 475,983 | 9.1 |

Source: Calculated from MITI (1984; 1986; 1989a; 1992b)

Due to the large number of small family businesses, Census figures concentrate on the number of outlets rather than businesses, and on the number of full-time employees as a measure of outlet size. In 1991, around 75 per cent of all wholesale outlets employed fewer than ten people (see Table 3.3). Between 1982 and 1985, the number of outlets employing either one or two people or more than 100 people, that is the smallest and the largest categories, both decreased by more than 5 per cent. Since 1985, the overall number of wholesale outlets has recovered.

The number of businesses can be estimated from tables 17 and 21 of the first volume of Census statistics (MITI, 1992b). In 1991, unincorporated businesses operated a quarter of all wholesale outlets, but accounted for only slightly more than 1 per cent of total sales (Table 3.4). Outlets in unincorporated businesses averaged sales of only ¥63.5 million, compared to ¥1,565 million for those in incorporated businesses.

This is an important difference and relates to the continuing survival of so many wholesale outlets. Because of their small share of sales, outlets in unincorporated wholesale businesses appear to play only a minor role, and Table 3.4 shows that it is the unincorporated businesses that are in decline. They survive, however, for two main reasons.

First, wholesaling is an easy business to enter. Opening a retail shop requires some investment in shop fitting and display, but a wholesale outlet requires only storage space. Some 55 per cent of employees in outlets of unincorporated businesses are unpaid family members (MITI, 1992b: 547), and many small wholesalers are family businesses, which simply use free space in the home.

Second, manufacturers and retailers still demand the services of small wholesalers. Manufacturers use them to supply small retailers, and small retailers rely on them for frequent, prompt supply of goods. Consequently, the proportion of wholesale sales from unincorporated businesses is highest in less affluent, rural prefectures such as Wakayama, Nara or Saga, where retailers are more remote and difficult to access.

Understanding the role of small outlets is crucial to understanding distribution in Japan. They are important in both the wholesale and the retail sectors, although as the number of small retailers decreases, significant falls in the number of small wholesalers are likely too.

Table 3.5 presents a breakdown of the wholesale industry by business sector (MITI, 1992a: 12–13). Expansion in the number of

Table 3.4 Structure and trends in incorporated and unincorporated wholesale business

| | 1982 | % change 82/79 | 1985[a] | % change 85/82 | 1988 | % change 88/85 | 1991 | % change 91/88 |
|---|---|---|---|---|---|---|---|---|
| Businesses | 314,835 | 11.7 | 302,439 | -3.9 | 313,009 | 3.5 | 333,808 | 6.6 |
| incorporated businesses | 186,488 | 12.1 | 186,150 | -0.2 | 196,391 | 5.8 | 221,339 | 12.4 |
| unincorporated businesses | 128,347 | 11.1 | 116,289 | -9.4 | 116,118 | -0.1 | 112,469 | -3.1 |
| Number of outlets | 428,858 | 16.3 | 413,016 | -3.7 | 436,421 | 5.7 | 475,983 | 9.1 |
| in incorporated businesses | 297,395 | 18.8 | 294,199 | -1.1 | 317,876 | 8.0 | 361,614 | 13.8 |
| in unincorporated businesses | 131,463 | 11.2 | 118,817 | -9.6 | 118,545 | -0.2 | 114,369 | -3.5 |
| Number of employees | 4,090,919 | 11.4 | 3,998,437 | -2.3 | 4,331,727 | 8.3 | 4,772,709 | 10.2 |
| in incorporated businesses | 3,679,622 | 12.1 | 3,622,147 | -1.6 | 3,957,607 | 9.3 | 4,442,792 | 12.3 |
| in unincorporated businesses | 411,297 | 5.0 | 376,290 | -8.5 | 374,120 | -0.6 | 329,917 | -11.8 |
| Sales (¥ million) | 398,536,234 | 45.2 | 427,750,891 | 7.3 | 446,483,972 | 4.4 | 573,164,699 | 28.4 |
| in incorporated businesses | 390,900,622 | 45.9 | 421,046,732 | 7.7 | 439,267,615 | 4.3 | 565,901,288 | 28.8 |
| in unincorporated businesses | 7,635,612 | 16.2 | 7,243,924 | -5.1 | 7,216,356 | -0.4 | 7,263,411 | 0.7 |

[a] Sales figures for 1985 are as according to the original Census.
Source: Calculated from MITI (1984; 1986; 1989a; 1992b)

Table 3.5 The wholesale sector by product type, 1982–91

| Industrial classification | 1982 Outlets | % change 82/79 | 1985 Outlets | % change 85/82 | 1988 Outlets | % change 88/85 | 1991 Outlets | % change 91/88 |
|---|---|---|---|---|---|---|---|---|
| 49 General merchandise wholesalers[a] | 50 | -3.8 | 985 | n.a. | 824 | -16.3 | 706 | -14.3 |
| 50 Materials and parts wholesalers | 213,419 | 20.5 | 205,577 | -3.7 | 219,692 | 6.9 | 243,355 | 10.8 |
| 501 Textile products | 11,964 | 10.0 | 12,044 | 0.7 | 12,055 | 0.1 | 12,419 | 3.0 |
| 502 Chemicals and related products | 15,341 | 16.5 | 15,546 | 1.3 | 16,924 | 8.9 | 18,141 | 7.2 |
| 503 Metal and minerals | 21,229 | 16.8 | 21,017 | -1.0 | 21,041 | 0.1 | 22,655 | 7.7 |
| 504 Machinery and equipment | 86,788 | 24.9 | 85,072 | -2.0 | 94,775 | 11.4 | 111,052 | 17.2 |
| 505 Building supplies | 60,031 | 17.3 | 56,029 | -6.7 | 59,877 | 6.9 | 63,886 | 6.7 |
| 506 Recycled materials | 18,066 | 27.2 | 15,869 | -12.2 | 15,020 | -5.4 | 15,202 | 1.2 |
| 51 Finished goods wholesalers | 213,253 | 12.3 | 204,936 | -3.9 | 214,976 | 4.9 | 230,705 | 7.3 |
| 511 Apparel and accessories | 31,205 | 9.7 | 28,960 | -7.2 | 30,180 | 4.2 | 32,330 | 7.1 |
| 512 Farm, livestock and marine products | 39,827 | 8.1 | 39,193 | -1.6 | 41,071 | 4.8 | 43,332 | 5.5 |
| 513 Food and beverages | 54,205 | 8.3 | 54,082 | -0.2 | 54,996 | 1.7 | 56,658 | 3.0 |
| 514 Drugs and toiletries | 16,933 | 22.9 | 16,809 | -0.7 | 18,525 | 10.2 | 21,320 | 15.1 |
| 515 Furniture and fittings | 23,592 | 15.5 | 21,354 | -9.5 | 22,117 | 3.6 | 23,436 | 6.0 |
| 516 Other wholesale | 47,491 | 17.9 | 44,538 | -6.2 | 48,087 | 8.0 | 53,629 | 11.5 |
| 52 Agents and brokers | 2,136 | 28.8 | 1,518 | -28.9 | 929 | -38.8 | 1,217 | 31.0 |
| Totals | 428,858 | 16.3 | 413,016 | -3.7 | 436,421 | 5.7 | 475,983 | 9.1 |

a Counting for general wholesalers changed in 1985, figures incompatible.
Source: Calculated from MITI (1984; 1986; 1989a; 1992b)

wholesale outlets in 1991 is clear for all sectors except general merchandise. This growth was due to a booming economy and the expansion of larger, corporate wholesalers (MITI, 1992b).

Most of the 706 general merchandise wholesale outlets were trading companies, including major trading houses such as Mitsubishi and Sumitomo.[6] In 1988, these companies were responsible for 34.6 per cent of all transactions made by Japanese companies overseas (MITI, 1989a: 676). The number of trading companies is now declining due to increased specialisation within distribution. Other firms, notably large retailers, now prefer to handle their own overseas trading and are large enough to do so.

Similarly, the number of outlets acting purely as agents or brokers declined by 28.3 per cent from 1985 to 1991. Many wholesalers frequently act as brokers (Miyashita, 1992). A wholesaler may arrange sale and supply of merchandise between two other channel members, without ever handling goods at any time (MITI, 1989b). Recently, although large retailers negotiate directly with manufacturers, some manufacturers prefer to have intermediary wholesale agents handle paperwork and delivery. This provides a buffer between themselves and the more powerful retailers should problems arise.

One final general aspect of wholesaling is the considerable concentration of sales into the three main urban areas of Tokyo, Osaka and Nagoya in Aichi (see Chapter 2). Table 3.6 shows that these prefectures account for 33 per cent of outlets and just under 60 per cent of all sales. Moreover, this share is slowly increasing. For any single wholesale sector, no less than 10 per cent of outlets and 16 per cent of sales are concentrated in Tokyo, with 80 per cent of general merchandise sales there. Tokyo also accounts for more than 30 per cent of sales in four other sectors. The Osaka and Aichi areas have similarly high concentrations of wholesale sales.

The large number of small wholesale outlets supports the system of distribution in Japan. In 1990, there were around 878,000 manufacturing businesses, 86 per cent of which employed fewer than twenty people (Chūshō Kigyō Chō, 1992b: statistical appendix, 3–5). Because most manufacturers and most retailers are small, they rely on wholesalers to handle physical distribution and storage of goods. Some large retailers also use the skills of smaller wholesalers (see pages 89–92 below), but, on the whole, the fragmented wholesale system exists to supply the even more fragmented retail system.

Table 3.6 Geographical concentration of wholesale sales, 1991

| Industrial classification | % of total outlets | | | | % of total sales | | | |
|---|---|---|---|---|---|---|---|---|
| | Tokyo | Osaka | Aichi | Total | Tokyo | Osaka | Aichi | Total |
| 49 General merchandise wholesalers | 11.6 | 10.9 | 8.2 | 30.8 | 80.0 | 12.6 | 3.2 | 95.8 |
| 50 Materials and parts wholesalers | 14.7 | 11.1 | 7.2 | 33.0 | 25.9 | 17.4 | 13.5 | 56.8 |
| 501 Textile products | 17.6 | 21.5 | 11.0 | 50.1 | 16.2 | 45.7 | 10.4 | 72.3 |
| 502 Chemicals and related products | 19.6 | 15.3 | 8.9 | 43.8 | 35.9 | 26.2 | 11.3 | 73.4 |
| 503 Metal and minerals | 17.3 | 14.7 | 7.5 | 39.4 | 30.2 | 17.0 | 12.3 | 59.5 |
| 504 Machinery and equipment | 15.9 | 11.0 | 7.4 | 34.3 | 24.9 | 14.5 | 16.5 | 56.0 |
| 505 Building supplies | 10.1 | 7.4 | 5.8 | 23.3 | 19.6 | 10.5 | 7.5 | 37.5 |
| 506 Recycled materials | 12.7 | 9.2 | 6.9 | 28.8 | 18.0 | 14.2 | 10.1 | 42.3 |
| 51 Finished goods wholesalers | 16.4 | 10.9 | 6.5 | 33.7 | 24.6 | 13.4 | 8.1 | 46.1 |
| 511 Apparel and accessories | 26.4 | 19.4 | 6.9 | 52.6 | 34.7 | 25.8 | 8.8 | 69.3 |
| 512 Farm, livestock and marine products | 12.0 | 7.3 | 5.5 | 24.9 | 19.9 | 9.6 | 6.8 | 36.3 |
| 513 Food and beverages | 11.0 | 7.6 | 5.9 | 24.5 | 19.7 | 10.7 | 7.2 | 37.6 |
| 514 Drugs and toiletries | 11.7 | 8.9 | 6.0 | 26.6 | 18.5 | 11.8 | 7.9 | 38.1 |
| 515 Furniture and fittings | 16.0 | 10.6 | 8.2 | 34.7 | 23.1 | 15.7 | 9.5 | 48.3 |
| 516 Other wholesale | 21.7 | 12.9 | 7.0 | 41.5 | 34.3 | 15.2 | 10.3 | 59.9 |
| Total | 15.5 | 11.0 | 6.9 | 33.3 | 34.7 | 15.1 | 9.8 | 59.6 |

Source: Compiled from MITI (1992b)

### The structure of the retail industry

In 1991, there were 1.6 million retail stores operated by 1.3 million businesses, and employing almost 7 million people (see Table 3.7). Total retail sales were ¥140 billion,[7] generated from some 110 million square metres of sales floor space. Individual shops are small in terms of both the number of full-time employees per outlet and floor size. In 1991, the average store employed four people and had an annual turnover of about ¥88 million and sales space of less than 70 square metres.

Retail stores are so numerous for several reasons. Starting a retail store is only a little more difficult than starting a wholesale business. Retailing is the single largest employment sector in the economy with 11 per cent of the full-time labour force. In addition, small retailers are a large, powerful political lobby, and various legislation both supports and encourages their survival (see Chapter 4).

On the demand side, consumers are used to having many small shops near their doorstep. Most shopping is done on foot or by bicycle, and shopping frequency is high (see Chapter 2). Small stores survive for these reasons. There are small stores everywhere, and where there are no shops, there are vending machines (see pages 99–100).

Again, using number of full-time employees as a measure of size,[8] outlets in the retail sector are even smaller than in wholesaling (see Table 3.8). Over 50 per cent of retail stores employ fewer than three people full-time, with more than 90 per cent employing fewer than ten. Most of the smallest stores are family run. Like small wholesalers, many small shops are part of the family home. Often the head of the household holds a separate full-time job. The rest of the family, grandmother, grandfather and housewife, are the shop assistants. In unincorporated retail businesses almost 62 per cent of employees are unpaid family members (MITI, 1992b: 569). These stores make little money, even though the family do not normally draw salaries.

Between 1982 and 1991, there was a net decline of some 130,000 retail outlets, but this decline was solely among the very smallest stores. Stores employing four or more people all recorded net increases in the same period. The smallest stores, those employing only one or two people, declined by almost 190,000 outlets, or 18 per cent, in nine years.

Figure 3.1 shows the percentage contribution to this total decline for each store size category from 1982 to 1991. In the 1985, 1988 and 1991 Censuses, the smallest stores accounted for all of the total

*Table 3.7* Summary statistics for the retail industry, 1982–91

| | 1982 | % change 82/79 | 1985 | % change 85/82 | 1988 | % change 88/85 | 1991 | % change 91/88 |
|---|---|---|---|---|---|---|---|---|
| Businesses | 1,482,516 | 1.1 | 1,386,891 | −6.5 | 1,348,100 | −2.8 | 1,294,532 | −4.0 |
| Outlets | 1,721,465 | 2.9 | 1,628,644 | −5.4 | 1,619,752 | −0.5 | 1,591,223 | −1.8 |
| Employees[a] | 6,369,426 | 6.9 | 6,328,614 | −0.6 | 6,851,335 | 8.3 | 6,936,526 | 1.2 |
| Sales space (sq m) | 95,430,071 | 11.3 | 94,506,983 | −1.0 | 102,050,766 | 8.0 | 109,911,315 | 7.7 |
| Sales (¥ million) | 93,971,191 | 27.7 | 101,718,812 | 8.2 | 114,839,927 | 12.9 | 140,638,104 | 22.5 |
| Averages per business | | | | | | | | |
| Outlets | 1.16 | 1.8 | 1.17 | 1.1 | 1.20 | 2.3 | 1.23 | 2.3 |
| Employees | 4.30 | 5.7 | 4.56 | 6.2 | 5.08 | 11.4 | 5.36 | 5.4 |
| Sales space (sq m) | 64.37 | 10.1 | 68.14 | 5.9 | 75.70 | 11.1 | 84.90 | 12.2 |
| Sales (¥ million) | 63.39 | 26.4 | 73.34 | 15.7 | 85.19 | 16.1 | 108.64 | 27.5 |

[a] Full-time only

*Source:* Calculated from MITI (1984; 1986; 1989a; 1992b)

Table 3.8 Retail outlets by number of full-time employees, 1982–91

| No of full-time employees | 1982 | | 1985 | | 1988 | | 1991 | |
|---|---|---|---|---|---|---|---|---|
| | Outlets | % change 82/79 | Outlets | % change 85/82 | Outlets | % change 88/85 | Outlets | % change 91/88 |
| 1–2 | 1,036,046 | 1.4 | 940,023 | −9.3 | 874,377 | −7.0 | 847,185 | −3.1 |
| 3–4 | 412,701 | 2.9 | 408,178 | −1.1 | 422,067 | 3.4 | 416,940 | −1.2 |
| 5–9 | 187,898 | 6.8 | 190,434 | 1.3 | 213,046 | 11.9 | 214,007 | 0.5 |
| 10–19 | 54,156 | 13.8 | 57,911 | 6.9 | 70,394 | 21.6 | 71,905 | 2.1 |
| 20–29 | 14,776 | 14.2 | 15,340 | 3.8 | 19,186 | 25.1 | 20,202 | 5.3 |
| 30–49 | 9,494 | 16.0 | 10,035 | 5.7 | 12,250 | 22.1 | 12,850 | 4.9 |
| 50–99 | 4,519 | 12.4 | 4,764 | 5.4 | 5,362 | 12.6 | 5,851 | 9.1 |
| 100 or more | 1,875 | 11.5 | 1,959 | 4.5 | 2,070 | 5.7 | 2,283 | 10.3 |
| Total | 1,721,465 | 2.9 | 1,628,644 | −5.4 | 1,619,752 | −0.5 | 1,591,223 | −1.8 |

Source: Calculated from MITI (1984; 1986; 1989a; 1992b)

decline in numbers. As Table 3.8 and Figure 3.1 show, larger stores increased in number. Stores employing between ten and forty-nine employees increased by about a third between 1982 and 1991, and stores employing fifty or more employees increased by over 27 per cent.

Figure 3.2 shows number of retail stores by employees per outlet. In 1991, stores employing fewer than ten people accounted for over 92 per cent of stores, and about 60 per cent of both total employee numbers and sales space.

In contrast, these smallest stores accounted for only 47 per cent of sales. Over the 1980s, larger stores took an increasing share of sales. In 1982, stores with more than ten employees made over 45 per cent of total sales. By 1991 this had increased to over 52 per cent. The sales share of stores with fewer than ten employees decreased in each Census. There are census data on retail sales space, but these are less accurate with over 207,000 outlets omitted from the 1991 figures.[9] The available data show the same predominance of tiny shops, and re-emphasise that only the very smallest stores are in the sharpest decline (see Chapter 4, pages 112–17).

Despite the decline in the number of the smallest stores, the overall number of outlets is still large. Demand for small, local retailing means that many independent retailers are replaced by new small outlets operating within chains of convenience stores and speciality stores. In the 1980s, many stores ceased trading as independent businesses, and were either bought or franchised by retail chains. With some refurbishment and new management techniques, many of the smallest stores which closed simply moved to a larger category. They are still small stores, but now employ more full-time employees.

Nevertheless, the overall trend is a decrease in store numbers. Table 3.9 gives figures from a survey of medium and small retailers that asked for possible reasons for future business problems (Chūshō Kigyō Chō, 1988a). Around 40 per cent of all respondents saw static or declining sales as the greatest threat to their businesses. Other reasons, however, differed between small and medium store operators.

Some 37 per cent of small retailers cited the owner's old age as a reason to quit. Related to this, a further 33.6 per cent also noted that they had no willing successor to take over the business. Economic factors such as competitors, looming bankruptcy and high land prices were of less concern to small retailers, but, combined with the lack of a successor, poor and worsening sales put considerable pressure on older stores. Medium sized retailers suggested the strength of

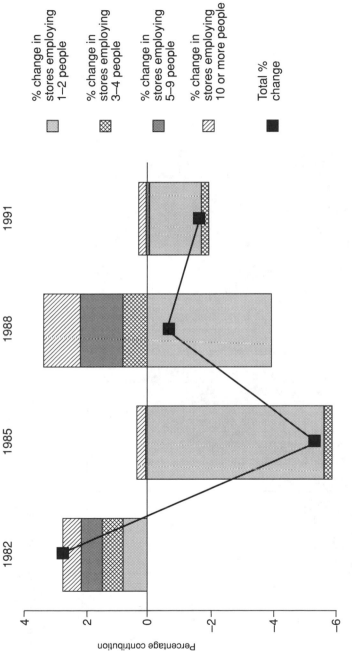

*Figure 3.1* Percentage contribution to overall change in store numbers, by full-time employees per store, 1982–91
*Source*: Adapted from MITI (1992b: 43)

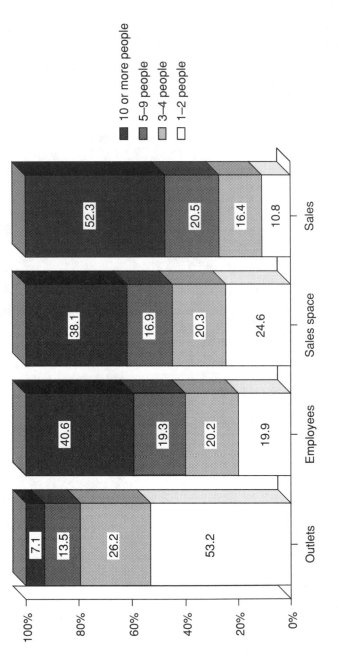

*Figure 3.2* Shares of total store numbers, employees, sales space and sales, by full-time employees per store, 1991
*Source*: Compiled from MITI (1992b)

*Table 3.9* Reasons for business failures among medium and small stores

| | % of responses | |
|---|---|---|
| | *Small stores (1–4 employees)* | *Medium stores (5–49 employees)* |
| Sales static or declining | 39.9 | 41.2 |
| Shop owner's old age | 37.2 | 14.1 |
| No successor to take over | 33.6 | 21.2 |
| Merchandise sector is poor | 28.2 | 29.4 |
| Local customers declining | 18.5 | 17.6 |
| Change to chain businesses | 16.4 | 16.4 |
| Competitors too strong | 15.4 | 40.0 |
| Move to new business | 8.1 | 15.3 |
| Likely bankruptcy | 6.7 | 10.6 |
| High land prices | 3.4 | 5.9 |

Survey of existing retailers considering closure or retirement.

*Source*: Chūshō Kigyō Chō (1988a)

competitors was the second largest threat to their business. They were more concerned with economic factors than were the small retailers, but significant proportions did note that old age (14 per cent) and no successor (21 per cent) could also become problems.

Secondary problems for both medium and small store operators were the growth of convenience store and supermarket chains, and declines in the number of local customers. In rural areas small stores are disappearing as store owners retire or as the local economy declines (Hatakeyama, 1989; Okumura, 1989; Takayama, 1989), but, where the large chains have penetrated, the situation is worse as these quickly draw customers away from local stores.

As in the wholesale sector, there is geographical concentration in retailing too. Ten prefectures account for around 50 per cent of the retail market. Over 20 per cent of all retail outlets and around 24 per cent of both retail employees and retail sales were in Tokyo and the three surrounding prefectures. This share increased slowly over the 1980s. The Osaka area accounted for a further 14 per cent of stores, and similar shares of employees and sales, with Aichi, Hokkaido and Fukuoka each accounting for between 4 and 6 per cent. Tokyo and Osaka also account for significant shares of the large store market. Thirty-eight of the nationwide total of 455 department stores are located in central Tokyo.

Table 3.10 Number of retail outlets by merchandise sector, 1982–91

| Industrial classification | 1982 Outlets | % change 82/79 | 1985 Outlets | % change 85/82 | 1988 Outlets | % change 88/85 | 1991 Outlets | % change 91/88 |
|---|---|---|---|---|---|---|---|---|
| 53 General merchandise | 4,219 | 16.2 | 3,531 | −16.3 | 3,843 | 8.8 | 4,347 | 13.1 |
| 531 Department stores | 1,754 | −11.7 | 1,827 | 4.2 | 1,911 | 4.6 | 2,004 | 4.9 |
| 539 Other | 2,465 | 49.8 | 1,704 | −30.9 | 1,932 | 13.4 | 2,343 | 21.3 |
| 54 Clothing, accessories | 242,866 | 2.5 | 229,606 | −5.5 | 234,527 | 2.1 | 240,989 | 2.8 |
| 541 Japanese clothing | 59,662 | 1.5 | 54,234 | −9.1 | 50,322 | −7.2 | 47,802 | −5.0 |
| 542 Men's apparel | 40,984 | −4.3 | 35,929 | −12.3 | 35,026 | −2.5 | 34,935 | −0.3 |
| 543 Women's, children's apparel | 66,502 | 15.1 | 70,814 | 6.5 | 83,468 | 17.9 | 94,947 | 13.8 |
| 544 Footwear, hosiery | 30,712 | −6.6 | 27,649 | −10.0 | 25,333 | −8.4 | 23,302 | −8.0 |
| 549 Other | 45,004 | 0.8 | 40,980 | −8.9 | 40,378 | −1.5 | 40,003 | −0.9 |
| 55 Food and beverages | 725,585 | −1.2 | 671,190 | −7.5 | 650,110 | −3.1 | 622,751 | −4.2 |
| 551 General foods | 90,604 | −6.0 | 92,602 | 2.2 | 77,468 | −16.3 | 68,913 | −11.0 |
| 552 Beverage, seasonings | 109,621 | 2.2 | 106,693 | −2.7 | 107,665 | 0.9 | 106,650 | −0.9 |
| 553 Meat, poultry | 41,371 | −5.7 | 36,171 | −12.6 | 32,936 | −8.9 | 28,792 | −12.6 |
| 554 Fresh fish | 53,133 | −6.1 | 46,638 | −12.2 | 43,890 | −5.9 | 41,204 | −6.1 |
| 555 Cured food | 11,850 | −10.2 | 9,419 | −20.5 | 9,128 | −3.1 | 8,141 | −10.8 |
| 556 Vegetables, fruit | 58,785 | −4.8 | 50,871 | −13.5 | 49,863 | −2.0 | 46,700 | −6.3 |
| 557 Confectionery, bakery | 175,941 | −2.1 | 150,416 | −14.5 | 139,794 | −7.1 | 126,194 | −9.7 |
| 558 Rice, barley, other cereals | 42,467 | 0.1 | 41,167 | −3.1 | 40,435 | −1.8 | 37,098 | −8.3 |
| 559 Other | 141,813 | 6.2 | 137,213 | −3.2 | 148,940 | 8.5 | 159,059 | 6.8 |

| | | | | | | | |
|---|---|---|---|---|---|---|---|
| 56 Motor vehicles, bicycles | 84,988 | 14.9 | 83,931 | −1.2 | 89,292 | 6.4 | 93,230 | 4.4 |
| 561 Motor vehicles | 47,652 | 24.5 | 47,686 | 0.1 | 53,491 | 12.2 | 59,126 | 10.5 |
| 562 Bicycles, motorcycles | 37,336 | 4.7 | 36,245 | −2.9 | 35,801 | −1.2 | 34,104 | −4.7 |
| 57 Furniture, household goods | 189,404 | 3.4 | 172,686 | −8.8 | 164,833 | −4.5 | 158,104 | −4.1 |
| 571 Furniture, fixtures, tatami | 62,527 | 2.5 | 55,183 | −11.7 | 51,602 | −6.5 | 49,031 | −5.0 |
| 572 Hardware, kitchenware | 36,038 | −0.4 | 32,373 | −10.2 | 29,902 | −7.6 | 27,070 | −9.5 |
| 573 China, glassware | 10,259 | 4.5 | 8,970 | −12.6 | 8,782 | −2.1 | 9,052 | 3.1 |
| 574 Household appliances | 78,943 | 6.1 | 74,386 | −5.8 | 72,958 | −1.9 | 71,203 | −2.4 |
| 579 Other | 1,637 | 12.7 | 1,774 | 8.4 | 1,589 | −10.4 | 1,748 | 10.0 |
| 58 Other retailers | 474,405 | 7.5 | 467,700 | −1.4 | 464,796 | −0.6 | 471,765 | 1.5 |
| 581 Drugs, toiletries | 82,855 | 9.8 | 85,181 | 2.8 | 86,342 | 1.4 | 90,845 | 5.2 |
| 582 Farm, garden supplies | 22,367 | 6.0 | 21,428 | −4.2 | 21,156 | −1.3 | 20,702 | −2.1 |
| 583 Fuel, gasoline | 75,045 | 6.2 | 74,470 | −0.8 | 73,540 | −1.2 | 72,807 | −1.0 |
| 584 Books, stationery | 78,427 | 8.2 | 78,186 | −0.3 | 76,903 | −1.6 | 76,730 | −0.2 |
| 585 Sports goods, toys, musical | 46,708 | 6.6 | 43,138 | −7.6 | 41,801 | −3.1 | 43,465 | 4.0 |
| 586 Cameras, photographic | 18,657 | 22.7 | 18,625 | −0.2 | 15,781 | −15.3 | 13,486 | −14.5 |
| 587 Watches, optical goods | 24,641 | −3.4 | 22,622 | −8.2 | 21,835 | −3.5 | 21,565 | −1.2 |
| 588 Second-hand stores | 5,158 | 4.0 | 5,014 | −2.8 | 5,903 | 17.7 | 6,428 | 8.9 |
| 589 Other | 120,547 | 7.6 | 119,036 | −1.3 | 121,535 | 2.1 | 125,737 | 3.5 |
| Totals | 1,721,465 | 2.9 | 1,628,644 | −5.4 | 1,607,401 | −1.3 | 1,591,186 | −1.0 |

Source: MITI (1984; 1986; 1989a; 1992b)

Table 3.10 provides a detailed breakdown of retail stores by merchandise type. The food and beverages sector was by far the largest, accounting for around 40 per cent of all stores. Fresh food retailers accounted for 8 per cent of the total in 1991, a higher proportion than found in most Western nations (MITI, 1989a: 69), meeting consumer demand for a large proportion of fresh produce (see Chapter 2).

The decline in store numbers between 1982 and 1991 was spread across most merchandise sectors, but the food sector saw the greatest fall as it has the most small stores. Over 90 per cent of dried foods, bakery, and rice and cereal retailers employ fewer than five people.

Stores in only eight of the thirty-two subcategories increased during the same period. Motor vehicle agents and second-hand stores grew by more than 20 per cent, but the largest increase was in the women's and children's apparel sector, which increased by almost 43 per cent, or by some 30,000 outlets. This was largely due to the expansion of fashion shopping centres and the booming economy of the 1980s.

Overall, while the decline in the very smallest stores is rapid, the number of surviving small stores is far larger. Small retailing is not yet a thing of the past. Rather there is a shift towards more corporate retail chains (see pages 92–6 below). There are more larger retail formats, but the Large Store Law (see Chapter 4) and demand for small convenient formats restrict their growth. Relaxation of restrictive legislation will mean more large outlets in the future, but small stores are still a major part of the retail environment. For this reason alone, Japanese distribution remains different from most Western systems. To understand how small outlets have survived and how the rest of the distribution system works to support them, it is necessary to consider other aspects of the system in more detail.

## DISTRIBUTION PROBLEMS IN JAPAN

### Multiple wholesale layers

Even in modern Japanese distribution, merchandise commonly passes through several wholesale stages between manufacturer and retailer. Because of this, wholesale turnover is almost four times that of retailing. Multiple wholesale levels make the distribution system complex, and are one of the reasons why consumer prices are so high – the more wholesale margins included, the higher the final retail price (Czinkota and Woronoff, 1986; 1991; Economist, 1981).

Table 3.11 shows details of wholesale transactions in 1988. A large proportion of wholesalers deal with other wholesalers in almost all product categories. Excluding general wholesalers, on average, 36 per cent of purchase transactions made by industrial wholesalers came from other wholesalers. The proportion was similar for consumer goods wholesalers (31 per cent). Overall 35 per cent of wholesale sales were to other wholesale firms.

There are other anomalies. Wholesalers of processed materials make almost 73 per cent of their purchases from other wholesalers. In addition, agricultural and marine products have the second longest distribution channels of all, with just under 49 per cent of both purchases and sales being through other wholesalers. Government protection of farmers and control of channels by large agricultural buying co-operatives are the causes of this, and it is the reason why food prices are particularly high.

MITI classifies wholesaling into primary, secondary and tertiary levels, and Figure 3.3 illustrates the complex relationship between them (Chūshō Kigyō Chō, 1989: 2). Primary wholesalers buy goods directly from manufacturers or overseas, and supply either end users or other wholesalers. They are usually large scale businesses, and most are located in the main commercial areas of Tokyo, Osaka and Nagoya, as well as in key regional centres such as Sapporo, Sendai, Hiroshima and Fukuoka. They deal mainly with larger manufacturers.

Secondary wholesalers buy products from other wholesale companies, and supply wholesalers at the next level of distribution. Tertiary wholesalers buy products from other wholesale companies, and supply retailers, industrial end users or overseas buyers. Secondary and tertiary wholesalers have fewer direct links with manufacturers and producers. Most are small or medium sized companies, and operate as regional businesses.

Most wholesalers operate at one of the three levels, but not all the time (Chūshō Kigyō Chō, 1989; Uno et al., 1988: 211). Larger primary wholesalers make transactions in all three roles, and secondary and tertiary wholesalers respectively purchase 17.1 per cent and 9.6 per cent of their merchandise directly from manufacturers. A wholesaler may act as a primary wholesaler when dealing in one product, but as a secondary wholesaler when dealing in another

Table 3.11 Wholesale suppliers and customers by merchandise product, 1988 (% of total sales)

| Wholesale sector | Suppliers (total = 100%) | | | | | Customers (total = 100%) | | | | | |
|---|---|---|---|---|---|---|---|---|---|---|---|
| | Manu-facturers | In-house purchase | Over-seas | In-house manu-facture | Other whole-saler | Retailers | In-house sale | Overseas | Industrial con-sumer | Other whole-saler | General con-sumers |
| 49 General merchandise wholesalers | 33.4 | 5.8 | 19.0 | 0.0 | 41.8 | 5.9 | 3.2 | 20.7 | 40.9 | 29.3 | 0.0 |
| 50 Materials and parts wholesalers | | | | | | | | | | | |
| 501 Textile products | 43.0 | 14.0 | 5.7 | 0.4 | 36.9 | 14.5 | 2.3 | 5.9 | 21.8 | 55.3 | 0.2 |
| 502 Chemicals and related products | 38.2 | 34.8 | 3.4 | 0.5 | 23.1 | 8.6 | 2.9 | 2.1 | 45.9 | 40.3 | 0.2 |
| 503 Metal and minerals | 25.2 | 37.6 | 5.3 | 0.2 | 31.7 | 19.5 | 5.3 | 4.1 | 36.1 | 34.3 | 0.7 |
| 504 Machinery and equipment | 34.8 | 46.4 | 2.1 | 0.3 | 16.4 | 21.7 | 8.3 | 11.2 | 32.8 | 24.9 | 1.1 |
| 505 Building supplies | 35.8 | 25.0 | 1.8 | 0.8 | 36.6 | 17.6 | 2.3 | 0.6 | 40.8 | 38.3 | 0.4 |
| 506 Recycled materials | 16.9 | 7.2 | 2.0 | 1.0 | 72.9 | 3.4 | 1.3 | 0.7 | 58.9 | 35.5 | 0.2 |
| 51 Finished goods wholesalers | | | | | | | | | | | |
| 511 Apparel and accessories | 45.3 | 16.0 | 2.5 | 1.5 | 34.7 | 58.8 | 11.0 | 1.0 | 3.7 | 25.0 | 0.5 |
| 512 Farm, livestock and products | 25.7 | 23.0 | 2.2 | 0.5 | 48.6 | 34.2 | 10.3 | 0.6 | 5.5 | 48.9 | 0.5 |
| 513 Food and beverages | 32.7 | 35.5 | 1.4 | 0.6 | 29.8 | 42.1 | 6.0 | 0.4 | 8.7 | 42.1 | 0.7 |
| 514 Drugs and toiletries | 34.7 | 47.7 | 1.7 | 0.3 | 15.6 | 28.9 | 6.2 | 0.4 | 24.8 | 39.4 | 0.3 |
| 515 Furniture and fittings | 45.0 | 26.9 | 1.6 | 1.1 | 25.4 | 42.1 | 5.0 | 3.2 | 15.0 | 33.5 | 1.2 |
| 516 Other wholesale | 37.9 | 22.9 | 3.8 | 0.7 | 34.7 | 30.1 | 6.8 | 2.1 | 23.9 | 36.2 | 0.9 |
| Total wholesale industry | 33.0 | 27.6 | 6.1 | 0.4 | 32.9 | 22.9 | 6.1 | 7.4 | 28.0 | 35.0 | 0.6 |

Source: MITI (1990a: 92)

product. This situation arises when one primary wholesaler has better links with the manufacturer of the product that another wholesaler wishes to purchase. Such a relationship acts in exclusion of other primary wholesalers. This type of exclusive dealing also forces large retailers to buy certain brands from particular whole-salers. Examples of manufacturers who operate exclusive wholesale networks include Matsushita and Canon in electronics, and Kao in toiletries (Ejiri, 1988: 17).

Figure 3.3 summarises the various layers of the distribution system. Under 31 per cent of primary wholesale turnover was direct to retailers, with over 33 per cent, the largest proportion, going to secondary and tertiary wholesale levels. Most of the remainder went to industrial consumers and overseas, and under 2 per cent was direct to consumers. Some goods also pass back to primary wholesalers from secondary and tertiary wholesalers, and other data suggest that approximately 0.5 per cent of retail sales also pass back to whole-salers and manufacturers (MITI, 1989a: 677).

The diagram only accounts for 84.7 per cent of turnover originating from tertiary wholesalers. The remaining 15 per cent goes to yet more wholesale layers, making four or even more levels in some instances (Chūshō Kigyō Chō, 1989: 3). The average number of steps between manufacturer and retailer is between 1.03 and 2.6 depending on product sector (Chūshō Kigyō Chō, 1990: 149). These multiple wholesale layers make the system complex.

On the other hand, some Japanese observers are keen to point out that distribution channels for imports are no longer than for domestic products (EPA, 1986; JETRO and MIPRO, 1985). They claim that multiple wholesale layers are necessary in the Japanese case (Ejiri, 1980; Maruyama, 1989; Maruyama et al., 1989), arguing that, as wholesale and retail companies are too small to provide compre-hensive services, the system relies on numerous small firms to provide complementary services and functions. As a suggestion of an ideal system, this ignores both the efficiency of large wholesalers, and the recent expansion and wider functions of larger retailers, but it does offer an explanation for multiple wholesale layers in the present system. Secondary layers of small wholesalers supply small, relatively isolated groups of retailers with a limited assortment of products and services. They allow small retailers to survive.

On the other hand, multiple layers are becoming less important because the situation is changing. Manufacturers encouraged this complexity in order to maintain control over distribution channels

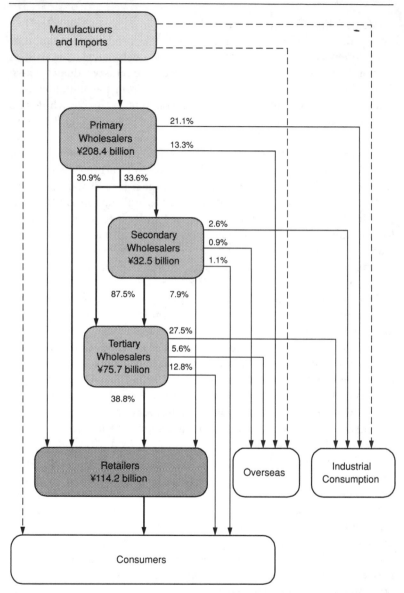

*Note*: Figures in the boxes represent total sales at each stage, percentages represent proportions of that figure to go to next stage, dotted lines indicate very small proportions

*Figure 3.3* Multi-layered distribution channels: percentage shares, 1986
*Source*: Adapted and translated from Chūshō Kigyō Chō (1989: 2)

and keep a distance between themselves and retailers. Now, as the buying power of retailers grows, in practical terms manufacturers can no longer avoid dealing directly with the largest chains.

Multiple wholesale channels still exist, but are becoming less common due to the increasing power of large retail companies. The one remaining role of multiple layers is to provide a wide ranging distribution network, and supply the thousands of surviving small retailers. As small retailers decline, so will the complex wholesale system.

## The power of manufacturers in the distribution channels

The success of the Japanese economy is largely due to strong, innovative and aggressive manufacturing companies (for details see Abegglen and Stalk, 1987; Clark, 1987; McMilan, 1984). Today, hundreds of Japanese companies are famous for successful export strategies, but they are equally dominant within the domestic economy and in distribution channels. Some manufacturers, notably those in the home electrical, cosmetics and automobile sectors, even developed their own chains of outlets known as retail *keiretsu*.

In Japanese, a *keiretsu* is a group of companies led by a single dominant firm. The word *keiretsu* is now familiar to scholars and businessmen in the West (Czinkota and Woronoff, 1986; 1991: 47–64), where the word first gained notice because companies within a *keiretsu* often have no formal connection, but co-operate as a single concern, sometimes like a cartel.

There are two main types: enterprise keiretsu (*kigyō keiretsu*) and distribution keiretsu (*ryūtsū keiretsu*). Enterprise keiretsu are a system of numerous small companies, supplying one large manufacturing company with parts and materials. The automobile and electronics industries are examples of this. Distribution keiretsu consist of numerous wholesale and retail outlets that sell the products of a single manufacturer on an exclusive or semi-exclusive basis.[10]

Distribution keiretsu were established in the early 1960s so that manufacturers could control their distribution channels. Through this system, they were able to dictate and monitor sales methods, marketing and promotion, customer service and even prices (JFTC, 1988; Niwa, 1988; Tajima, 1988). Member wholesalers and retailers receive wide ranging support, including regular supply of new models and products, temporary assistants from the manufacturer or wholesaler, display and promotional materials, and even full shop fronts and fittings. Keiretsu stores are also eligible for special loans, discounts, rebates and sales bonuses. Some store owners even receive a guaranteed monthly income. Keiretsu outlets rely on this support, allowing manufacturers to demand good or 'required' performance. The largest retail keiretsu are in the electrical, cosmetics and automobile sectors, with Matsushita, Toshiba, Hitachi, Shiseido, Kao, Toyota and Nissan all operating large chains. The Matsushita chain alone has around 15,000 retail outlets (Shiraishi and Sato, 1992).

Some authors claim that distribution keiretsu are 'Japanese' vertical marketing systems, and are an efficient way for manufacturers to supply a wide geographical area, while providing a high level of customer service (Ejiri, 1988: 70–9; Miwa, 1992: 189–92). On the other hand, the temptation for manufacturers to indulge in anti-competitive practices, notably price maintenance, is well known (Czinkota and Woronoff, 1986; Flath, 1989; Fujigane and Ennis, 1990; Imai, 1980; JFTC, 1988; Kawade, 1980; Nishimura, 1986; also see pages 85–7).

As with multiple wholesale layers, distribution keiretsu are gradually changing. Hitachi, for example, no longer refer to their store chain as a keiretsu due to the stigma now attached to the name (Fujigane and Ennis, 1990). In any case, maintaining adequate stocks in large chains of small stores is expensive and unnecessary with large retailers now providing a more effective sales route. Consequently, keiretsu chains have been significantly cut back in recent years (Fujigane and Ennis, 1990; Nihon Keizai Shinbun, 1990e; Shiraishi and Sato, 1992).

Manufacturers cannot afford to keep their products out of large chains just in order to avoid discounting (Kishi, 1989). This was not always the case. In 1964, Matsushita stopped all shipments to Daiei after the retailer sold Matsushita products at 20 per cent below the manufacturer's 'recommended' retail price. As of 1993, Matsushita still refuses to supply Daiei directly. Matsushita's National and Panasonic brands are sold in Daiei stores, but these products are supplied via an intermediary distributor – a dummy sales company set up by Matsushita (Shiraishi and Sato, 1992).

Retail price maintenance has been illegal in Japan since 1965, but manufacturers are still able to apply their recommended prices quite strictly. Technically, this is the manufacturer's 'desired retail price' (*kibō kouri kakaku*), but consumers and stores more commonly refer to it as the 'set price' (*teika*). Manufacturers usually print prices on packages.

This too is changing. Some department stores still adhere to set prices, buying their merchandise through the traditional manufacturer–wholesaler system rather than direct from producers, and most smaller retailers do not have the buying power to make demands of the still powerful manufacturers. Other larger retail chain companies, however, insist on controlling their own pricing (Nikkei Ryūtsū Shinbun, 1992: 33–4). Again, the increased power of the major retailers is changing the distribution system.

## Anti-competitive business practices and customs

Over the decades, manufacturers came to provide various services to retailers in order to maintain control over channels. Many of these services are now expected by retailers and wholesalers to the point that they are often referred to as business customs (*shōkankō*). Without this help, many small retailers could not continue in business (Itozono, 1988). On the other hand, these business customs also reduce the level of competition.

Most customs originate with manufacturers and are passed down the distribution channel via wholesalers. Small retailers and wholesalers receive support in various forms including:

• long credit periods for payment on goods
• financial help for expansion
• financial help during slump periods
• marketing advice and promotional materials
• liberal rights to return unsold goods
• performance-related incentives and bonuses.

English sources have already described these customs and practices in some detail.[11] Now, due both to criticism from overseas and to advances within retailing, they are becoming less important.

As noted above, distribution businesses provide each other with mutual support in order to survive. This support is based on strong personal relationships between individual managers, and it means that, even in times of crisis, companies may prefer to stay with a known supplier rather than find new ones. Business relationships may take precedence over purely economic considerations of profit or loss. When looking for new merchandise, a company may ask for an introduction from an existing supplier rather than make an approach itself. For example, recently a retailer cancelled an order I had placed three months earlier, because the company's existing supplier could not obtain the goods. The retailer refused to look for a different supplier, preferring to lose the order instead.

In one survey, suppliers claimed that rebates and discounts were objective rewards for good performance such as high sales volume, but the personal discretion of managers is often more important than economic performance and other objective guidelines (Shimaguchi, 1977: 86–7). Manufacturers and wholesalers offer such discounts, rebates and loans as a means to maintain control over channel members. While small retailers claim that these are all that stand between their survival and bankruptcy, these incentives are rarely seen by consumers in terms of lower prices.[12] Distribution control rather than marketing promotion or competition is the primary motivation.

Some distribution business practices are of more direct benefit to consumers, but even these invariably provide an improved level of service rather than reduction in price.

For example, manufacturers and wholesalers commonly send loan shop assistants, called *hakken ten'in*, to smaller businesses further down the channel (EPA, 1986: 34–5). The suppliers pay for these loan assistants. They are common in various large store departments, selling foods, cosmetics, jewellery and kimonos. Theoretically, such assistants have specialised knowledge of the merchandise. They are highly motivated, and contribute directly to the sales performance of suppliers as well as the retailer. The retailer reduces staffing costs, but in a large, mixed merchandise store these assistants can be overly biased towards their own goods. Retailers can come to rely on this service, leaving their own employees with insufficient product knowledge or experience. Such reliance on these assistants may also make retailers dependent on a single supplier, reducing the range and variety of goods that it handles (Shimaguchi, 1977: 57–8, 93–5).

For department stores, loan assistants usually work in only a small section and affect only a small part of the sales space and merchandise. They come from various different suppliers and compete with each other in the store. In the past, in smaller speciality stores such as electrical stores, loan assistants came from only one supplier and there was little competition. Manufacturers could control the store by providing the most knowledgeable shop assistants. The Japan Fair Trade Commission introduced guidelines to reduce use of loan assistants in small stores in 1991 as a result.

Another practice allows free return of unsold merchandise. This is sometimes in the form of consignment sales, whereby the retailer only pays for goods that sell, but also sometimes means that retailers can return goods they have already taken possession of. Where this operates, consumers can also return goods for almost any reason they wish. All department stores offer this service. Retailers return goods to wholesalers, and, in turn, wholesalers to manufacturers. Suppliers resell these goods in other areas of Japan, release them into the discount market or possibly recycle or destroy them. The consumer pays for a liberal return privilege through higher overall prices.

Again, by accepting the return of unsold goods, manufacturers discourage discounts on unsold merchandise, and maintain prices. As this practice is so widespread, suppliers also offer financial incentives for not returning goods (Shimaguchi, 1977: 52–3, 114–15). This has led to electrical retailers, for example, buying in bulk to gain volume discounts and rebates, and then, knowing that they cannot sell such volumes themselves, immediately releasing excess stock to discount chains. Manufacturers dislike this, but these retailers are now too large to be cut from the channel.

### Retailers dismantling unfair business practices

The kind of business practices which control prices and restrict supply are illegal under the Japanese anti-monopoly law. On the other hand, the Japanese Fair Trade Commission (JFTC: *Kōsei Torihiki Iinkai*) has little political power because, behind the scenes, any activity which restricts Japanese business is seen as bad for the economy (Economist 1989f; Imogawa, 1992). Occasionally, the JFTC makes an example of a company that draws complaints, but this is relatively rare (see Flath, 1989; Hanada, 1985; Kobayashi, 1988; Watanabe and Suzuki, 1988).

This situation is changing, albeit slowly. Since the 1989 SII trade talks, the JFTC has introduced various guidelines to control and reduce some of the most restrictive distribution business practices (Nikkei Ryūtsū Shinbun, 1991: 11–13; 1992: 72–5). They have succeeded in reducing loan assistants and 'sale-or-return' agreements. The Commission is now studying ways to remove or simplify rebate and discount systems.

In addition to the efforts of the JFTC, these practices are being changed by developments within the distribution system itself. Originally these customs were a means of support for small retailers while protecting the interests of manufacturers (Czinkota and Woronoff, 1986: 86; Shimaguchi, 1977: 115), but today it is the larger retailers and wholesalers who demand the highest discounts and rebates (Ejiri, 1985; Matsuzaka, 1993a; Nikkei Ryūtsū Shinbun, 1990b). Neither manufacturers nor small retailers like this situation, and they have begun to dismantle the old systems.

In 1993 there were two significant cases of retail chains fighting large manufacturers' control over channels.

The first case concerned Aoyama Shoji, a successful men's clothing retailer (see Chapter 5). The company bought most of its supply of suits from the top manufacturer, Onward Kashiyama, who also supplies major department stores. Aoyama's marketing strategy included opening stores in exclusive fashion areas such as Ginza and Shibuya in Tokyo, and, in the opening promotion, selling suits for as little as ¥1,000 apiece. Not only that, Aoyama also claimed that their suits only differed from those sold in department stores by price and by the brand label. This upset both Onward Kashiyama and department stores and the manufacturer now refuses to supply Aoyama (Sato, 1993; Yamanaka, 1993).

The second case was Kawachiya, a small cosmetics retailer. Kawachiya began discounting products from Shiseido, the top cosmetics manufacturer, in 1993. Shiseido immediately stopped supplying the store, and other big manufacturers, Kao and Kanebo, then did the same (Economist, 1993; Holyoke, 1993). Kawachiya complained to the JFTC, and with discounting currently popular, the incident received a lot of publicity. At present the case is awaiting judgement from the JFTC (Matsuzaka, 1993b; 1993c). The store is still selling Shiseido merchandise at a discount, but buying stocks from independent suppliers.

Many unusual and undesirable business practices continue to exist in Japanese distribution. As these final two examples illustrate, however, one factor is changing the internal structure of the industry more than any other. That is the increasing willingness of larger retail companies to determine their own strategies.

## AREAS OF DISTRIBUTION CHANGE

While the number of wholesale and retail outlets is declining, the number of incorporated businesses and the size of these businesses are increasing. Census data still put emphasis on outlets rather than businesses due to the large total number of stores, but, combined with other data, it is easy to see the growing importance of larger businesses. In addition, retailers are taking a more prominent role within distribution channels, and wholesalers are changing in order to compete and survive. This section looks at general aspects of these changes. It also briefly introduces non-store retailing as an additional aspect of the system.

### New wholesale sector functions

The function of wholesalers is changing in response to advances in the retail sector. With the exception of the largest wholesale businesses, the intermediary function of wholesalers is declining. The number of wholesale outlets remains high, but they are operated by a smaller number of increasingly large companies. In addition, many wholesalers are beginning to focus on physical distribution skills rather than traditional wholesale buying and selling.

Greater competition in distribution has pushed larger wholesalers towards rationalisation. In particular, the largest wholesalers are attempting to control regional markets. Table 3.12 shows the top wholesalers by turnover in 1992–3. In the late 1980s, the top three food wholesalers, Kokubu, Ryōshoku and Meidiya, were all involved in takeover activity, and all three were looking to improve services to regional areas – previously a function of smaller, secondary intermediaries (Nihon Keizai Shinbun, 1990d; *Nikkei Ryūtsū Shinbun*, 1989a: 17–18). Large wholesalers compete with manufacturers and retailers who wish to dictate and control the wholesale stage of the distribution channel. They need both physical size and technical ability in order to survive.

In addition, manufacturers and retailers remain reluctant to vertically integrate and take over physical distribution functions. Physical distribution is difficult and costly due to the high cost of land and a poor transport infrastructure. Large retailers are keen to reduce physical distribution costs, and all the top companies are involved directly in physical distribution to some degree. But with wholesalers operating existing networks and facilities, most retailers prefer to use these rather than incur the expense of developing their own facilities.

This provides many medium wholesalers with the opportunity to survive by offering specialised services, but it also means they can no longer rely on special relationships with retailers to win contracts. Rather they must provide cost performance (Chūshō Kigyō Chō, 1992a: 3–4). The skills and services they offer are a result of both experience and technological investment.

For example, small wholesalers have always provided small

Table 3.12 Leading wholesale companies in 1992–93

| Company | Merchandise sector | Sales (¥ million) | % change 93/4 | Pre-tax operating profit (¥ million) | % change 93/4 | % profit margin |
|---|---|---|---|---|---|---|
| 1 Kokubu | Foods | 756,661 | 3.5 | 3,659 | 0.8 | 0.00 |
| 2 Tohan | Books and CDs | 672,224 | 5.2 | 6,453 | -9.7 | 0.01 |
| 3 Nihon Shuppan Hanbai | Books and CDs | 639,727 | 5.7 | 1,401 | -49.3 | 0.00 |
| 4 Suzuken | Pharmaceuticals | 507,281 | 13.1 | 16,368 | 41.0 | 0.03 |
| 5 Nintendo[a] | Toys | 503,510 | n.a. | 156,247 | n.a. | 0.31 |
| 6 Ryōshoku | Foods | 496,589 | 9.5 | 3,713 | 68.8 | 0.00 |
| 7 Meidiya | Foods | 460,316 | 0.3 | 1,092 | -36.3 | 0.00 |
| 8 Nihonshi Pulp Shoji[a] | Paper | 377,271 | n.a. | 3,820 | n.a. | 0.01 |
| 9 Nihon Shurui Hanbai | Liquor | 302,055 | -1.7 | 3,854 | -7.5 | 0.01 |
| 10 Matsushita Suzuki | Foods | 270,531 | 5.6 | 2,430 | 14.1 | 0.01 |
| 11 Kuraya Yakuhin | Pharmaceuticals | 263,938 | 10.5 | 4,449 | 23.0 | 0.01 |
| 12 Koami | Liquor | 261,787 | -1.5 | n.a. | n.a. | n.a |
| 13 Onaga Shi Tsusho[a] | Paper | 257,045 | n.a. | 610 | n.a. | 0.00 |
| 14 Katō Sangyō | Foods | 235,564 | 7.7 | 4,213 | 15.8 | 0.02 |
| 15 Sanseido | Pharmaceuticals | 228,181 | 8.1 | 6,292 | 6.2 | 0.03 |
| 16 Renown[a] | Apparel | 221,418 | n.a. | -8,224 | n.a. | n.a |
| 17 Sanmikku Tsusho[a] | Paper | 213,317 | n.a. | 681 | n.a. | 0.00 |
| 18 Sega Enterprises[a] | Toys | 212,090 | n.a. | 33,484 | n.a. | 0.16 |
| 19 Takisada | Fabrics | 199,935 | -4.3 | 6,203 | -32.0 | 0.04 |
| 20 Onward Kashiyama | Apparel |  | -6.2 | 16,879 | -29.3 | 0.11 |

a Figures for 1992–3 not available, 1991–2 figures used.

Source: Compiled from Nikkei Ryūtsū Shinbun (1992: 338–67; 1993d: 299–328)

retailers with frequent, small-volume deliveries at short notice – maybe a single carton delivered immediately after a phone call (Shimaguchi, 1977: 54). In this way, wholesalers acted as back-room inventory space for small retailers.

Modern, large retailers require this kind of service as the basis of just-in-time delivery systems (Ito, 1987). The best example is the convenience store business (see Chapter 5) which employs controlled, frequent delivery of perishable goods in small units to keep store inventory at an optimal minimum at all times. Such systems are retailer controlled, and based on centralised distribution facilities, but most chains also employ independent regional suppliers for a proportion of their perishable items.

Between 1989 and 1990, the overall number of frequent, small-unit deliveries increased (Aruta, 1988; Chūshō Kigyō Chō, 1992a: 4–5; MITI, 1989a: 27; Sasaki, 1988). More precisely:

- deliveries of non-perishable household items from small wholesalers increased from 3 to 3.3 times a week
- the proportion of items delivered six times a week or more rose from 14.9 per cent to 20.2 per cent
- average lead time between receiving the order and making the delivery decreased from 28.2 hours to 25.8 hours
- the number of deliveries of one case or less increased from 63.4 per cent to 68.4 per cent of all deliveries
- small processed-food wholesalers delivered up to four times a day, with as little as fifteen minutes' allowance in the delivery schedule laid down by the retailer before incurring penalties.

Large retailers pushed small and medium wholesalers to make these changes. This, however, is not always easy to do. Small companies cannot afford the necessary level of investment. For example, Katō Sangyō, only the fourteenth largest wholesaler, invested ¥2,300 million in new facilities in 1990 alone (Nikkei Ryūtsū Shinbun, 1992). To match this kind of investment, groups of smaller companies, including wholesalers, trucking companies and packaging companies, are developing joint facilities. In one example (Chūshō Kigyō Chō, 1992a: 12–15), fifty-four companies operate a jointly built and funded central distribution centre, sharing the cost and labour of arranging orders, sorting and labelling products and delivery to stores. Use of the centre increased average loads in delivery vehicles from 30 per cent to over 80 per cent capacity in the first year.

In this way, small wholesalers co-operate to survive. Standardisation of systems is also improving, with significant efforts to standardise pallett, container and truck sizes and specifications, as well as racks, conveyors, automatic sorting machinery and so on (see Chūshō Kigyō Chō, 1992a). In addition, a long overdue standardisation of paperwork, logistics codes, product codes, and various data formats is also taking place.

The other major form of rationalisation within the wholesale sector is the widespread introduction of information systems. Even the smallest distributors are investing in computers. In 1985, over 45 per cent of all computers used in Japanese business were employed in wholesaling and retailing (MITI, 1989a: 44).

In the mid-1970s wholesalers developed electronic ordering systems (EOS), beginning simply by leasing terminals to individual retailers. This increased order speed, but was inefficient as orders were still taken from each individual store. Following privatisation of the telephone system in 1985, companies set up 'value added networks' (VANs). With forty networks in operation by 1992, medium and small wholesalers rely increasingly on regional VANs (Chūshō Kigyō Chō, 1992a: 89). Large wholesalers use their own dedicated systems.

VANs allow orders from numerous retail outlets to be processed centrally, with consolidated orders then being sent to appropriate wholesale outlets within the network. Today regional VANs can handle data for several hundred wholesale and retail outlets, including outlets of various sizes and for various merchandise types. These systems make taking and filling orders both faster and more accurate.

In Japan the sheer number of outlets makes distribution especially complex. Information systems help to reduce this complexity, and the number of companies using such networks is growing monthly. Even the smallest wholesalers recognise the need to participate in this development. It is often the only way to remain competitive in a system that places ever greater emphasis on speed and efficiency.

## Changes in the type and number of retail businesses

The Census employs general definitions of retail formats based on store size and sales technique (Table 3.13).[13] Table 3.14 uses these definitions to show the number of stores in each format. It again illustrates the large number of small-format stores. Larger outlets, including general merchandise superstores and department stores,

Table 3.13 Definitions of retail business formats used in the census of commerce: proportion of sales by merchandise

| Store format | Apparel | Food | Household | Number of employees | Sales space (sq m) | Self-service | Business hours/day | Other points |
|---|---|---|---|---|---|---|---|---|
| **1.0 Department stores** | | | | | | | | |
| 1.1 Large stores | 10%~70% | 10%~70% | 10%~70% | Over 50 | Over 1,500[a] | no | | |
| 1.2 Others | 10%~70% | 10%~70% | 10%~70% | Over 50 | Under 1,500[a] | no | | |
| **2.0 General superstores** | | | | | | | | |
| 2.1 Large stores | 10%~70% | 10%~70% | 10%~70% | Over 50 | Over 1,500[a] | yes | | |
| 2.2 Medium stores | 10%~70% | 10%~70% | 10%~70% | Over 50 | Under 1,500[a] | yes | | |
| **3.0 Other general stores** | Under 50% | Under 50% | Under 50% | Under 50 | | yes | Under 12[b] | |
| **4.0 Large speciality stores** | | | | | | | | |
| 4.1 Apparel superstores | Over 70% | | | | Over 500 | yes | | |
| 4.2 Food superstores | | Over 70% | | | Over 500 | yes | | |
| 4.3 Household superstores | | | Over 70% | | Over 500 | yes | | |
| **5.0 Convenience stores** | | | | | | | | |
| 5.1 Specific CVS | | | | | 50~500 | yes | Over 12[c] | |
| **6.0 Other large stores** | | | | | | yes | | Not included in 1 to 5 |
| **7.0 Speciality stores** | | | | | | | | |
| 7.1 Apparel stores | Over 90% | | | | | no | | |
| 7.2 Food stores | | Over 90% | | | | no | | |
| 7.3 Household stores | | | Over 90% | | | no | | |
| **8.0 General retailers** | | | | | | | | |
| 8.1 General | Under 50% | Under 50% | Under 50% | Under 50 | | no | | |
| 8.2 Apparel | Over 50% | | | Under 50 | | no | | |
| 8.3 Foods | | Over 50% | | Under 50 | | no | | |
| 8.4 Household | | | Over 50% | Under 50 | | no | | |
| **9.0 Other retailers** | | | | | | | | Not included in 1 to 8 |

[a] 3,000 sq.m. in large cities; [b] or closing before 9 pm; [c] or closing after 9 pm
Source: MITI (1992a: 6)

Table 3.14 Number of retail stores by retail type, 1988–91

| Type of store | Outlets | % change 91/88 | Employees | % change 91/88 | Sales (¥ million) | % change 91/88 | Sales space (sq m) | % change 91/88 |
|---|---|---|---|---|---|---|---|---|
| Department stores | 455 | 5.1 | 207,275 | 7.3 | 11,414,025 | 25.9 | 6,834,119 | 11.2 |
| Large stores | 426 | 4.7 | 203,292 | 6.5 | 11,220,583 | 24.8 | 6,819,625 | 11.4 |
| Others | 29 | 11.5 | 3,983 | 77.3 | 193,442 | 179.2 | 17,464 | -25.0 |
| General superstores | 1,549 | 4.8 | 220,138 | 9.8 | 8,159,582 | 22.9 | 9,172,447 | 12.5 |
| Large stores | 1,404 | 7.8 | 208,603 | 11.5 | 7,812,705 | 25.1 | 8,905,478 | 13.8 |
| Medium stores | 145 | -17.6 | 11,535 | -14.9 | 346,876 | -11.1 | 266,969 | -18.1 |
| Others | 375 | 0.5 | 3,566 | -6.7 | 117,378 | 5.4 | 148,286 | -2.1 |
| Speciality superstores | 7,130 | 11.5 | 261,006 | 8.7 | 8,002,595 | 25.2 | 7,776,850 | 17.9 |
| Apparel superstores | 618 | 8.2 | 15,475 | -2.4 | 482,429 | 12.6 | 907,644 | 12.1 |
| Food superstores | 5,185 | 6.3 | 210,398 | 4.9 | 6,182,350 | 19.4 | 5,078,679 | 9.8 |
| Household superstores | 1,327 | 39.8 | 35,133 | 48.6 | 1,337,816 | 69.7 | 1,790,527 | 54.3 |
| Convenience stores | 41,847 | 21.1 | 355,529 | 16.3 | 6,984,858 | 39.3 | 5,643,016 | 23.7 |
| Specific CVS | 31,305 | 26.2 | 286,070 | 18.3 | 5,461,996 | 44.3 | 4,132,592 | 27.8 |
| Other superstores | 67,473 | 25.3 | 403,945 | 9.8 | 9,666,270 | 24.5 | 9,014,319 | 16.8 |
| Speciality stores | 1,000,166 | -0.8 | 3,814,613 | 1.2 | 64,607,844 | 24.5 | 43,292,737 | 6.2 |
| Apparel | 154,656 | 2.2 | 463,648 | 2.3 | 7,679,223 | 24.0 | 8,680,292 | 12.1 |
| Foods | 283,570 | -3.3 | 951,457 | -3.5 | 10,337,361 | 11.0 | 8,483,884 | 2.8 |
| Household | 561,940 | -0.2 | 2,399,508 | 2.9 | 46,591,260 | 28.1 | 26,128,561 | 5.5 |
| General retailers | 470,289 | -8.4 | 1,659,426 | -5.9 | 31,450,539 | 13.0 | 27,859,698 | -0.1 |
| Miscellaneous goods | 1,890 | 13.7 | 8,108 | 15.6 | 194,023 | 29.6 | 180,460 | 9.6 |
| Apparel | 76,903 | -2.2 | 287,521 | -4.0 | 5,782,976 | 15.0 | 6,947,543 | 0.0 |
| Foods | 224,756 | -11.3 | 693,981 | -8.3 | 10,540,683 | 10.1 | 10,080,359 | -4.2 |
| Household | 166,740 | -7.2 | 669,816 | -4.3 | 14,932,857 | 14.2 | 10,651,336 | 2.9 |
| Other retailers | 1,939 | 21.7 | 11,028 | 54.4 | 235,014 | 71.1 | 160,025 | 61.1 |
| Total | 1,591,223 | | 6,936,526 | | 140,638,105 | | 109,901,497 | |

Source: Calculated from MITI (1984; 1986; 1989a; 1992b)

accounted for less than 10 per cent of the total in 1991. The largest proportion of stores, 62 per cent, were speciality stores, followed by general retailers (30 per cent). Similarly, speciality stores generated over 45 per cent of sales, and general retailers over 33 per cent. Department stores, despite their small number, had an 8.1 per cent share in the same year. Large superstores, speciality supermarkets and convenience stores, accounted for roughly 5 per cent each.

There were 1.3 million businesses operating retail stores in 1991. The overall number declined between 1982 and 1991 (see Table 3.15), but the gross decrease was far greater in the unincorporated business sector, with incorporated businesses actually increasing in number. In 1982 there were some 1.2 million unincorporated retail businesses, but this figure fell 19 per cent to a little under 1 million by 1991. The number of incorporated businesses increased 17 per cent from 248,000 to 291,000.

Table 3.15 Numbers of new stores and store closures, 1979–91

|  | 1979–82 | 1982–5 | 1985–8 | 1988–91 |
|---|---|---|---|---|
| (A) **New stores** | 209,518 | 155,223 | 156,727 | 172,132 |
| In incorporated businesses | 66,535 | 59,852 | 70,065 | 91,098 |
| In unincorporated businesses | 142,983 | 95,371 | 86,662 | 81,034 |
| (B) **Store closures** | 167,642 | 249,135 | 168,393 | 200,764 |
| In incorporated businesses | 13,572 | 46,647 | 16,380 | 30,222 |
| In unincorporated businesses | 154,070 | 202,488 | 152,013 | 170,542 |
| (C) **Unknown** | 5,922 | 1,101 | 2,764 | 93 |
| In incorporated businesses | 1,886 | 292 | 724 | 38 |
| In unincorporated businesses | 4,036 | 809 | 2,040 | 55 |
| **Total change** (A – B + C) | 47,798 | –92,811 | –8,902 | –28,539 |

Source: Calculated from MITI (1984; 1986; 1989a; 1992b)

As in the wholesale sector, there are significant differences between retail outlets in incorporated businesses and those in unincorporated businesses. Unincorporated businesses operated about 65 per cent of outlets in 1991, with 61 per cent being single-store businesses. Incorporated businesses, however, account for over 60 per cent of employees and sales space. The 35 per cent of outlets that operate in incorporated businesses also account for some 82 per cent of sales.

Shimaguchi (1993) suggests that retailing has a dual structure, with a large number of small, inefficient independent stores on the one hand, and a small number of efficient, technically advanced multiple retail businesses on the other. These large companies are changing the industry as a whole, and most of the remainder of this book describes their activities.

There are a number of universal trends that do not fit into discussion of any one of the main retail formats. These include the introduction of information technology in retailing in line with the same activity in the wholesale industry, and the additional topic of non-store retailing.

### Information technology in retailing

The introduction of information technology, especially electronic ordering systems and point-of-sale (*POS* in Japanese) information systems, has been rapid and wideranging (Asano, 1989; 1993). Table 3.16 shows the rise in the number of point-of-sale terminals and the number of stores using this technology.

*Table 3.16* Introduction of bar codes and POS information systems

|  | Manufacturers using allocated bar codes | Retail stores with POS terminals | Number of POS terminals |
|---|---|---|---|
| 1979 | 27 | 1 | 3 |
| 1980 | 53 | 2 | 17 |
| 1981 | 86 | 25 | 154 |
| 1982 | 217 | 91 | 406 |
| 1983 | 1,744 | 1,909 | 4,740 |
| 1984 | 5,231 | 2,725 | 7,255 |
| 1985 | 11,016 | 4,212 | 12,196 |
| 1986 | 19,250 | 7,930 | 29,706 |
| 1987 | 26,440 | 11,711 | 40,691 |
| 1988 | 32,537 | 21,348 | 63,981 |
| 1989 | 38,449 | 42,880 | 119,137 |
| 1990 | 44,723 | 70,061 | 183,497 |
| 1991 | 50,560 | 92,461 | 245,254 |
| 1992 | 66,345 | 122,141 | 311,405 |
| 1993 | 68,854 | 149,638 | 374,864 |

*Source*: Figures courtesy of the Japan Distribution Code Center

In 1979 there were only twenty-seven manufacturers using product codes and only one store with a Japan Article Number (JAN) POS system. By 1993, almost 150,000 stores had these systems, with just under 375,000 POS terminals in use. In addition, 69,000 manufacturers had registered article number codes.

Large retailers have used these systems to rationalise their overall operations. Convenience store chains rely on POS data and Electronic Ordering Systems (EOS) to control just-in-time delivery, and maintain low in-store inventory. POS data are also used to adjust merchandise mix in order to keep product turnaround high (see Chapter 5). Large retail stores use the same systems to control their large, diverse inventories and to maintain close links with suppliers. The same systems allow the overall improvement in the speed and efficiency of distribution (Asano, 1993).

From the retail point of view, information systems gave multiple retail companies the opportunity to take control over merchandise policy. Through POS data, large retailers know what is being sold and where. They can decide the best type and the most suitable volume of merchandise and use this information to negotiate with manufacturers. In addition to the competitive size of these companies, multiple retailers have gained new strength and control within distribution channels as a result of information systems.

Table 3.17 shows the penetration of POS scanning terminals by store type. Taking definitions of store types introduced in Table 3.13, roughly half of all convenience stores use POS scanning terminals, where they are essential for daily operation. Other than this, the highest penetration rates are in large-store retail businesses such as department stores, general merchandise stores and supermarkets. More speciality stores operate POS terminals than any other sector, but, because of the large number of speciality stores (see Table 3.14), the rate of penetration is not high. Table 3.17 shows that the number of terminals per store is static for this store type, as the increasing number of terminals in use is spread over a larger number of speciality stores every year. The same is true for general retailers.

In addition to overseas computer companies such as NCR and IBM, all of the largest Japanese computer manufacturers are involved in developing information systems for the distribution market. Some of the hardware is very advanced. The leading convenience store chain, Seven-Eleven, uses hand-held scanners and portable, graphic ordering terminals for stock control and ordering. Ito-Yokado, the Seven-Eleven parent company, has linked its store chain into a single ISDN (integrated services digital network) real-time data transfer network, which the company claims is the largest in the world. This

Table 3.17 Number of POS terminals and number of stores using POS by store type

| | 1991 | | | 1992 | | | 1993 | | |
|---|---|---|---|---|---|---|---|---|---|
| | POS terminals | Stores using POS | Terminals per store | POS terminals | Stores using POS | Terminals per store | POS terminals | Stores using POS | Terminals per store |
| Department stores | 2,898 | 180 | 16.1 | 4,176 | 238 | 17.5 | 6,908 | 291 | 23.7 |
| General merchandise stores | 57,211 | 4,175 | 13.7 | 67,834 | 5,388 | 12.6 | 75,953 | 6,174 | 12.3 |
| Supermarkets | 60,678 | 16,290 | 3.7 | 72,348 | 19,965 | 3.6 | 83,193 | 23,309 | 3.6 |
| Convenience stores | 34,714 | 20,110 | 1.7 | 41,089 | 23,993 | 1.7 | 48,537 | 27,927 | 1.7 |
| Agricultural co-op stores | 3,861 | 1,045 | 3.7 | 4,464 | 1,249 | 3.6 | 5,037 | 1,444 | 3.5 |
| Co-operative society stores | 8,354 | 1,440 | 5.8 | 10,461 | 1,794 | 5.8 | 11,269 | 2,041 | 5.5 |
| Shopping centres | 2,399 | 634 | 3.8 | 3,124 | 720 | 4.3 | 3,735 | 788 | 4.7 |
| Home centres | 1,773 | 368 | 4.8 | 3,269 | 746 | 4.4 | 5,236 | 1,103 | 4.7 |
| Speciality stores | 52,095 | 39,209 | 1.3 | 66,220 | 50,831 | 1.3 | 79,721 | 60,224 | 1.3 |
| General retail stores | 3,701 | 2,544 | 1.5 | 4,367 | 3,099 | 1.4 | 5,959 | 4,149 | 1.4 |
| Other stores | 17,570 | 6,466 | 2.7 | 23,155 | 9,843 | 2.4 | 27,553 | 13,501 | 2.0 |
| Total | 245,254 | 92,461 | 2.7 | 300,507 | 117,866 | 2.5 | 353,101 | 140,951 | 2.5 |

Source: Figures courtesy of the Japan Distribution Code Centre

gives head office access to stock and sales information for every store in the chain at any time.

Because of the enthusiastic and widespread use of bar codes, there is already a shortage of bar code numbers to allocate to products (*Asahi Shinbun*, 1991). The International Article Numbering Association allocated not one but two country codes to Japan (*Tokyo Shinbun*, 1991), which allows up to 200,000 companies to register products for codes. This will come into effect when the number of registered manufacturers that use bar codes exceeds 70,000, which will almost certainly occur in 1994. Each company can register up to 100,000 product types; but, with the vast range of seasonal products as well as normal lines (see Chapter 2 on gift giving), some confectionery and cosmetics companies have already exceeded this limit. The Japan Distribution Code Center is now working on various ideas to alleviate this problem, including two-dimensional bar codes in order to allow more available numbers (Seki, 1993).

This form of innovation will be a major driving force in the distribution system over coming years. Most importantly, the increase in the use of information technology is led largely by the retail business, giving large retailers ever increasing strength within distribution channels.

### The expansion of non-store retailing

Non-store retailing is a separate but important part of the distribution system. It is important in three ways. First, it is a growing sector. Second, it has several minor but unusual characteristics that relate to Japanese culture and the existing distribution system. Third, non-store retailing also uses advanced information technology, and will continue to expand the use of new distribution techniques.

Non-store retailing takes three main forms: direct sales including door-to-door and catalogue sales, automatic vending machines, and home buying clubs. In total, they accounted for 21.6 per cent of retail sales in 1991. Of this 12 per cent arose from direct door-to-door sales, 1.5 per cent from catalogue sales, 1 per cent from vending machines and 7.1 per cent from buying clubs.

Home buying clubs are mostly groups of housewives who club together to purchase groceries in bulk. This is a system run by all the regional consumer co-operative societies, some of which do not operate retail outlets at all.

Catalogues are especially popular due to the demand for convenience shopping (see Chapter 2). The increasing number of women returning to the work force have less time to shop in stores, and many turn to catalogues (Otomo, 1993). Young men also like to shop by catalogue (*Nikkei Trendy*, 1993b). Young women enjoy catalogue shopping as a simple form of leisure. In recent years, catalogue companies have made efforts to improve the speed and accuracy of delivery services and provide fast, friendly after-sales back-up. Consumers trust catalogue shopping more and more as a result. The catalogue sales business has been helped by the increase and improvement in fast delivery services and the increase in the number of consumer data bases, for example from credit cards.

Door-to-door and home party sales are common, but not growing as quickly as catalogue sales. They are aimed at the non-working housewife, and sell various items including household goods such as cleaning materials, cosmetics (see Traeger, 1982) and toiletries. More recent developments are an increase in television and telephone marketing (Hulme, 1993). Most local stations include a couple of hours of television sales every day, usually interleaved between programmes.

The vending machine business accounts for only 1 per cent of retail sales, but it is an interesting and innovative part of the retail environment. A low crime rate and low incidence of vandalism mean that vending machines are almost as safe and reliable as shops. There are vending machines everywhere, and they sell an amazing range of products. The most common are canned drinks and cigarettes, but Japanese vending machines go much further, selling alcohol, bouquets of fresh flowers, 10 kg bags of rice, soft pornography, vegetables, diamond jewellery, underwear and even cuts of beef! The machines are very sophisticated. By law, alcoholic beverage machines should shut down at 11 pm, for example. Coca Cola Japan has experimented with on-line machines which tell the supplier the level of stock, and allow electronic advertising to be piped to the machine over the same lines. These are good examples of new technology and Japanese retail culture creating unusual innovations.

The main future growth in non-store retailing will be in catalogue sales. The largest companies, including Cecile, Mutō and Senshukai, are now well established and continue to grow every year. Most of the largest retail companies, notably Takashimaya, Mitsukoshi, Saison Group and Daiei Group, all have successful and growing catalogue sales divisions too.

## RETAILING AND DISTRIBUTION IN THE YEAR 2000: SOME HINTS

The decline in the number of the very smallest wholesale and retail outlets will continue well into the future. The falls in the 1980s were cushioned within a very large number of stores overall and a relatively high replacement rate. Small, independent businesses will find it increasingly difficult to compete. Many will retire, and increases in the number of incorporated businesses will bring even more pressure.

Shortly before the publication of the 1991 Census, the Commercial System Research Center (Ryūtsū Sābisu Shinbun, 1993) estimated that the number of outlets will fall by over 300,000 during the 1990s. The Center believes that the decline will continue among small stores employing fewer than five full-time employees. If this prediction is correct, these small stores will fall by a further 10 per cent to under 70 per cent of the total in less than ten years.

The report also suggested stores employing between five and forty-nine employees will expand by over 90,000 outlets. This means new physically small outlets such as speciality stores and convenience stores, as well as new large-format stores. Depending on the state of the Japanese economy, the relaxation of the Large Store Law will also allow larger stores to quickly increase in number.

With the decline in the number of small retailers, the number of wholesale outlets is also likely to decline. The economic recession of the early 1990s is hurting many small wholesale companies. Growth in large retailing also reduces the need for the smallest wholesalers to remain in business.

On the other hand, large numbers of small wholesalers will continue to do business for the reasons outlined in this chapter. To survive, they will need the foresight and the financial strength to change their operations in line with demands from the new channel leaders – the large retailers. Many wholesalers will become specialist distribution companies, storing, sorting and distributing merchandise between factory and store (Higuchi et al., 1993). Most will come to rely more on orders placed by retailers than on the patronage of manufacturers.

The most recent changes in the retail sector have been carried through into distribution as a whole. Distribution in Japan remains very different from what is often expected in the West. In the 1960s, when superstore chains such as Daiei and Ito-Yokado first grew in strength, academics talked of a distribution revolution, but, at the time, little really changed. Similarly in the 1990s, so-called traditional business practices are becoming less relevant, the power of manufacturers in the distribution channel is declining, and retailers are stronger than ever. This too has been called a revolution. Again this is going a little too far, but it is true that the evolution of the distribution system has suddenly increased in speed.

## CONCLUSION: THE REIGN OF THE SMALL STORE CONTINUES

This chapter took a brief statistical look at the overall structure of distribution in Japan. While the Census of Commerce recorded large net falls in the number of retail stores during the 1980s, most of this decline was among the very smallest wholesalers and retailers. Small outlets continue to dominate distribution channels by numbers, but not by strength or importance.

In Japan, there are still three clearly distinguished parts to the distribution channel. Manufacturers were the traditional channel leaders, and in some sectors they are still the dominant players. Wholesalers have continued to survive in large numbers as they act as natural intermediaries, working to help manufacturers maintain tight distribution control on the one hand, and providing thousands of small retailers with essential services on the other. Wholesalers also help alleviate inherent difficulties with physical distribution. Retailers continue to exist in large numbers because of a demand for small stores, and because the established base is so large.

Nevertheless, changes are now taking place. Primarily, larger, more professional and technically skilful retail companies are emerging at the other end of the scale from traditional small stores. They are challenging the dominance of large manufacturers within distribution channels, and demanding that wholesalers provide improved, economically sound distribution services. They lead the introduction of information technology throughout the industry, and have begun to dismantle or make obsolete many of the questionable customs used to control channels in the past.

Retail companies in Japan are still not as dominant as in some Western countries. There are still too many independent retailers, too many wholesale companies, and manufacturers are loath to see retailers grow too powerful. The corporate sector has split retailing into the small traditional part, and the new sophisticated part. Large retail companies will lead the distribution industry into the twenty-first century and bring many improvements that Western observers will welcome. Many of these are already in place.

For too long, the Japanese distribution system has been seen as archaic in Western eyes. In reality, while some aspects of the system are out of date, others are very modern indeed.

The following chapters describe a situation in which, although many small independent retailers continue to survive, large multiple chains are becoming more and more important. These are the future of the distribution industry in Japan, just as similar companies are now the most important in many Western systems.

# Chapter 4

# The Large Store Law

Chapter 3 introduced various controversial and unusual aspects of the distribution system in Japan. There is one more which is controversial both in Japan and abroad: the Large Store Law (LSL).[1] Arguably, the LSL has been one of the largest influences on the development of macro level retailing in twentieth-century Japan.

The LSL aims to protect small independent retailers from the competitive power of large retail companies. It does this by controlling the opening and expansion of large retail outlets. Companies continue to open large stores, but the law restricts both the size of the stores and the speed at which they can expand their chains.

Despite the LSL, Chapter 3 showed a large ongoing fall in the number of small stores starting in the 1980s. It is possible that without the LSL small stores would be disappearing even more rapidly. Also as the previous chapter showed, the very smallest stores were replaced by stores that are only a little larger. This is mainly because the LSL discouraged chain store companies from opening larger outlets. In this way the LSL contributed to the rapid growth of convenience stores and speciality stores in the 1980s.

It is not only the type of restrictions that the LSL imposed, but also the way this was done, that make the law a controversial issue. A chief aim of the American negotiators during the 1989 SII (Structural Impediments Initiative: see Chapter 3) talks was to obtain the abolition of this law. Similar demands have been made within Japan (see Asahi Shinbun 1990a; Nakauchi, 1989; Takaoka, 1989; TBT, 1989a; 1989b), but independent retailers continue to expect the protection that the LSL provides. In addition, those large retailers which operate existing large stores are reluctant to criticise the law as it serves to protect their stores from new competition. True critics, however, are scathing (see Mishima, 1988a; 1989; Mori *et al.*, 1989; Nakaoka, 1989; Niwa, 1988).

## AN OVERVIEW OF THE LARGE STORE LAW

The origins of the LSL stretch back to 1937 (Larke and Dawson, 1992; Suzuki, 1993). It was abolished during the American occupation following the Second World War, only to be reintroduced in a slightly altered form in 1956. It was then completely revised and strengthened in 1974, and the same legislation was still in force in the early 1990s. One result of the SII talks in 1989 was a major revision of the LSL in 1992. Further revision was implemented in May 1994.

The LSL exists because of loud and effective political lobbying by small, independent retailers. Up to 1993, a single political party, the Liberal Democratic Party (LDP), formed every government for over thirty years (see *Economist*, 1988c; 1988j; 1988m). The LDP relied on the electoral support of more traditional and conservative sectors of society, including farmers and independent shopkeepers. Around 1.6 million people were working in unincorporated retail outlets as owners or unpaid family employees in 1991, making this a significant voting segment (MITI, 1992a: 568). This political lobby was largely responsible for the original legislation and continues to call for protection against the growth of large retailers. The political reasoning behind the LSL was summarised by the Japanese Chamber of Commerce and Industry:

> If the opening of large-scale retail stores, with their ability to attract great numbers of customers, is not coordinated in an orderly fashion, it can create financial difficulties for many small neighbourhood stores and is likely to adversely affect the stability of local communities.
>
> (JCCI, 1989: 19)

As with numerous aspects of Japanese law, the operation of the LSL is more controversial than its effect. The operation of the law was always ambiguous and, arguably, inconsistent. Several revisions and amendments only made this situation worse, and it was the operation of the law which attracted the most criticism.

In its simplest form, however, the LSL requires developers and operators of large retail stores to submit a series of detailed proposals and plans to local authorities prior to opening a new store. One or more committees are given an opportunity to scrutinise and criticise these plans. Members of the committees often include local small retailers and others who may be adversely affected by the opening of the new store. A company must submit nearly 200 application forms, related to nineteen laws, and in connection with forty-two goverment-controlled licences (Nakauchi, 1993). Through this procedure, the law aims to produce a consensus of agreement to the plans before the proposal can progress and the store is opened.

The LSL is very careful not to call this an 'application process', although the need for consensus effectively makes it precisely that. Under the constitution of Japan, no official body may actually refuse a company permission to open a new store. Rather, the law provided a means for those opposed to the new store to force changes to the original plans, for example reducing the sales area in the store, and, most significantly, delaying the opening of the store. Under the 1974 law and its later revisions, this delay could be for years, if not indefinitely.

Following the second introduction of such legislation in 1956, the various revisions and amendments sought only to strengthen the LSL. In 1989, however, the American government made a direct demand for the LSL to be abolished (see *Economist*, 1989b; Rodger, 1990). Overseas observers argued that larger stores, with their greater sales space, sold more imported goods than did smaller stores, therefore the LSL was a barrier to trade as it restricted the opening of large stores. The Japanese government refused to comply with the American demand to abolish the law, but, as a result of this pressure, MITI began positive moves to clarify and simplify the law. This was the first significant relaxation in the law since its inception. Large-store retailers saw the early 1990s as a period of opportunity, and the number of proposals to open new large stores increased dramatically after 1989.

There is considerable misunderstanding surrounding the LSL, and few reasonable explanations of the law exist in English (see Dawson and Sato, 1985; Kirby, 1984; Larke and Dawson, 1992). This is partly due to a lack of information. On the other hand, the political and, from a Western viewpoint, unusual nature of the LSL means that there is wide scope for bias. This is equally true for some Japanese accounts, which can often be unthinkingly defensive or totally evasive. This chapter gives a brief description of the development of the LSL and various controversial aspects of the operation of the law. It then looks at the situation up to 1993, and the effects of the 1990 and 1992 revisions.

## A BRIEF HISTORY OF THE LARGE STORE LAW

### Early restrictions on large stores

The history of the LSL began before the Second World War. Large department stores became the dominant form of retailing in Japan during the early part of the century, expanding rapidly in the 1920s and 1930s (see Chapter 6).[2] Fierce competition between department stores affected small retailers over a wide geographical area. In addition to large multi-regional chains of department stores which emerged for the first time, single-outlet regional department stores were the main retailers in their local markets. The big Tokyo and Osaka department stores sent their salesmen to regional areas to provide a form of 'door-to-door' retailing for wealthy customers, so spreading their influence across the country (see Chapter 6, page 192).

This expansion brought considerable opposition from small retailers in many parts of the country, to such an extent that it became a political problem. In the mid-1930s, under the guidance of the Japan Department Store Association (Nihon Hyakkaten Kyōkai), department stores imposed voluntary restraints on this expansion. These proved too half-hearted to satisfy the small shopkeeper community, and, in 1937, the first 'Department Store Law' (Hyakkaten Hō) was introduced (Takaoka and Koyama, 1970). This law was abolished during the American occupation (1945–56), but re-enacted in a similar form in 1956. This second law was also called the Department Store Law (1956) (Hayashi, 1980).

### Retail development in the 1960s and the Large Store Law

As department stores were the only significant large retailers until the mid-1950s, the earlier legislation aimed specifically at these. The true objective of the legislation, however, was to restrict the activities of large retailers in general. The 1956 Law restricted the opening of new department store outlets and the expansion of existing stores. Large retail businesses were required to obtain special licensing for any such developments. The Law defined a large retail business as 'a retail business operating within a single store, which takes up 1,500 square metres of store space and provides a wide variety of goods'. (Nihon Keizai Shinbun, 1988: 238).

In the 1950s and 1960s, the first supermarket and superstore chains emerged and expanded across Japan. Table 4.1 shows the leading retail companies by sales from 1960 to 1990. Until 1972, department stores were the largest retail companies. Most have histories that stretch back to the nineteenth century, with some much older (for example, Larke and Nagashima, 1992; also see Chapter 6).

In 1972, Daiei, a general merchandise chain store founded as recently as 1957, overtook Mitsukoshi as the largest company. This was a shock to the industry. The Mitsukoshi department store group is one of the oldest retailers in Japan, with a history stretching back over 300 years (see Chapter 6), and, arguably, one of the most respected by both consumers and other retail companies. In only fifteen years of business, Daiei surpassed a national institution.

By the time Daiei became the top retail company, there were three other chain store companies in the top ten. Over the next twenty years, the position of these general merchandise retailers continued to improve, with only the largest and most prestigious department stores holding their own. In 1990, five of the top ten retailers were department stores, but only four of these were traditional, high-prestige companies that led the industry in the 1960s. All of the largest four companies were general merchandise chain stores.

Technically, the 1956 Department Store Law applied to any retail business with a sales floor space of 1,500 square metres or more. The emphasis on retail *business*, however, provided a loophole which chain stores were quick to exploit. The general merchandise chains bypassed the Department Store Law by opening shopping buildings in which each floor, part of a floor or store section was operated as a separate business. Each separate 'business' operated up to, but did not exceed, the regulation 1,500 square metres (Czinkota and Woronoff, 1986: 111–12; Larke and Dawson, 1992; Nihon Keizai Shinbun, 1988: 239; Suzuki, 1993).

By exploiting this loophole, general merchandise store chains expanded rapidly throughout the 1960s. The traditional department stores which the 1956 law aimed to restrict were more conservative in their business and more carefully scrutinised, so they could not take advantage of the same loophole. The new general merchandise chains became known as *giji hyakkaten* or 'pseudo-department stores' (Nihon Keizai Shinbun, 1988: 239). Their rapid and relatively unhindered expansion soon made them the new targets for complaint

Table 4.1 Leading retail companies in Japan, selected years, 1960–91

| | 1960 | | | 1972 | | | 1980 | | | 1990 | | |
|---|---|---|---|---|---|---|---|---|---|---|---|---|
| Company | | Sales (¥'000 million) | Stores | Company | | Sales (¥'000 million) | Stores | Company | | Sales (¥'000 million) | Stores | Company | | Sales (¥'000 million) | Stores |

| Company | | Sales (¥'000 million) | Stores | Company | | Sales (¥'000 million) | Stores | Company | | Sales (¥'000 million) | Stores | Company | | Sales (¥'000 million) | Stores |
|---|---|---|---|---|---|---|---|---|---|---|---|---|---|---|---|
| 1 Mitsukoshi | D | 45 | 10 | Daiei | G | 305 | 90 | Daiei | G | 1,134 | 169 | Daiei | G | 1,842 | 191 |
| 2 Daimaru | D | 45 | 4 | Mitsukoshi | D | 292 | 12 | Ito-Yokado | G | 688 | 102 | Ito-Yokado | G | 1,355 | 140 |
| 3 Takashimaya | D | 39 | 3 | Daimaru | D | 213 | 6 | Seiyu Stores | G | 599 | 149 | Seiyu | G | 1,048 | 201 |
| 4 Matsuzakaya | D | 37 | 5 | Takashimaya | D | 199 | 4 | Jusco | G | 554 | 133 | Jusco | G | 995 | 172 |
| 5 Toyoko | D | 30 | 3 | Seiyu Stores | G | 167 | 96 | Mitsukoshi | D | 546 | 15 | Seibu | D | 985 | 17 |
| 6 Isetan | D | 23 | 2 | Seibu | D | 155 | 10 | Nichii | G | 455 | 155 | Mitsukoshi | D | 867 | 14 |
| 7 Hankyu | D | 21 | 4 | Jusco | G | 155 | 131 | Daimaru | D | 421 | 7 | Takashimaya | D | 768 | 10 |
| 8 Seibu | D | 19 | 2 | Matsuzakaya | D | 149 | 6 | Takashimaya | D | 415 | 5 | Nichii | G | 708 | 149 |
| 9 Sogo | D | 15 | 3 | Nichii | G | 144 | 156 | Seibu | D | 375 | 10 | Daimaru | D | 607 | 7 |
| 10 Matsuya | D | 12 | 3 | Uny | G | 126 | 108 | Uny | G | 126 | 108 | Marui | D | 566 | 33 |

Key: D = department store company, G = general merchandise store company.
Source: Nikkei Ryūtsū Shinbun (1991: 258)

from small and medium independent retailers. Department stores were also not opposed to new restrictions to stop the growth of chain stores.

To meet these new complaints and to bring the general merchandise chains under the law, the basis of the present LSL was introduced in 1974. Rather than targeting retail businesses, the new LSL focused on the actual stores, requiring companies to submit plans to build new stores or to expand existing ones. By making the store the target of regulation, the LSL effectively closed the loophole in the previous legislation, and became applicable to both department stores and general merchandise store chains.

The 1974 LSL required companies to gain approval for any new store with 1,500 square metres sales space or more (3,000 square metres in the eleven largest cities). This was the same measure used in the 1956 law. In both pieces of legislation, the choice of 1,500 square metres as the point of regulation was purely arbitrary. The new 1974 LSL also required stores to conform to various restrictions on opening times and a minimum number of closing days per month.

## Further amendments up to 1992

The LSL was amended in 1979 and the operation of the law was adjusted in 1982. In the mid- and late 1970s, the speed with which large retailers opened stores under the law was still too quick to satisfy the small retailer lobby (Saeki, 1981; 1982). In May 1979, the LSL was amended to take in any proposed new store over 500 square metres – not particularly 'large' at all. In addition, since 1979, all submissions for new stores with sales space between 500 and 1,500 square metres (or 3,000 square metres in the largest cities) were dealt with by prefectural government, with those above these limits referred to the Minister for Trade and Industry in Tokyo.

These two categories of store size were Type 1 Large-Scale Retail Stores (*Dai-isshu daikibo kouri tenpo*: 1,500 or 3,000 square metres or greater), and Type 2 Large-Scale Retail Stores (*Dai-ni shu daikibo kouri tenpo*). Because of the different regulations in the largest cities, Type 2 Large-Scale Retail Stores were in effect all non-Type 1 stores over 500 square metres.

Still this new level of regulation was not enough. In 1982, after studying the expansion of large-scale stores, MITI concluded that many regional towns and cities had achieved 'a desirable' level of Type 1 store concentration (Nihon Keizai Shinbun 1988: 241).

Consequently, the Ministry introduced guidelines that made two significant amendments to the existing LSL. They allowed additional local authority restrictions on large stores in particular areas of the country, and added a further preliminary investigation stage to the process for obtaining approval for a new store. Both guidelines were originally introduced for a two-year period, but both remained in force up to the 1992 revision of the LSL. Neither of these additions was ever part of the formal legislation, being introduced solely as guideline procedures to alter the operation of the law. In effect, they served to increase the complexity and ambiguity of the LSL, and were some of the aspects that Japanese critics were most opposed to.

These new guidelines extended the power of local authorities to restrict the opening of large stores in regional areas. In addition, they required large retail corporations, especially companies controlling national chains of stores, to display self-restraint and avoid opening new stores in areas designated as already having a high concentration of large stores. These amendments brought a total freeze on large store applications in hundreds of cities, including such major centres as Kyoto and Shizuoka.[3]

Local authorities took the opportunity to introduce or toughen their own autonomous restrictions on the opening of new stores. Many local authorities imposed restrictions on any new stores with sales floor space below 500 square metres, some cities requiring approval for stores as small as 100 square metres (Nihon Keizai Shinbun, 1988).

A 1989 survey suggested that some 1,031 local authorities in various cities, towns and boroughs imposed additional restrictions over and above those laid down in the formal LSL (Takahashi, 1991). In some cities a freeze on large store developments was still in operation in the late 1980s (Nikkei Ryūtsū Shinbun, 1989a: 69–74).

The second 1982 amendment altered the approval process itself. It introduced a new stage to the approval process called the *jizen setsumei* or 'preliminary explanation'. The guidelines stated that this explanatory meeting had to be convened prior even to the first submission of plans for development of a new retail site – that is before the formal approval process was ever begun. The official aim of this new procedure was to allow interested parties time to reach a consensus before any official investigation (see Dawson and Sato, 1985; Larke and Dawson, 1992). But, without consensus at this explanatory meeting, the official approval process under the formal LSL could not begin.[4]

This additional guideline, unrecognised in the formal law, became the most controversial factor in whole process. It allowed local storekeepers and other opposing groups to block progress by actively avoiding consensus. They avoided a consensus by not convening the explanatory meeting, and they could do this simply by not turning up at an appointed time or place. Without completing the preliminary explanation, developers could not submit even the basic plans, and the official, legal process of gaining approval could not begin. Consequently, most proposals submitted in the 1980s took years to gain approval, with an unknown number being delayed to the extent that the plans were abandoned altogether.

## CRITICISMS OF THE LARGE STORE LAW

From 1974 to 1992, the LSL placed strict controls on the opening of large retail stores. From its original promulgation in 1974 until the first notable relaxation in 1990, this law was responsible for limiting expansion in all large-store retail sectors. The continuing survival of many small stores is at least partly due to the LSL, although the significant fall in their numbers after 1982 shows that the law was not sufficient to protect small stores in an absolute sense.

Table 4.2 summarises changes in the number of retail outlets by sales space between 1982 and 1991. As Chapter 3 described, there were significant declines in the smallest stores during the 1980s. On the other hand, all categories of store larger than 50 square metres increased in number. This increase was highest in two categories, stores with sales space between 200 and 499 square metres and those between 1,000 and 1,500 square metres.

Naturally, the LSL did not stop retailers from trying to open new larger stores. The concentration of growth around 500 and 1,500 square metres shows that companies opened stores up to, but within, the limits of the LSL in most cases. Both the complexity of the law and the difficulty of the approval process for new stores encouraged companies to restrict new outlets to within these boundaries wherever feasible.[5]

Table 4.3 shows the number of stores that opened after 1978 which fall under the LSL. Up to 1988, retail companies had opened only 16,000 stores with sales space over 500 square metres, representing less than 1 per cent of total retail outlets. The figure for existing stores over this size is even less, because a few of these have since gone out of business.

Table 4.2 Number of retail outlets by sales space, 1982–91

| Store size (sq m) | 1982 | | 1985 | | 1988 | | 1991 | |
|---|---|---|---|---|---|---|---|---|
| | Outlets | % Change 82/79 | Outlets | % Change 85/82 | Outlets | % Change 88/82 | Outlets | % Change 91/88 |
| Less than 50 | 1,194,937 | -1.6 | 1,057,355 | -11.5 | 998,614 | -5.6 | 918,528 | -8.0 |
| 50–199.99 | 339,294 | 14.7 | 351,973 | 3.7 | 367,487 | 4.4 | 391,438 | 6.5 |
| 200–499.99 | 38,708 | 16.3 | 36,350 | -6.1 | 48,423 | 33.2 | 56,490 | 16.7 |
| 500–999.99 | 8,913 | 5.6 | 8,161 | -8.4 | 8,408 | 3.0 | 8,799 | 4.7 |
| 1,000–1,499.99 | 3,730 | 30.3 | 3,400 | -8.8 | 3,888 | 14.4 | 4,358 | 12.1 |
| 1,500 or more | 3,275 | 11.5 | 3,890 | 18.8 | 4,154 | 6.8 | 4,640 | 11.7 |
| Unknown | 132,608 | 14.3 | 167,515 | 26.3 | 188,778 | 12.7 | 206,970 | 9.6 |
| Total | 1,721,465 | 2.9 | 1,628,644 | -5.4 | 1,619,752 | -0.5 | 1,591,223 | -1.8 |

Source: Compiled from MITI (1984 1986, 1989a, 1992b)

*Table 4.3* New large stores and sales space, 1978–88

| | Type 1 stores | | Type 2 stores | |
|---|---|---|---|---|
| | New stores | New sales space (000 sq m) | New stores | New sales space (000 sq m) |
| To 1978 | 2,556 | 16,513 | – | – |
| 1979 | 219 | 1,433 | 8,994[a] | – |
| 1980 | 234 | 1,934 | 787 | 10,203[b] |
| 1981 | 247 | 1,287 | 476 | 563 |
| 1982 | 190 | 903 | 332 | 314 |
| 1983 | 218 | 1,060 | 223 | 255 |
| 1984 | 100 | 1,095 | 209 | 268 |
| 1985 | 105 | 470 | 180 | 234 |
| 1986 | 98 | 651 | 171 | 260 |
| 1987 | 150 | 1,194 | 207 | 265 |
| 1988 | 130 | 859 | 170 | 254 |
| Total | 4,247 | 27,399 | 11,749 | 12,616 |

[a] Figure to 1978
[b] Figure to 1980
*Source*: Adapted from MITI (1989a: 90, 190)

As noted earlier, in addition to the physical restrictions that the LSL imposed, the operation of the law was unclear, slow and often ambiguous. The process of gaining permission to open new stores over 500 square metres was long and unpredictable. The requirement for a consensus between developers, existing shopkeepers and other people affected by the opening of a new store meant that, if these people opposed the opening, they could delay or even force cancellation of the plans simply by failing to attend meetings. There was no guarantee how the approval procedure would progress.

Figure 4.1 is a flow chart showing the stages in the approval process up to the introduction of new guidelines in 1990. The diagram immediately shows the complexity of the process. Approval began with the preliminary explanation meeting (*jizen setsumei*), an aspect not even recognised under the formal legislation, and one which could take years to complete. It then progressed through at least seven, but usually up to sixteen, different stages before final approval was forthcoming. At several of the stages, opposing parties could hold up applications or force developers to redraw plans and schedules.

For example, in September 1981, Life Stores, a large supermarket chain, announced plans to build a store in Shiki, Saitama Prefecture.

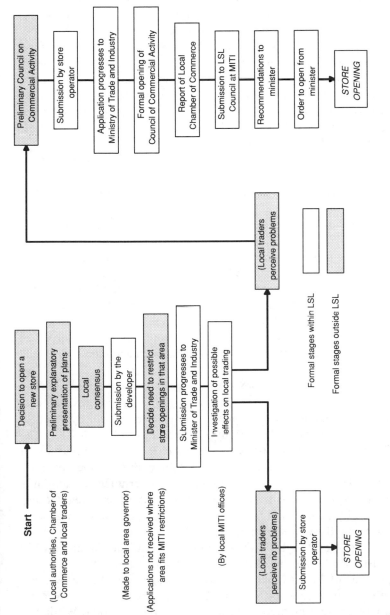

Start

(Local authorities, Chamber of Commerce and local traders)

Decision to open a new store

Preliminary explanatory presentation of plans

Local consensus

(Made to local area governor)

Submission by the developer

Decide need to restrict store openings in that area

(Applications not received where area fits MITI restrictions)

Submission progresses to Minister of Trade and Industry

Investigation of possible effects on local trading

(By local MITI offices)

(Local traders perceive problems)

(Local traders perceive no problems)

Submission by store operator

STORE OPENING

Preliminary Council on Commercial Activity

Submission by store operator

Application progresses to Ministry of Trade and Industry

Formal opening of Council of Commercial Activity

Report of Local Chamber of Commerce

Submission to LSL Council at MITI

Recommendations to minister

Order to open from minister

STORE OPENING

Formal stages within LSL

Formal stages outside LSL

*Figure 4.1* Approval and consensus-building process for Type 1 retail stores to 1990
Source: Adapted from Nihon Keizai Shinbun (1990e)

Nine years later, the company had still failed to persuade relevant parties to attend the required preliminary explanation meetings. Life Stores never even began the formal procedure for approval to develop the site, because they could not overcome the preliminary, unofficial hurdle of explanatory meetings (Nihon Keizai Shinbun, 1990e: 64–9). As a consequence, the company began legal action against MITI. The grounds for the suit were that this process of delay and non-cooperation which the LSL allowed constituted refusal to approve the new store – in effect an unconstitutional act (*Asahi Shinbun*, 1990b; Rodger, 1990). The action was later dropped when it became clear that MITI aimed to clarify the operation of the LSL (see pages 117–22 below).

There are no official figures that indicate how long the process of opening a new store could take, but discussions with various industry experts and officials suggest that few approval procedures took less than one year, and most took five or more. Overseas journalists have been quick to note the time-consuming nature of the application process, with some suggesting that ten years was a typical time span from beginning the process to obtaining approval (for example, Rodger, 1990; YRI 1990). But, as the law only existed in its most ambiguous form from 1979 to 1989, this is misleading. Although the approval procedure was unnecessarily long, plans were approved after several years or were never approved at all. It is probable that a significant number of proposals were shelved or totally abandoned due to the length of time and related cost of the approval procedure.

The length of the LSL procedure was not the only criticism. The additional regulations imposed by city and prefectural governments were usually even more stringent than those laid down by the LSL (Mori *et al.*, 1989; Nikkei Ryūtsū Shinbun, 1989a: 58–100). The problem of local restrictions was a difficult one. The abolition of local regulations was proposed by MITI in the summer of 1989 (MITI, 1989a), but some local prefectural governments, claiming a constitutional right to handle their own planning and regulations, successfully forced MITI to back down (Hirono, 1989; Kitamatsu, 1989; Shōgyōkai, 1989; Sugioka, 1989).

Criticism of the LSL also came from outside Japan, mostly because of a belief that the law indirectly restricted the volume of imports available in Japanese shops (see page 106). Some overseas politicians even believed that the LSL discriminated against overseas retailers, preventing their entry into the Japanese market. While this point was refuted by the existence of large overseas companies in the market, C&A for example, it is true that the LSL acted as a major disincentive, and provided the possibility of discrimination. If Japanese retailers could be prevented from opening large stores, so could overseas companies.

In October 1989, the American multinational retailer Toys'R'Us announced its desire to open a store in the provincial city of Niigata in north-eastern Japan, along with five or six stores in other regions by 1991 (Anzai, 1990; *Asahi Shinbun*, 1990c; Graven, 1990; Nihon Keizai Shinbun, 1990c; 1990e; Sekiguchi, 1990; Shale, 1990). The Toys'R'Us announcement coincided closely with the beginning of the US–Japan SII negotiations in the autumn of 1989. Whether by plan or accident, Toys'R'Us executives and American diplomats were seeking the same goal. Although some Japanese had also long been critical of the LSL (see Mori *et al.*, 1989; Nakauchi, 1989), the SII brought heightened public interest in the LSL issue, considerable sympathy for the plight of small retailers, but greater understanding of the needs of large retail businesses.

## RELAXATION OF THE LARGE STORE LAW IN THE 1990S

The highly critical approach adopted by the Americans in the SII talks won them few supporters in Japan, and the Japanese government refused to abolish the LSL. Many observers considered this the correct decision in the face of such US pressure (see Thomson, 1990b). On the other hand, the pressure was enough to force MITI to implement changes. In the summer of 1989, MITI published its *Vision for Distribution in the 90s* (MITI, 1989a). Partly in anticipation of the SII, in it were published a number of proposals for relaxation of the LSL. These became formalised in May the following year at the end of the first stage of the SII trade talks (*Nihon Keizai Shinbun*, 1990a; *Nikkei Ryūtsū Shinbun*, 1990a).

Apart from during the period of postwar occupation, this 1990 directive was the first relaxation of legislation restricting the expansion and operations of large retail stores for more than fifty years. It contained four main points. Existing stores were allowed to increase their sales space by 10 per cent or up to 50 square metres without needing approval, to extend their opening hours from 6 o'clock to 7 o'clock and to reduce the minimum number of closing days per year from forty-eight to forty-four. Far more significantly, however, the new initiative introduced a maximum period of eighteen months for the approval of new store plans. Also MITI called for the relaxation of additional local authority restrictions.

These guidelines represented the most MITI could do without taking the issue to parliament. The government of Prime Minister Kaifu formally amended the legislation a year later in May 1991, and included additional changes to related laws, and two new laws. These amendments came into effect in January 1992 (Nihon Keizai Shinbun, 1990e). They are based on the May 1990 initiative, but are both more positive and far reaching. The major points are shown in Table 4.4.

The single most important change was the further reduction of the official approval process to a maximum of just one year. This was done by simplifying the investigation process as a whole, doing away totally with the preliminary explanation stage and amalgamating the roles of other approval committees prescribed under the previous LSL into a single body. Other important changes were the removal of additional restrictions imposed by local authorities, and the increase in the size of Type 1 stores from 1,500 square metres to 3,000 square metres or more (6,000 metres or more in designated cities).

Figure 4.2 illustrates the new one-year process introduced in 1992. Comparing this diagram with the one in Figure 4.1, the simplification of the whole procedure is clear. There is a maximum of seven stages and the largest potential bottleneck, that is hearings and consideration by local interest groups and officials, is amalgamated into a single part of the process. MITI defined the time limits for each stage clearly.

The approval process now begins with the submission of plans by the developer of the site. Although the preliminary explanatory meetings have been removed, within the four months following this submission, the law still requires developers to conduct an explanatory meeting with interested parties in the area. Some critics worry that this provides new opportunities for delay (Nihon Keizai Shinbun, 1990e), but the stated limitation of this stage to four months means that local authorities must act to avoid such delays.

In the revised LSL, MITI has the power to intervene should an application be held up for a period longer than that laid down in the law. The emphasis, however, remains on the formation of a consensus among various local interest groups, including the developer. If a consensus still seems unlikely two months before the specified time limits at each stage, the law requires that MITI or chairmen of the local investigating bodies construct a list of the delaying problems

*Table 4.4* The 1992 revision of the Large Store Law and related legislation

---

**1  Amendments to the Large Store Law**

- The maximum time period for the investigation process was reduced to one year, starting from receipt of submission of papers from the site developer
- The preliminary explanatory meeting was removed from the process, with the investigation beginning from the time of submission of plans by the site developer
- The investigation process was simplified, with various committees being unified into a single formal body
- Additional regulations applied by local authorities were restricted
- The size limit for Type 1 stores was to be raised from 1,500 to 3,000 square metres, and from 3,000 to 6,000 square metres in the largest cities

---

**2  Exceptional Law Regarding Sales Areas for Imported Goods[a]**

- Speciality sales areas dedicated to the sale of imported goods can now be opened without restriction up to a maximum of 1,000 square metres
- Such sales areas are subject to recommendations or orders to improve their operation, with penal measures available should an order be ignored

---

**3  Amendment to the Small and Medium Retail Promotion Law[b]**

- Grants are now available to help shopping street associations (*shōtengai*) increase efficiency through the introduction of computer technology, new community centres, parking areas and other facilities

---

**4  Amendment to the Law for Promotion of Private Enterprise Facilities[c]**

- A financial body is planned to supply interest-free loans for the construction of commercial facilities that will be for the cooperative use of both large and small retailers

---

**5  A New Law for the Development of Commercial Facilities[d]**

- Funds are now available to encourage the establishment and improvement of commercial facilities in cities, town and villages, with particular emphasis on developments jointly involving large and small retail businesses

---

[a] Japanese: Yunyū hin Uriba ni kan suru Tokurei Hō.
[b] Japanese: Chūshō Kouri Shōgyō Shinkō Hō.
[c] Japanese: Minkan Jigyō no Nōryoku no Katsuyō ni yoru Tokutei Shisetsu no Seibi no Sokushin ni Kan suru Rinji Sochi Hō.
[d] Japanese: Tokutei Shōgyō Shūseki Seibi Hō.
*Source*: Adapted from MITI (1989a: 90, 190)

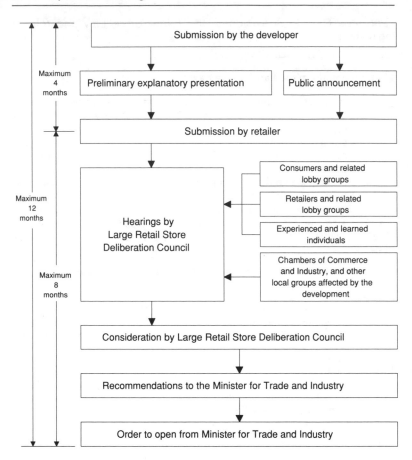

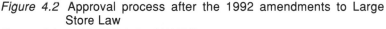

*Figure 4.2* Approval process after the 1992 amendments to Large
            Store Law
*Source*: Adapted from *Takahashi* (1991)

and a timetable for reaching a consensus within the remaining two
months. Where the earlier stages are completed ahead of the time
limits, the time saved can be added to the later stages if problems
arise, so long as the maximum period of one year is not exceeded
(MITI, 1990b: 214–15).

As the length of the approval process was the main restriction
within the LSL in the 1980s, specification of the maximum time for
granting approval is an important change. On the other hand, to

enforce such time limits, direct intervention by MITI at the prefectural level becomes a necessity. This leads to the possibility of complaints of unconstitutional practice from local authorities.

Moreover, the conditions under which store opening plans would be amended, or, conceivably, even refused, are still unclear. Previously, the stronger the local opposition to a proposed store, the longer the approval process could become. If MITI guarantees a maximum approval time of one year, does it mean that new store applications will always succeed if companies persevere for this length of time?

This point remains unclear, but to date it has not been a problem. Some 44 per cent of plans were amended and redrawn as a result of the application process, but the new regulations allowed plans to proceed on schedule (Nikkei Ryūtsū Shinbun, 1993e).

There are two reasons why the LSL has not caused problems in its new form. First, the political and common popularity of new large stores has risen, and the level of opposition is now lower in many cities than at any time in the past. Second, despite the first point, poor economic conditions in the early 1990s have led retailers to reduce the number of applications for new stores (see pages 122–5).

Due to the number of additional restrictions commonly employed by local authorities, the unification of the LSL across regional areas is also an important move. Whereas local administrations could bypass the 1990 MITI directive, the new 1992 amendment to the LSL itself clarified and strengthened MITI's position, making local restrictions more difficult to impose.

In addition to the amendments to the LSL itself, the government also introduced new legislation and amended other laws in order to encourage small retail business (see Table 4.4). The Law for the Development of Commercial Facilities (Tokutei Shōgyō Shūseki Seibi Hō) and the Exceptional Law Regarding Sales Areas for Imported Goods Yu'nyū Hin Uriba ni kan suru Tokurei Hō) were both newly introduced.

The former aims to encourage the development of new retail facilities. It provides funding and other help for groups of small retailers to join together to develop and build regional shopping centres and other facilities. This law also has provisions for joint developments including small local retailers and large national chains (MITI, 1991b: 12–14). By 1993 there were already a small number of these developments in regional areas (Nikkei Ryūtsū Shinbun, 1993f).

The second law aims to encourage the development of special sales areas exclusively for imported goods. Stores can open sales space up to 1,000 square metres to be used for imported goods only, without formal approval under the LSL. This piece of legislation was largely conciliatory towards American demands for more imports to Japan. Some retailers may have taken advantage of the opportunity, but there has been little media interest, and probably few examples. A store selling only imports in 1,000 square metres of sales space is often impractical. Even the new Toys'R'Us outlets sell a significant proportion of domestically produced Japanese products in their stores.

A further revision of the LSL is due to come into effect in 1994. The main point of this minor revision was to raise the minimum sales space for a Type 2 store from 500 square metres to 1,000 square metres. The minimum number of required closing days was reduced to 28 – from 44, and the latest closing time increased to 8 pm – from 7 pm.

## THE EFFECTS OF THE NEW LARGE STORE LAW

Although the 1992 amendments to the LSL were far reaching, actual implementation and results of these amendments can only be judged in the fullness of time. The Nihon Keizai Shinbun (1990e) suggested that new, unofficial preliminary stages could well arise to slow the process down once more. It is also possible that, where there is serious opposition to a new store, local authorities will try to alter and restrict plans to a greater extent than before. This could become just another way of damaging the feasibility of store applications.

This all remains to be seen. What is sure, however, is that the Large Store Law presents fewer restrictions to opening new large retail stores now than at any time for over twenty years.

Multiple retail businesses quickly recognised this. In 1990 alone, after the first MITI initiative, there was an increase of over 40 per cent in the number of new store proposals submitted to the authorities (see Table 4.5). The number of submissions for the larger Type 1 stores increased by 254 to 586, a jump of 77 per cent on 1990, and the highest number in a single year since the LSL was introduced in 1974. There were also 516 submissions for Type 2 stores in 1990, making 1,102 plans submitted altogether.

The total number of plans submitted in 1991 and 1992 exceeded

*Table 4.5* Submissions of plans for new large retail stores, 1974–93

|  |  | Type 1 stores | Type 2 stores | Total |
|---|---|---|---|---|
| *Existing stores*[a] |  | 1,846 | 9,754 | 11,600 |
| Plans submitted in year | 1974 | 399 | – | – |
|  | 1975 | 281 | – | – |
|  | 1976 | 264 | – | – |
|  | 1977 | 318 | – | – |
|  | 1978 | 243 | – | – |
|  | 1979[b] | 576 | 1,029 | 1,605 |
|  | 1980 | 371 | 424 | 795 |
|  | 1981 | 194 | 308 | 502 |
|  | 1982 | 132 | 270 | 402 |
|  | 1983 | 125 | 276 | 401 |
|  | 1984 | 156 | 288 | 444 |
|  | 1985 | 158 | 349 | 507 |
|  | 1986 | 157 | 369 | 526 |
|  | 1987 | 203 | 365 | 568 |
|  | 1988 | 244 | 408 | 652 |
|  | 1989 | 332 | 462 | 794 |
|  | 1990 | 586 | 516 | 1,102 |
|  | 1991 | 427 | 580 | 1,007 |
|  | 1992[c] | 297 | 1,142 | 1,439 |
|  | 1993 | 251 | 600 | 851 |

[a] Pre-1974 for Type 1, and pre-1979 for Type 2 stores.
[b] Type 2 store classification began in 1979. Type 2 figures 1974–9 inclusive.
[c] Applicable size of Type 1 store classification doubled in 1992.
*Source*: Compiled from Honma (1992); Otani (1991), author's calculations

1,000 in both years. The alteration in size categories in January 1992 means that the statistics after this point are incompatible with those before. In the twelve months February 1992 to January 1993, retailers submitted 297 plans for the new Type 1 stores, now 3,000 square metres or more, and 1,142 plans for Type 2 stores with more than 500 square metres.[6] Many of the Type 2 store plans would have been classified as Type 1 in the previous year. The total number in 1992, 1,439, was the highest since 1979, and around twice the number for most years in the mid-1980s.

There are significant differences in the number of submissions by prefecture (see Figure 4.3). There were only twenty-two submissions for new stores in Tokyo. This reflects the very high cost of land and the lack of good available sites. The highest number of submissions,

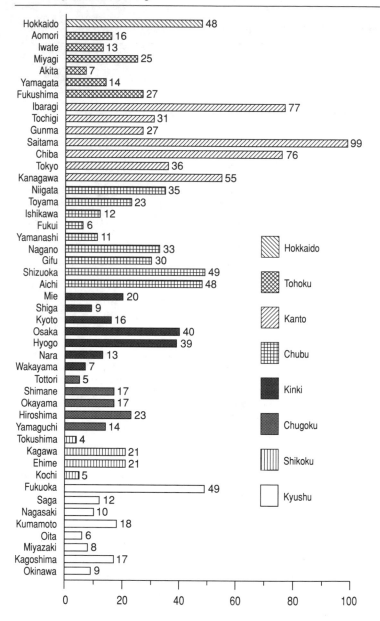

Figure 4.3  Type 1 store applications by prefecture and region, 1991–3
*Source: Nikkei Ryūtūsu Shinbun* (various issues 1991–3)

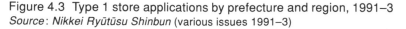

however, were in Saitama, Chiba and Kanagawa, the prefectures surrounding the capital and in Ibaragi Prefecture, further to the north, which saw a large number of submissions as the Tokyo population shifted further and further away from the centre so as to avoid the high land prices in the capital.

Retailers are confident that opposition to the opening of new stores is now reduced. Academics who are directly involved in the development and application of the new policy agree with this. Already Mitsukoshi, the leading department store, has opened a new annexe building in Shinjuku in central Tokyo, with a sales space of 20,000 square metres. In the mid-1990s, rival company Takashimaya plans to open a new store on land owned by the national railways only 100 metres away. For Takashimaya, this opportunity comes about forty years since the same company was denied the chance to build in Shinjuku by the earlier Department Store Law. Both developments represent the first major new department stores in central Tokyo for many years.[7]

## THE FUTURE OF THE LARGE STORE LAW

In the further review of the LSL in 1994, the government will again face conflicting pressures. Large retail companies and politicians from overseas will demand the abolition of the LSL, while the small-retailer lobby will campaign for its continuation and strengthening. The most likely outcome, as I noted earlier, is greater relaxation and simplification of the existing LSL, but not its total abolition. This leaves the possibility of returning to a tougher policy in the future.

All the largest multiple retail companies have submitted more plans for new stores since 1992 than for several years previously. It is natural that they take advantage of the new opportunity to increase their chains of large-format stores after years of restriction.

There will be two other barriers to this expansion. First, the economic downturn of the early 1990s has put considerable pressure on the largest retailers. Department stores (see Chapter 6) are finding that their more conservative business methods are ineffic-ient in an economic recession. General merchandise store chains are also suffering falls in sales. This will slow the number of new stores opened.

In addition, as the number of large stores increases, good locations will become increasingly rare. This may well lead to a reshaping of the retail industry overall. As the best sites are taken by competing companies, small and medium retailers may become targets for takeover. In 1993, there were several examples of mergers and takeovers between competing chains. If this activity increases, weaker multiple chains are likely to add their support to small retailers, and call for a return to a more conservative, restrictive policy.

Only time will tell whether such conservative policies will return, or whether a rapid change in the Japanese retail environment will make restrictions no longer necessary. In the meantime, the LSL affects the whole of the Japanese retail industry, and will continue to do so for the foreseeable future.

# Chapter 5

# Types of small-format retail organisation in Japan

Small shops dominate the retail environment in Japan simply through their sheer numbers. Some 90 per cent of all retail shops employ fewer than ten people (see Chapter 3), and 75 per cent have less than 100 square metres of sales space (Chapter 4). There were 1.3 million retail businesses in Japan in 1991. Of these, 970,000 were unincorporated, and 704,000 were single-outlet businesses employing only one or two people. These are the smallest independent family retail businesses.

There are several important types of small-store retail organisations, but most fall into one of two main groups. They are either organisations of independent retail businesses, such as voluntary chains, or actual chains of stores within or directly linked to a single retail company, such as speciality chains. One significant effect of the Large Store Law was to encourage large retail corporations to move into small-format retailing, developing new corporate chains of small stores in the speciality store and convenience store sectors. These were the fastest growing chains in the 1980s. They are successful not only because of the skills of large companies, but also because small-unit retailing is popular among consumers, and an enduring part of the retail environment.

Today, chains of retailer-organised small stores, including convenience stores and speciality stores, are the most important type of small-format retailing in terms of their business expansion and sales. On the other hand, manufacturers and wholesalers continue to organise small, independent retailers. The *keiretsu* chains are one such type of organisation, operating under the umbrella of large manufacturers (see Chapter 3). There are also a number of wholesaler-operated voluntary chains. Spar, a voluntary chain organisation originating in Europe, has a number of regional chains in Japan. On the whole, however, wholesalers are not keen to enter the retail market, and voluntary chains are fewer and smaller than retailer-operated organisations (Efuji, 1982). Independent retailers often organise themselves into street or local area associations. Such associations are very common, and a unique aspect of Japanese retailing.

This chapter considers both independent and multiple chain organisations. Not all speciality retail store chains operate strictly small-format stores, but most do, and this is a good place to introduce and describe the large speciality stores sector. Also, most convenience stores are either franchises or members of voluntary chains, so remaining, in theory, partly in the independent retail sector; leading franchisors keep a tight control over their member stores, meaning they are independent in terms of ownership, but not management.

Convenience stores and speciality stores were the most successful retailers in the 1980s. This was a result of well developed management techniques, capital backing from the largest retail groups, the opportunity for growth, which was blocked by the Large Store Law for larger formats, and consumer demand for small-format retailing. While large-format stores offer the possibility of economies of scale within a single outlet, companies gained economies of replication and standardisation through opening numerous small outlets. In most cases franchising was popular because it is cheaper than direct operation, and helps to give the franchisee the feeling that he keeps his independence.

Third, the chapter looks at shopping centres. Because there are relatively few large stores in Japan, small stores, with their large numbers, form the most usual source of competition to large outlets in any one area. Even companies operating mainly larger-format stores such as department stores recognise the popularity of small stores. In order to get the best of both worlds, some companies developed multi-storey speciality shopping buildings in the 1970s which house hundreds of small tenants. These are an extension of the small-format retail chain organisation. They provide the facilities of a large store with the ambience of small-unit retailing, and are very popular. They are now the most common form of shopping centre in Japan, and have many unique characteristics.

No matter what form of organisation they operate in, small retailers as a whole are able to compete with large corporations in terms of merchandise variety. At the individual store level they provide a specialised personal service which many consumers prefer and many large stores attempt to match. In the same way that personal relationships are important in general business (see Chapter 3), the personal relationship between neighbourhood retailers and local customers is important in Japan (Larke, 1988). Newer small-format multiples attempt to build the same kind of relationships at the store level.

All these factors mean that small-format retailing continues to survive and prosper, and it is the type of organisation that the retailers belong to which is changing. This chapter covers these points.

## THE ORGANISATION OF SMALL INDEPENDENT RETAILERS

### The role of small stores

Chapter 3 described how small, independent family-run stores dominate the overall structure of retailing. Most independent retailers are unincorporated businesses. Table 5.1 shows that almost 50 per cent of unincorporated retail businesses were founded before 1965. A fifth began business before the end of the war, and only around 30 per cent were opened since 1975. Newer retail businesses tend to take an incorporated format which requires greater capital and faces greater legislative controls, while providing limited liability.

The majority of these small, independent retailers sell food (see Chapter 3). On the other hand, taken as a collective group, small retailers sell an almost unlimited range of products. They sell the same kinds of merchandise and brands as do superstores and department stores, ranging from the most exclusive, high-quality brands down to the most common and cheapest craft products.

Small stores also sell products which large companies will not or can not. They sell in smaller volumes and can give a more specialised service. Such products include traditional Japanese items that have been used for hundreds of years. Few traditional products are suitable for mass production, many being handmade and sold in relatively small volumes. For example, traditional confectionery, rice products, wooden utensils, furniture items, toys and even large items such as tatami matting have become almost the exclusive province of both small producers and small stores.

As in many countries, large retailers do not compete on price as

Table 5.1 Year of opening for retail outlets in 1991 by number of employees and business type

| | Pre-1944 | % of total | 1945–54 | % of total | 1955–64 | % of total | 1965–74 | % of total | 1975–84 | % of total | After 1984 | % of total | Unknown | Total | % of total |
|---|---|---|---|---|---|---|---|---|---|---|---|---|---|---|---|
| **Outlets in unincorporated businesses** | | | | | | | | | | | | | | | |
| 1–2 | 132,603 | 54.9 | 100,547 | 50.5 | 122,220 | 54.3 | 141,806 | 47.8 | 141,997 | 41.8 | 94,596 | 32.7 | 38 | 733,807 | 46.1 |
| 3–4 | 51,028 | 21.1 | 35,755 | 18.0 | 34,360 | 15.3 | 37,681 | 12.7 | 37,047 | 10.9 | 27,663 | 9.6 | 12 | 223,546 | 14.0 |
| 5–9 | 8,687 | 3.6 | 6,353 | 3.2 | 6,706 | 3.0 | 8,414 | 2.8 | 10,917 | 3.2 | 10,524 | 3.6 | 3 | 51,604 | 3.2 |
| 10–19 | 880 | 0.4 | 597 | 0.3 | 958 | 0.4 | 1,583 | 0.5 | 3,148 | 0.9 | 4,337 | 1.5 | 2 | 11,505 | 0.7 |
| 20–29 | 235 | 0.1 | 150 | 0.1 | 292 | 0.1 | 535 | 0.2 | 961 | 0.3 | 1,099 | 0.4 | | 3,272 | 0.2 |
| 30–49 | 226 | 0.1 | 95 | 0.0 | 239 | 0.1 | 401 | 0.1 | 641 | 0.2 | 384 | 0.1 | | 1,986 | 0.1 |
| 50–99 | 90 | 0.0 | 30 | 0.0 | 111 | 0.0 | 206 | 0.1 | 256 | 0.1 | 107 | 0.0 | | 800 | 0.1 |
| 100 or more | 6 | 0.0 | 5 | 0.0 | 11 | 0.0 | 21 | 0.0 | 12 | 0.0 | 6 | 0.0 | | 61 | 0.0 |
| Subtotal | 193,755 | 80.1 | 143,532 | 72.1 | 164,897 | 73.3 | 190,647 | 64.2 | 194,979 | 57.4 | 138,716 | 48.0 | 55 | 1,026,581 | 64.5 |
| **Outlets in incorporated businesses** | | | | | | | | | | | | | | | |
| 1–2 | 6,644 | 2.7 | 9,417 | 4.7 | 9,965 | 4.4 | 19,400 | 6.5 | 31,624 | 9.3 | 36,318 | 12.6 | 10 | 113,378 | 7.1 |
| 3–4 | 20,281 | 8.4 | 21,929 | 11.0 | 21,572 | 9.6 | 35,258 | 11.9 | 46,058 | 13.6 | 48,290 | 16.7 | 6 | 193,394 | 12.2 |
| 5–9 | 15,360 | 6.4 | 17,202 | 8.6 | 18,783 | 8.3 | 31,417 | 10.6 | 39,262 | 11.6 | 40,367 | 14.0 | 12 | 162,403 | 10.2 |
| 10–19 | 3,992 | 1.7 | 4,994 | 2.5 | 6,263 | 2.8 | 11,937 | 4.0 | 16,336 | 4.8 | 16,869 | 5.8 | 6 | 60,400 | 3.8 |
| 20–29 | 849 | 0.4 | 1,069 | 0.5 | 1,592 | 0.7 | 3,727 | 1.3 | 5,083 | 1.5 | 4,610 | 1.6 | | 16,930 | 1.1 |
| 30–49 | 478 | 0.2 | 623 | 0.3 | 1,160 | 0.5 | 2,562 | 0.9 | 3,491 | 1.0 | 2,549 | 0.9 | 1 | 10,864 | 0.7 |
| 50–99 | 221 | 0.1 | 274 | 0.1 | 608 | 0.3 | 1,246 | 0.4 | 1,771 | 0.5 | 931 | 0.3 | | 5,051 | 0.3 |
| 100 or more | 167 | 0.1 | 105 | 0.1 | 201 | 0.1 | 539 | 0.2 | 795 | 0.2 | 415 | 0.1 | | 2,222 | 0.1 |
| Subtotal | 47,992 | 19.9 | 55,613 | 27.9 | 60,144 | 26.7 | 106,086 | 35.8 | 144,420 | 42.6 | 150,349 | 52.0 | 38 | 564,642 | 35.5 |
| Total | 241,747 | 100.0 | 199,145 | 100.0 | 225,041 | 100.0 | 296,733 | 100.0 | 339,399 | 100.0 | 289,065 | 100.0 | 93 | 1,591,223 | 100.0 |

Source: Compiled from MITI (1992b)

much as location and merchandise mix. Consumer prices in Japan are high. In some Western nations price competition from cost-efficient, bulk-buying multiples has hurt the independent retail sector. In Japan, the overall level of high prices means that this is far less of a factor. Many small stores are little more expensive than supermarket chains, and usually cheaper than convenience stores.

On the other hand, while they survive collectively, the accelerating expansion of large-scale corporate retail businesses puts more and more pressure on small stores. Increasingly, it is only in isolated regions or in protected environments that independent stores are able to operate without some element of specialisation or differentiation. Where large superstores and supermarkets have opened, small retailers have altered their merchandise lines, extended their business hours or in some way provide a specialised and competitive service.

In the centres of major urban areas such as Tokyo and Osaka, housewives no longer visit local independent stores every day to buy basic necessities. Some small stores do continue to survive as greengrocers, fruiterers, fishmongers and butchers. Others hold special licences to sell liquor or rice, and provide special delivery services to the local area for these products. Few, however, make more than a basic living. Some supply local restaurants with fresh produce on a daily basis, or simply provide friendly, personal service and make the most of their convenient locations.

Many stores rely on protection from local authority legislation, and on the encouragement and support of their local fellow retailers. They are surprisingly well organised. The most common form of organisation for truly independent retail stores is a street or area association. These are everywhere in Japan, and a unique part of the retail environment.

### The *shōtengai*: retail street associations

The association of groups of stores within a single street or shopping area is common in many countries. In Japan it is predominant. Japanese sociology emphasises group orientation, co-operation and interdependence. Small shopkeepers are an example of this phenomenon, frequently co-operating within a group of neighbouring stores.[1] These associations are called *shōtengai* – literally 'commercial shop streets'.

The overall number of such street associations is unclear. Many are formal associations with a leader and letters of association, but the level of formality varies greatly between different groups. There is a large literature on *shōtengai* in Japanese, although I have yet to find work that provides an accurate figure as to their overall number. The best estimates range from 14,000 to 18,000 nationwide (Akabane, 1986; Nihon Keizai Shinbun, 1988: 223; Nikkei Ryūtsū Shinbun, 1993d: 15).

The Census of Commerce defines a commercial district as having a street association, and an area with a street association as a commercial district (MITI, 1988).[2] While this provides some ambiguous results, for example numerous 'associations' with only one member store, it does give a comprehensive list of these commercial districts across the whole country. There is some overlap between formal street associations and stores that are simply located in the same place.

Unfortunately the Census includes some buildings and areas that are not strictly amalgamations of stores into a single co-operative street, and does not provide overall summary statistics for all commercial districts. The total list included some 21,000 streets and associations in the 1988 survey, most of which would have been *shōtengai*.[3] Whatever the true figure, there are a lot of street associations in Japan. Many have long histories, and play a major role in their local retail environment. Collectively, street associations are what give a political voice to the independent retail lobby.

The largest district in 1988 was the Ginza area in central Tokyo, with over 600 stores, most of which were members of the Ginza Shopping Association. The smallest associations have just two or three members, often as a result of other members going out of business.

## Activities of typical *shōtengai*

The activities of formal street associations range from co-operative promotion and development of the street or area to political lobbying at local and national level. The degree of co-operation varies greatly between one association and another. At the very least, members co-operate to clean the street at New Year, but in many cases, with co-operation and financial support from government and private sources, associations make their street into a pedestrian area, often with a roof. The only place they are not evident is central Tokyo, where the level of congestion and the concentration of large-store retailing has led to the physical break-up of many streets. Associations in Tokyo like the one in Ginza have no single physical presence.

With the one exception of Tokyo, roofed shopping streets are everywhere. Even the large cities of Osaka, Yokohama and Nagoya all have such streets in or very near their city centres. The main retail area of Osaka, Japan's second largest city, is based on a series of joining *shōtengais* stretching down a single narrow street for almost three kilometres. The main shopping area is the Shinsaibashi *shōtengai*. Osaka has some of the largest street associations in Japan.

Shopping streets and their street associations vary greatly in their sophistication and mix of retail types. The Shinsaibashi *shōtengai* includes a full range of formats from small traditional stores selling rice crackers to two major department stores. There are several international retailers in the street too, including C&A and Hunting World. The street itself, while roofed for most of its length, is narrow, no more than eight metres wide in places. Having grown organically over many years, the quality of the paving and lighting varies between different parts and the mixture of retail and merchandise types is also somewhat random.

This type of street and area development is the main function of most associations. It brings together its various members to clean, decorate, promote and develop their common facilities. This may be in the form of regular seasonal events or major street redevelopments, usually with the approval and encouragement of local authorities.

These shopping streets vary from those that have received less planning than the Osaka example to those that have received much more. Some street associations have their own specially designed shopping bags and wrapping paper. Some also provide piped background music through loudspeakers along the street. Street ornaments such as benches, statues and flowers, and public amenities such as telephones and toilets, are also often organised and planned by the street association (Chūshō Kigyō Chō, 1988b).

In the smallest regional towns and cities, it is common to find small groups of stores selling mainly fresh foods and daily apparel. In many cases, these were once members of a periodical town market that gradually developed into a single shopping facility. Some are no more than a metre wide, roofed in a haphazard way with corrugated iron sheeting and lit by single electric bulbs.

At the other end of the scale are the street associations of Sendai and Yokohama. The main Sendai *shōtengai* is similar to Osaka's Shinsaibashi, only a little smaller and better planned. The main pavements are between twenty and thirty metres wide. The retail mix ranges from the usual local stores to a large department store and a superstore branch of Daiei. Lighting is carefully planned and well designed. Members of the street co-operate to organise and run regular events to attract customers, just as would happen in a more conventional modern shopping centre.

The Motomachi *shōtengai* in Yokohama is untypical in that it has no roof, but is very much a single planned street of stores. The Motomachi street concentrates strongly on fashion apparel. It has decorative, well designed pavements and street lighting, and has its own information signs and boards. The members of the Motomachi association also co-operate and arrange joint events in the same way roofed streets do.

## Development of the *shōtengai* and its problems

Street association members are, however, the same small, independent retailers that are declining in number. While the largest streets continue to prosper in the same way as new shopping centres, smaller streets, especially those with relatively poor locations away from city centres, or those that are old and badly organised have suffered because of the expansion of new retail facilities elsewhere.

The old Large Store Law aimed to protect small stores from the competitive pressures of larger retail companies, but organised street associations are the focus for the new 1992 policy to encourage small stores to modernise and improve their business. With their organised structure, street associations are ideal bodies through which authorities can channel funding for regional development. As small local businesspeople, often with some experience, they offer the foundation for new ideas and new facilities, and encourage the private sector. For this reason, medium sized and small but well organised and progressive street associations have been the focus of retail redevelopment. Their organisation also helps to gain support from wholesalers and other suppliers (Kunie, 1989).

One government policy supplies grants and low-interest loans for refurbishment, and street organisations are given help to redesign facilities, improve the image of the street and modernise retail technology. Grants and loans for the introduction of electronic point-of-sale systems are especially popular and encouraged.

In some cases, groups of local independent stores have moved together into a purpose-built building, to form a new shopping centre.

These were mostly developed in the 1950s, were previously non-fixed, public markets, and are predominantly food based (Shiraishi, 1991). Following the opening of new multi-storey speciality shopping centres in the 1970s and 1980s (see pages 156–63 below), local authorities and street associations joined together to build similar shopping centres in which the tenants were local retailers. The mixture of retailers in these buildings is more varied than the older, public market buildings, and many include national speciality store chains as well.

The street association and other developers manage the building like a shopping centre. Unlike the chains of shopping centres described on pages 156–7, however, tenants are under less pressure to perform, as they are members of the association who have simply relocated to the new building.

Part of the revision of legislation relating to retail development in 1992 included provision of new funding for revitalisation of independent retailers. This was carried out through the Law for the Development of Commercial Facilities (Tokutei Shōgyō Shūseki Seibi Hō) as Chapter 4 described. As part of this law, an independent consultancy and advisory body was established in mid-1992 consisting of consultants and academics whose job it is to devise and supervise the building of new shopping developments involving independent stores in regional areas. By including some form of community facilities within the structure, existing street associations can receive large grants and interest-free loans to build new shopping centres and relocate their stores to the new centre. This policy is still in its infancy, but thirty independent stores in Toyama Prefecture have already relocated into a new structure sponsored through central and local government (Ito, 1993).

In addition to organising funding, street associations are the focus of the small-store political lobby. They campaign against large stores, the Consumption Tax[4] and other issues seen as a threat to the small retailer. One example was opposition of some associations to retail developments by consumer co-operative societies. Being under the jurisdiction of the Ministry of Welfare rather than MITI, co-operative society retailers do not come under the Large Store Law. Until recently, the movement concentrated on opening small-format stores, but, needing to compete with multiple supermarket retailers, the largest societies are beginning to open outlets of 3,000 square metres or more. Pressure from street associations forced the change of such plans for large co-op stores in western Tokyo and in

Yokohama in the 1980s. In Yokohama, street associations persuaded the co-operative society to reduce the size of the proposed store, and integrate the store into an existing *shōtengai* (Nikkei Ryūtsū Shinbun, 1989c: 96–8).

There are cases where the opposition of a street association to the opening of new large stores has proved misguided. Most multiple retailers have alternative sites in an area they wish to develop. In the face of opposition from local stores, a large retailer may open a store on a second-choice site a few kilometres away. The drawing power of a new large store often means that the original, opposing shopping street may rapidly lose customers. On the other hand, some street associations have used their combined influence to invite large retailers to open in their area, thus attracting more customers to their own facilities.

There are many problems with organising a group of independent retailers, not least the individual personalities of entrepreneurs within the group (Ishihara, 1985). Today there is a growing polarisation between successful, flourishing streets and unsuccessful, declining ones. Nine out of ten *shōtengai* are not optimistic about their future (Chūshō Kigyō Chō, 1988b: 3–4). The successful streets are usually better organised and larger and play a significant role in the overall retail structure of a city. Examples include those in Sendai, Osaka and Kobe. They have some form of organised street management, with regular meetings of member stores, and even employ consultants and advertising agencies.

For most shopping streets, however, decreases in membership, bankruptcy or simply arguments among members will cause long-term decline to continue.

## MULTIPLE CHAINS OF SPECIALITY STORES

There are a wide range of speciality stores in Japan. The Census of Commerce classifies any store that takes over 90 per cent of sales from a single form of merchandise as a speciality store. On this basis, speciality stores are the most common type of retailing, numbering just over 1 million outlets in 1991 (see Chapter 3). They range from small single-outlet independent stores to large nationwide chains, most of which operate small-format outlets because of the specialised nature of the merchandise they sell.

Speciality stores are narrowly focused on a particular type of merchandise. For example, the majority of fashion boutiques not only stock just a single type of clothing, such as women's clothing, but restrict their merchandise to a single brand. Speciality stores provide shopping advice to customers on detailed aspects of the merchandise, provide a full back-up service and arrange special or unusual orders.

Most independent retailers cannot afford to specialise too narrowly because of the high risk of poor sales, but manufacturers of specialised products prefer to offer different lines in separate retail outlets to create a more exclusive image for each individual product and brand.

In the fashion clothing industry, the same manufacturer often sells two different brands through different retail stores, even within the same shopping centre. For example, the Bigi design house operates separate stores for its Pink House, Melrose, Bigi, Men's Bigi and D Grace brands, to name only five. In some cases, customers do not know that two brands are actually manufactured by the same company.

The most preferred location for smaller speciality stores is as a tenant within a shopping centre. The increasing cost of buying or renting land makes free-standing outlets more expensive than the cost of renting space within a multi-store building. This is a supply side reason for the success of multi-storey shopping centres (see pages 156–61). In larger cities where suitable street-front sites with reasonable rents are hardest to find, most speciality store chain outlets locate in shopping buildings, department stores, shopping malls or even supermarkets. Free-standing stores are more common in smaller regional cities.

**Leading multiple speciality store chains**

Multiple speciality store chains accounted for about 6 per cent of total retail sales in 1992. Japan's leading financial newspaper, the *Nihon Keizai Shinbun*, or, more commonly, *Nikkei*, publishes annual listings of the top retail companies. The ranking uses a broad definition of speciality retailing that includes general merchandise discount stores and DIY home centres, but it is a useful source of summary statistics. In the 1993 survey, there were only eight speciality store chains among the top fifty retailers, but 190 in the top 500 (Nikkei Ryūtsū Shinbun, 1993d: 236–45).

Speciality store chains accounted for 20.3 per cent of retail sales among the top 500 companies, a small rise on 1992, and compared to only 18.6 per cent in 1991 (Figure 5.1). While department stores and superstores have larger single shares of the corporate retail market, speciality stores were the only sector to show marked growth throughout the 1980s and into the 1990s (Nikkei Ryūtsū Shinbun, 1992: 282).

On the other hand, the growth in the speciality store sector all but stopped in 1992. This was not only due to poor economic conditions. The two largest markets, clothing and electrical items, are now reaching saturation point. The form of speciality retailing which continues to expand is the opening of new stores in suburban areas. Most of these are on cheaper, roadside sites in city suburbs, and have more parking than is usual for most retailers. Speciality stores selling sports goods, books and car parts and accessories are all expanding into the suburbs. There is also growth in suburban discount men's clothing and electrical stores, even though more up-market stores are doing less well in the city centres (Nikkei Ryūtsū Shinbun, 1993d: 249).

Table 5.2 lists the top twenty corporate chains of speciality stores.[5] There is considerable difference between, for example, a chain of electrical stores and one of fashion boutiques. They differ by individual store size and sales per store because of the difference in the merchandise they sell. There is also significant difference between the companies in terms of business strategy. Most of the leading chains in 1992 took a discounting strategy, but the degree of discounting varies greatly between chains. Readers should view these consolidated figures with care for these reasons.

## Speciality electrical chains

Six of the top twenty store chains deal in electrical items, including the two leading chains. The leading company, Best Denki is based in Fukuoka in northern Kyushu, and most of the company's stores are in Kyushu and southern Honshu, although there are a small number of franchise outlets as far north as Nagoya. By the end of 1992, the company operated 453 stores, 317 of which were franchises. The average store had a sales space of 450 square metres, and parking space for up to fifty cars (Nihon Keizai Shinbun, 1992: 862–4). The company also runs a number of stores overseas, in a tie-up with the international Yaohan chain of supermarkets and shopping centres.

The other large electrical chains are similar to Best Denki. Joshin, the number two speciality store, operates some 184 stores, including

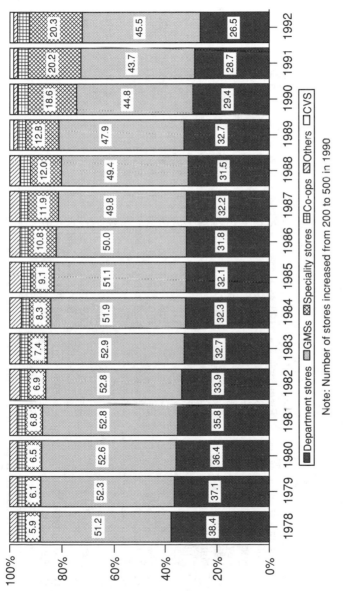

Figure 5.1 Sales of major retail formats in the annual *Nikkei* survey, 1978–92
*Source:* Compiled from Nikkei Ryūtsū Shinbun (1989c; 1992: 282; 1993g: 248)

Note: Number of stores increased from 200 to 500 in 1990

■ Department stores ▧ GMSs ⊠ Speciality stores ⊞ Co-ops ⊠ Others ☐ CVS

Table 5.2 Leading speciality store chains by sales volume 1992–3

| | | Product sector | Sales (¥ million) | % change 93/92 | Profits (¥ million) | % change 93/92 | Stores | Store no. change 93/92 |
|---|---|---|---|---|---|---|---|---|
| 1 | Best Denki | Electrical | 194,728 | −7.6 | 8,089 | −33.9 | 453 | +5 |
| 2 | Joshin | Electrical | 193,490 | −4.5 | 2,202 | −70.2 | 184 | +12 |
| 3 | Chiyoda | Shoes | 180,547 | 7.8 | 11,896 | −16.6 | 1,469 | +210 |
| 4 | Shoes Marutomi | Shoes | 154,796 | 19.1 | 5,731 | 15.7 | 1,608 | +351 |
| 5 | Aoyama | Men's | 150,908 | 29.3 | 30,211 | 11.9 | 441 | +90 |
| 6 | Daiichi | Electrical | 146,707 | −8.9 | 2,583 | −55.5 | 287 | +10 |
| 7 | Maruzen | Books | 124,795 | 2.9 | 2,202 | 0.5 | 38 | − |
| 8 | Alpen | Sports | 111,186 | 14.0 | 5,755 | −33.3 | 302 | +2 |
| 9 | Yodobashi Camera | Cameras | 110,030 | 9.9 | 2,300 | −12.1 | 16 | +2 |
| 10 | Suzutan | Ladies' | 102,910 | 2.5 | 5,325 | −17.5 | 620 | − |
| 11 | Kojima Denki | Electrical | 100,876 | 7.5 | 925 | 12.3 | 150 | −7 |
| 12 | Rerian | Ladies' | 100,386 | 5.1 | 5,393 | −4.9 | 444 | +23 |
| 13 | Kinokuniya | Books | 97,377 | 4.9 | 4,201 | 20.2 | 32 | +2 |
| 14 | Victoria | Sports | 94,357 | −0.9 | 367 | 27.9 | 156 | +22 |
| 15 | Bic Camera | Cameras | 92,759 | 40.6 | n.a. | n.a. | 9 | +2 |
| 16 | Matsuya Denki | Electrical | 89,661 | 2.2 | −221 | −131.3 | 286 | +0 |
| 17 | Laox | Electrical | 89,021 | −4.7 | 1,537 | −29.5 | 73 | −5 |
| 18 | Aoki International | Men's | 80,751 | 18.7 | 11,267 | 10.0 | 185 | +14 |
| 19 | Shinseido | Records | 80,338 | 3.8 | 2,829 | −8.7 | 291 | +14 |
| 20 | Shimashi | Furniture | 78,856 | 10.1 | 10,241 | −2.6 | 54 | +3 |

Source: Compiled from Nikkei Ryūtsū Shinbun (1992: 309–14; 1993d: 271–7)

thirty-two franchises, and averaging about 580 square metres of sales space each. Joshin stores are prominent in suburban areas around the Kansai area. The company also operates a small number in Tokyo suburbs.

Electrical chains suffered more than most in the economic downturn of the early 1990s. Large electrical manufacturers use their own *keiretsu* chains (see Chapter 3) to control the marketing and distribution of their latest models, but the speciality electrical chains provide access to the general mass markets, and manufacturers can no longer afford to ignore them.

Electrical chains sell goods below the manufacturer's price, but most are only pseudo-discounters. Most chains allow customers to negotiate a few more percentage points before purchase, but poor, inefficient cost structures mean that most chains must maintain high gross margins. For consumers, this is not a fair system, and with the electrical market now at saturation point, many are more careful about what they buy (see Chapter 2).

In addition, general merchandise discounters, which have efficient cost structures, are selling the same products at lower prices. To maintain profits, electrical chains rely on sales rebates from manufacturers and, previously, on other assistance such as loan sales assistants (see Chapter 3). These business practices are now unpopular and the largest chains have been forced to attempt to reduce costs. This change came late and profit levels for all the leading electrical chains fell in both 1991 and 1992. Consumers are less inclined to pay high prices for insignificant changes in product design, or for small, additional functions on electrical products.

### The leading speciality shoe chains

The third and fourth largest speciality companies are both chains of discount shoe shops. Along with convenience store chains, these are the only retailers with really large numbers of outlets that stretch across much of the country. In 1992, Chiyoda had 1,469 outlets, and Marutomi 1,608. Only one other company in the top fifteen, Suzutan, had more than 500 outlets. All 3,000 stores in Chiyoda and Marutomi are directly operated, with no franchise outlets, and both companies use formats averaging around 250 square metres. Both sell mainly footwear, but also accessories and some toys. Stores in both chains use discount, 'pile-it-high, sell-it-cheap' techniques, with no frills, and limited personal service. Both companies are publicly listed and pursue aggressive store expansion policies reminiscent of retail companies in the West.

Discounting is the key to the success of Chiyoda and Marutomi. It is interesting to compare discounting at these two shoe chains with the way electrical chains operate. While the electrical stores discount the manufacturers' recommended prices, these prices are so high that small percentage discounts are largely cosmetic.

Chiyoda and Marutomi buy in bulk and reduce costs through intensive use of information systems and by keeping labour costs to a minimum. They maintain close relations with mass production manufacturers and wholesalers, and import a lot of their merchandise through development imports from South-East Asia. The result of this strategy in 1992 was an 8 per cent growth in sales for Chiyoda and 19 per cent for Marutomi. On the other hand, costs rose for both chains. Marutomi invested in over 300 new outlets, and Chiyoda's profits suffered under strong price competition but were still the second highest amongst the top twenty chains (Nikkei Ryūtsū Shinbun, 1993d).

While these chains risk becoming too large to continue direct store operation only, they have so far pursued a successful strategy of rapid expansion which chains in other sectors look to emulate.

## Profits from men's suits

Discounting and low-price stores are the fastest growing areas of the speciality store business. Chiyoda and Marutomi are just the two largest examples of this trend. The other chains which achieved double-digit sales growth in 1992 were all discount stores.

Aoyama, the number five chain, is a men's clothing retailer with over a third of its sales coming from suits. It was the most profitable speciality store chain and the fourth most profitable retailer overall in 1992, with over ¥30,000 million in pre-tax profits. The company just missed achieving 30 per cent sales growth for the second year in succession (*Chain Store Age*, 1993).

Aoyama is one of several similar companies all selling men's suits and casual wear. Aoki International, the eighteenth largest chain in 1992, is its main rival. Again, Aoki stands out with high profits. Both Aoki and Aoyama were successful even in the poor economic climate (*Chain Store Age, 1993*).

The secret of their success again is discounting. Use of cheap suburban roadside locations, easily reached by car and with plenty of parking space, is a major part of their strategy (Nihon Keizai Shinbun, 1993b). This gives them cheaper rents than city-centre locations. In 1992, Aoyama had 441 stores averageing 430 square metres, and Aoki 185 stores with about 495 square metres of sales space each (Nihon Keizai Shinbun, 1992).

Like the shoe retailers, both Aoyama and Aoki sell cut-price goods, providing large stocks of cheaply made off-the-peg suits. Prices are well below those of the traditional sellers of suits, such as designer-brand speciality stores and department stores. Labour costs are kept as low as possible, with a single store employing perhaps only two full-time employees and other positions being filled by part-time workers. Most outlets employ fewer than three people full-time.

**Other speciality store chains and new developments**

Other chains use the same discount-oriented, roadside speciality format. Alpen and Victoria, the two largest sports retailers, are examples. The big electrical chains began to use a similar strategy in the late 1980s.

In a sudden change of strategy, in early 1993, Aoyama opened a store in Ginza – the most expensive shopping area in Japan. The company followed this with another store in Shibuya, also a high-class, exclusive area in Tokyo. Both stores have been a great success, selling cut-price suits next door to some of the most expensive department stores in the country.

New low-price stores like Chiyoda or Aoyama are finding success because they fill a pricing gap in the Japanese retail system. Consumers have long had access to high-price branded goods, and retailers like the electrical speciality stores offered some discounts on the top price range. True bargains were rare, however, even from so-called discounters, because retailers maintained high gross margins in order to cover high costs. Aoyama and Chiyoda are more concerned with controlling costs, and have begun to offer real discounts.

The economic downturn of the early 1990s made low-price retailers even more attractive to consumers who began to take greater care with their spending. Overall, the multiple speciality store chains who are still enjoying growth are the ones offering good value through both reasonable quality and prices.

## CONVENIENCE STORE RETAILING

Convenience stores, as their name suggests, offer convenience, but nowhere more so than in Japan. Among the various problems and criticisms surrounding the distribution system, the convenience store sector offers one area of great success and innovation. Arguably, convenience stores in Japan represent some of the most advanced retailing systems in the world.

Convenience stores were the major new retail format of the 1980s. Their success is due to highly efficient chain operations and popularity among consumers. The leading chains are part of the largest superstore groupings (see Chapter 7). Originally these large retail groups developed convenience stores as a means to open new business while avoiding the Large Store Law.

Convenience chains offer a wide range of basic goods and services that anyone may need at short notice at any time of day, and within easy reach of the home or office. Most chains base their merchandise mix on prepared foods and simple household goods like cleaning materials, stationery, toiletries and simple leisure products such as magazines.

Stores serve an immediate local area, usually within a 500 metre radius. They operate long hours. Both the Census of Commerce and *Nikkei* define convenience stores as opening for sixteen hours or more a day. Many, notably those located on busy inner-city roads, stay open twenty-four hours. Chains, therefore, provide convenience in terms of merchandise mix, close proximity to clientele and opening hours.

Convenience stores are close relations of small, independent neighbourhood stores. Previously, it was the neighbourhood store that provided similar convenience products and long business hours. Many small retailers still operate in this way.

### The leading convenience store chains

Today convenience store retailing is no longer the province of the local corner shop. The first convenience store chains were founded in the mid-1970s. In 1992, the three largest retail groups also operated the three largest chains of convenience stores. The top seven chains all operate over 1,000 outlets, and sales growth for the top seventy chains in 1992 was almost 17 per cent.

Most convenience stores are small, local shops run by big businesses. Nikkei Ryūtsū Shinbun (1988: 470) specified five criteria under which a chain of stores qualifies as a convenience store. To be a convenience store, the shop must:

- employ self-service
- operate more than sixteen hours a day
- have a sales floor space of less than 200 square metres
- take less than 30 per cent of total sales from fresh foods
- have fewer than two closing days a month.

Under this definition, the Nikkei Ryūtsū Shinbun rankings distinguish between convenience stores and mini-supermarkets, or *mini-sūpā*. A mini-supermarket is similar to a convenience store, except that it does not quite meet all of the above criteria. They are usually a little larger, operate slightly fewer hours or have more monthly closing days. In addition, perishable foods, especially fresh groceries, generally account for more than 30 per cent of the turnover of a mini-supermarket. Mini-supermarkets are more frequently independent stores or are part of voluntary chains linked to a large wholesaler. Convenience stores are more usually part of franchise chains managed by retail groups.

Table 5.3 provides the Nikkei Ryūtsū Shinbun ranking of the leading twenty convenience store chains by turnover for 1992–3. Sixteen of the top twenty were convenience stores as strictly defined. The remaining four were mini-supermarkets. This is the reverse of the situation in 1987 when there were only seven convenience stores in the top twenty chains, and illustrates the success of the convenience store format, and their use of franchising as a business organisation method. Most mini-supermarkets are voluntary chains, and there were only sixteen in the leading fifty chains, again compared to thirty-two in 1987.

Of the leading convenience and mini-supermarket chains, nine were retailer led, seven wholesaler led, with the rest independent or linked to manufacturers. Thirteen chains used a franchise system, and the other seven were voluntary chains. The largest voluntary chain operation in the world, Spar, was also well represented, with six regional chains in the top fifty.

Convenience stores and mini-supermarkets grew rapidly throughout the 1980s. Now, the rate of growth is slowing, having peaked at 28.8 per cent in 1982, and it was 10.7 per cent in 1992–3 (*Nikkei Ryūtsū Shinbun*, 1993g). The number of stores also grew by 9.7 per cent. The 1991 Census of Commerce (see Chapter 4), using a broader

Table 5.3 Leading convenience store chains by sales, 1992–3

| Store | Parent company | Format | Sales (¥ million) | % change 93/92 | % sales by chain type | | | Stores | Store no. change 93/92 |
|---|---|---|---|---|---|---|---|---|---|
| | | | | | Direct | FC | VC | | |
| 1 Seven-Eleven | Ito-Yokado | CVS | 1,194,913 | 10.4 | 1.9 | 98.1 | 0.0 | 5,058 | +429 |
| 2 Lawson/Sun Chain | Daiei | CVS | 666,400 | 11.3 | n.a | n.a | n.a | 4,448 | +378 |
| 3 Family Mart | Saison Group | CVS | 413,939 | 9.9 | 3.9 | 96.1 | 0.0 | 2,311 | +221 |
| 4 Sun-shop Yamazaki | Yamazaki Bread | CVS | 321,950 | 9.9 | 4.8 | 95.2 | 0.0 | 2,427 | +150 |
| 5 Zennishoku Chain | Zennihon Shokuhin | MS | 265,900 | 18.0 | 0.0 | 0.0 | 100.0 | 1,878 | +258 |
| 6 Circle K | Uny | CVS | 193,599 | 17.4 | n.a | n.a | n.a | 1,255 | +166 |
| 7 K-Mart | Kittaka | MS | 142,640 | –3.9 | 0.0 | 0.0 | 100.0 | 1,096 | –70 |
| 8 Sunkusu | Nagasakiya | CVS | 137,900 | 21.2 | 0.9 | 99.1 | 0.0 | 804 | +120 |
| 9 Community Store | Kokubu | CVS | 84,520 | 2.1 | 0.0 | 0.0 | 100.0 | 575 | +23 |
| 10 Monmāto | Monmāto Suto | CVS | 74,718 | 6.1 | 1.1 | 0.0 | 98.9 | 442 | +14 |
| 11 Mini-Stop | Jusco | CVS | 74,279 | 12.0 | 8.0 | 92.0 | 0.0 | 440 | +59 |
| 12 Hot Spar | Kasumi | CVS | 69,980 | 2.7 | 2.6 | 97.4 | 0.0 | 517 | +27 |
| 13 Seicomart | Nishio Maruyo | CVS | 68,100 | 9.7 | 0.0 | 100.0 | 0.0 | 425 | +41 |
| 14 Coco Store | Izumikku | CVS | 60,000 | 22.4 | 1.0 | 99.1 | 0.0 | 483 | +76 |
| 15 Spar/Hot Spar | Tōkan | MS | 43,991 | 0.4 | n.a | 0.0 | 85.9 | 190 | +30 |
| 16 3-8/Hi-Mart | Hiroya | CVS | 43,034 | 0.8 | 2.1 | 0.0 | 97.9 | 253 | +6 |
| 17 3-F | Fuji Shitio | CVS | 39,845 | 30.0 | 17.7 | 82.3 | 0.0 | 239 | +61 |
| 18 Sēbuon | Iseya | CVS | 37,770 | 27.5 | 29.4 | 70.6 | 0.0 | 366 | +98 |
| 19 Spar | Osaka Spar | MS | 33,778 | 4.3 | 0.0 | 0.0 | 100.0 | 131 | –2 |
| 20 Family Mart | Chubu Family Mart | CVS | 27,955 | 20.3 | 5.3 | 94.7 | 0.0 | 209 | –2 |

Key: CVS = convenience store, FC = franchise chain, MS = mini-supermarket, VC = voluntary chain.
Source: Compiled from Niikkei Ryūtsū Shinbun (1993g).

definition than that in the *Nikkei* survey, also recorded considerable growth in this sector, with a 24.4 per cent increase in store numbers from 1988–93.

The *Nikkei* survey covered 108 companies and included 24,556 outlets, 10 per cent of which were the broader mini-supermarket format. These companies had overall sales of ¥3.7 trillion in 1992, or about 2.6 per cent of total retail sales.

## The success of convenience store chains

These figures show rapid, marked success. What led to this success? Partly, convenience stores arrived in the Japanese market at the right time, fitting in well with urban consumer lifestyles. Equally, convenience stores are the competitive front line for the largest retail companies, leading aggressive expansion policies and providing innovation which companies translate back into their other store formats. Linked with this, the success of the largest convenience store chains lies in the development of efficient management systems.

In the late 1970s, powerful retail groups such as Ito-Yokado, Daiei and Saison used the know-how, experience and buying power of their large supermarket chains to build new convenience store chains. Starting from scratch so to speak, these new chains could ignore or bypass less efficient aspects of traditional distribution channels, such as dealing on the basis of personal relationships and relying on wholesale intermediaries. The smaller store format of convenience stores also offered greater flexibility in opening new stores, and the predominant use of franchising gave chains access to a wide range of locations.

Chains of convenience stores use one of three general chain management systems. Stores are operated directly by the parent company, as a franchise or as a voluntary store.

The largest convenience chains operate at least some of their stores directly. They do this for two reasons. First, a small pool of stores is useful for various training and experimental purposes. New products and management and customer service techniques are introduced into these stores, and information systems can be tested. Store personnel, field supervisors, general management personnel and prospective franchisees may receive their training in these stores. The number of directly operated stores in a chain generally depends on the size of the overall chain operation. For example, larger chains are developing their own retail brands, and use directly operated outlets to allow quick, accurate test marketing.

Alternatively, a franchisor may operate a store directly to take advantage of a good retail location when a suitable franchisee is unavailable. The search for new franchisees is slow and takes a lot of management time. Large chains may even rent or buy existing independent store premises, and convert them into a directly operated store. The parent company assigns an employee or an employee's family to the store as the store manager. These are called *itaku keiei ten* or 'trust-managed stores'. They are operated by personnel assigned by the franchisor or voluntary chain organiser rather than by the original owner of the store. Nevertheless, the original owner often retains rights to the store, land or parts of the building as with a full franchise agreement. This distinguishes the outlet from other directly operated stores.

Leading chains such as Lawson and Sun-shop Yamazaki use this method of site acquisition to achieve a rapid increase in the number and geographical spread of stores (MITI, 1989a: 284–5). Lawson also encourages employees from its parent retail group Daiei to operate their own businesses as franchisees. In keeping with the general principle of lifetime employment, the company helps willing middle-career employees to become convenience store franchisees in stores that were previously operated directly.

In addition to directly operated stores, twenty-seven of the top fifty chains ranked by the Nikkei Ryūtsū Shinbun 1992 survey were mainly voluntary chains. As in Europe, wholesalers organise and operate voluntary chains (Efuji, 1982). Members receive the advantages of a wide choice of goods at lower supply prices, while the wholesaler can buy in larger quantities because of its assured market.

Compared with many franchisees, voluntary chain members often receive a less sophisticated membership package. That is to say, there is less emphasis on new store fronts and design, store interior, logos, own brand labels, management supervision and store technology. On the other hand, members retain a greater degree of independence. Voluntary chain membership generally incurs a lower royalty charge than for franchise chains, but there are some major exceptions (MITI, 1989a: 476; Shōkuhin Shōgyō, 1987: 234–71).

Although five of the twenty chains shown in Table 5.3 are voluntary chains, the growth rates among these companies were well behind those using a franchise system. While only one of the largest companies suffered a decline in sales in 1992–3, average

sales growth for the top voluntary chains was 3.9 per cent compared
with 15.7 per cent for the franchise operators. The largest voluntary
chain in 1993 was Zennishoku with 1,878 stores, and sales of over
¥265,000 million.

Franchising is the third common form of convenience store
operation, and the most successful. Most of the largest and the fastest
growing companies use a franchise system. Usually, these systems
are highly controlled and automated. Franchisors provide everything
from shop fronts to employee manuals on how to wash their hands
and how to sweep the floor. As little as possible is left to the
franchisees to decide for themselves.

The rewards can be considerable for both chain and individual
franchise store. Efficient use of space and a rapid turnaround of
merchandise are the main objectives at store level. Through proper
training and advice from field supervisors, franchisees and store
managers carefully adjust a store's merchandise mix to attain a
rapid turnaround of stock, without either stock-outs or excess
inventory. To achieve this, companies use information on consumer
demand gathered at each and every store, and efficient physical
distribution systems.

### Use of information technology in convenience store chains

Convenience store chains are at the forefront in both information
technology and physical distribution systems in Japanese retailing.
They excel at both. Larger retailing groups pass successful developments on to other parts of their business such as supermarkets
and speciality stores.

By 1987, ninety-one of the top 102 chains were already using
electronic ordering systems (EOS) in their stores to make daily
ordering tasks fast and accurate (Nikkei Ryūtū Shinbun, 1989c: 480).
By the 1990s, most chains had an integrated information system for
both EOS and point-of-sale (POS) customer information gathering.

In the 1987 *Nikkei* survey, 14.8 per cent of convenience stores and
just 1.8 per cent of mini-supermarkets were also using POS terminals
throughout their store chains. By 1991, 53.4 per cent of convenience
store chains had POS technology in all their stores, and the proportion for all convenience store and mini-supermarket chains using
POS data in at least part of their chains was over 86 per cent.

The largest chain, Seven-Eleven Japan, has employed POS terminals in all its stores since the early 1980s (Seven-Eleven, 1989a,

1989b). Circle K (Japan) and Sunkusu completed installation of POS technology throughout their chains in 1988 (Nikkei Ryūtsū Shinbun, 1989c: 480). The other major chains installed it by the early 1990s. Now the largest and most advanced systems use real-time data exchange whereby head office knows the sales and stock situation in any of its members' stores at any time (see Chapter 3). In 1992, more than 10 per cent of convenience store chains were already using these advanced systems (Nikkei Ryūtsū Shinbun, 1993g).

This is used to keep a detailed track of merchandise inventory and sales, and to collect data on the customers using the store. Most systems use bar code scanning. For every sale, computers record the merchandise items sold and the time the sale was made, but many systems go further. The shop assistant who scans the items also keys in the sex of the customer and, in some cases, also a rough estimate of the customer's age.

With several thousand stores in a chain, this provides the largest convenience store companies with a huge volume of information. The information is used to fine-tune the merchandise mix for each store and for the overall chain. For its own 500-metre-radius trading area, each store knows what sells well and what does not. With the help of field supervisors dispatched from the franchisor, store managers carefully identify the best-selling products and the time of day when they sell. Products that sell poorly are watched and quickly replaced if poor performance continues.

Frequent delivery and knowledge of local demand mean inventory is tightly controlled. Most convenience stores are around 100 square metres in size, so shelf space is not wasted on items that are not likely to be sold within a relatively short period. The best-selling items are perishable prepared meals, so stores receive deliveries three or more times a day (see Figure 5.2). This is strict just-in-time delivery. Delivery vehicles have a timetable which may give them no more than a thirty-minute margin of error when delivering to a store. In some cases, if the delivery is late, stores can claim some form of compensation.

While there are differences between chains, most convenience stores carry around 3,000–4,000 product items. In the case of Seven-Eleven, the franchise offers member stores a pool of around 6,000 items and the average store carries 3,000. Using past experience, data from other similar outlets and then data generated with the store's own POS terminal, store operators and field supervisors tailor the merchandise mix for each individual store depending on its own

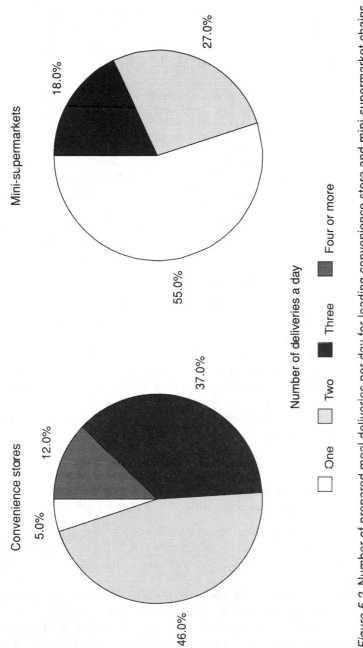

Convenience stores

5.0%
12.0%
37.0%
46.0%

Mini-supermarkets

18.0%
27.0%
55.0%

Number of deliveries a day

One    Two    Three    Four or more

Figure 5.2 Number of prepared meal deliveries per day for leading convenience store and mini-supermarket chains
Source: Nikkei Ryūtsū Shinbun (1992)

local circumstances. Some stores offer a small number of local products but 95 per cent is taken from a standard merchandise mix.

At the macro level, the franchisor uses data to identify macro trends. The company can identify geographical areas where more stores are likely to be successful, products that sell well and those that do not, and general trends in consumer behaviour. The largest chains use the data to develop and test their own new products and new store management techniques. Products are adapted and tested very quickly in this way.

The largest convenience store chains have instigated jointly operated distribution centres. Companies which jointly operate and use the centre may be from either the same retail group, or a group of the chain's suppliers, without the retailer being directly involved at all. Some convenience chains have the buying power to insist that competing suppliers co-operate to provide joint distribution services to the chain (Nikkei Ryūtsū Shinbun, 1992: 437; 1993d: 402–3).

**Convenience merchandise and services**

Consumers who have little time for mundane shopping like the long opening hours that convenience stores offer. These include working housewives and mothers, students and single workers. Convenience store operators are well aware of this, and merchandise and services reflect the needs of these groups. They provide a wide range of goods and a growing range of services which were previously available only in specialist stores.

Chains mainly offer four types of merchandise. In order of importance, these are:

- processed foods (liquors, seasonings, confectionery, etc.)
- daily foods (milk, dairy products, bread products, etc.)
- fast foods (prepared meals, salads, heated items, etc.)
- non-food items (magazines, toiletries, stationery, etc.)

recently, fast foods have become increasingly important to convenience stores. Three items are common to all outlets: prepared meals, called o-bentō, hot items from small, heated cabinets, and rice balls.

Prepared meals are rice-based dishes that come in an amazing number of types and varieties. Advances in packaging over recent years mean that most prepared meals can be reheated in the store microwave. Most chains offer a tray of o-den, a kind of Japanese stew, and a selection of hot steamed dumplings with various fillings to supplement the meals.

The single best-selling type of merchandise for many chains is their *o-nigiri* or rice balls. Convenience stores are responsible for many product innovations, but these are the most remarkable. Rice balls are the equivalent of the Western sandwich – another form of fast food that most stores also sell – and housewives make them at home for packed lunches and picnics. The convenience store version of these homely products is a neat triangle of rice filled with some tangy or spicy filling, then wrapped with a thin sheet of seaweed. Shop rice balls are packaged in such a way that the moist rice and filling are kept separate from the crisp, dry seaweed until the rice ball is actually unwrapped. Each chain has its own design, but the packaging allows rice balls to be unwrapped easily and quickly, with no sticky fingers, while leaving the seaweed crisp and fresh.

In addition to convenience products, chains now offer an increasing number of services. Nearly all stores act as agents for parcel delivery services, and most provide photograph developing. Other services include microwave ovens in the store to heat the ready-to-eat foods, sale of stamps, mail order, dry cleaning, hot food counters, picnic areas, sandwich making, made-to-order birthday cakes, photocopying and facsimile services. Beginning with the Seven-Eleven chain, some of the largest began to provide facilities for customers to pay gas, electricity and telephone bills at their stores. A future development is likely to be the amalgamation of convenience stores and larger services such as petrol stations, video rental stores and fast-food restaurants (MITI, 1989a: 288–9). Services accounted for less than 3 per cent of sales in 1990, but provide a useful means of drawing customers back to the store again and again.

## Dominance of leading chains

The largest four companies are now becoming increasingly dominant. The leading convenience store chain, Seven-Eleven, exceeded sales of ¥1.1 billion in 1992–3, with a chain of over 5,000 stores. By 1995, the chain had 5,500 outlets and is still growing despite the slowdown in the economy. Overall, the Seven–Eleven chain sells more food than any other retailer in Japan, outstripping even the largest superstore chain, Daiei (*Chain Store Age*, 1992).

Figures 5.3 and 5.4 illustrate the dominant position of the top convenience store chains. The second placed chain, Daiei Convenience

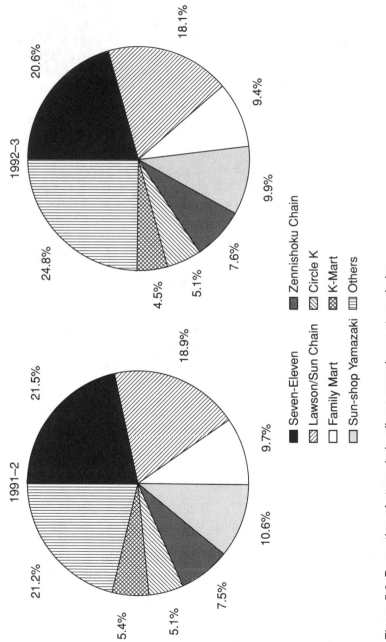

*Figure 5.3* Proportion of stores in leading convenience store chains
*Source*: Compiled from Nikkei Ryūtsū Shinbun (1993g)

90

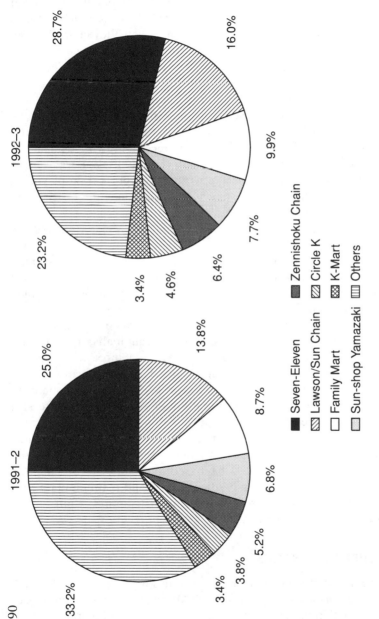

*Figure 5.4* Sales shares of leading convenience store chains
*Source*: Nikkei Ryūtsū Shinbun (1993g)

Systems, which includes both Lawson and Sun Chain stores, had a little over 4,000 stores and sales of ¥666,400 million. This is almost 45 per cent less than Seven-Eleven. In 1990, the parent company of Seven-Eleven Japan, Ito-Yokado, acquired 70 per cent of Southland Corporation of America, the owner of Seven-Eleven worldwide. Consequently, Ito-Yokado now controls over 13,000 convenience stores worldwide (Ito-Yokado, 1992; Kaletsky, 1990; Thomson, 1990a; Thomson and Kaletsky, 1990).

Leading convenience stores are very popular with consumers. The first convenience stores supplemented the service provided by supermarkets when they opened in the late 1970s (Dodwell Marketing Consultants, 1988: 38). Today they meet a growing demand for quick, convenient shopping in local communities. Large chains targeted new residential housing with a high proportion of young, dual-income couples, and student areas around universities and colleges (Seascope, 1989).

The front of the Shiogamaguchi campus of Meijo University in Nagoya is a striking example. There are no fewer than nine competing convenience stores within 300 metres of the university main gate: two Lawsons, two Circle K stores, two Coco Stores, one Dairy & Deli, one Mini-Stop and one Sun Chain store. A common strategy among all the top chains is to saturate city areas, aiming to have a store on every corner. In this way they keep out competitors. On the other hand, there is significant cannibalisation of sales between stores in the same chain that have to compete.

While growth in sales and store numbers among convenience store chains remains high, the sector is fast reaching maturity and the market is close to saturation in some areas. There still remains considerable scope for expansion in smaller cities and, to a lesser degree, some rural areas. The top chains will continue to increase their domination by both sales volume and store numbers. Competition will be based on the skill of adapting merchandise mix within individual stores, and maintaining a full, fresh stock of goods through efficient distribution. Both factors favour the larger companies.

## SHOPPING CENTRES

Shopping centres are another type of retail organisation with which small formats are strongly involved. Many are simply extensions of street associations, and some department stores and general merchandise stores are counted as shopping centres as they house a number of small stores.

There are a wide range of shopping centres in Japan, varying from the better organised shopping streets (see pages 129–36) to large, planned shopping developments, some of which exceed 100,000 metres in sales space. Some, like the Harborland complex in central Kobe, were built on the instigation of local government and include a number of large retailers. Most, however, are private developments, and all the largest retail companies have some interest in shopping centre development.

In 1992, the Japan Shopping Center Association (JSCA) had 1,695 member shopping centres (see Table 5.4). It is common for smaller stores to operate concessions within department stores and general merchandise stores, and most of the JSCA's members[6] are based around one of these two key formats. Table 5.4 shows a steady rise in new members throughout the 1980s. The growth of 114 new centres in 1992 reflects the relaxation of the Large Store Law in the previous year (see Chapter 4). Total sales for all JSCA members in 1991 were over ¥16.2 billion, or about 10 per cent of total retail sales. The large number of department stores and superstores who are key

*Table 5.4* Membership of Japan Shopping Center Association

| Year opened | New SCs | Tenants[a] | Sales space | Total sales (¥ million)[b] |
|---|---|---|---|---|
| Pre-1980 | 803 | 43,339 | 6,464,209 | 6,204.9 |
| 1981 | 84 | 3,860 | 769,977 | 8,094.1 |
| 1982 | 80 | 3,468 | 619,235 | 9,081.8 |
| 1983 | 56 | 2,097 | 386,235 | 9,173.2 |
| 1984 | 54 | 2,312 | 449,878 | 10,072.2 |
| 1985 | 52 | 2,506 | 444,005 | 10,620.7 |
| 1986 | 66 | 2,874 | 541,563 | 11,377.4 |
| 1987 | 68 | 3,144 | 568,774 | 11,895.4 |
| 1988 | 64 | 3,176 | 708,657 | 13,591.2 |
| 1989 | 87 | 4,427 | 822,330 | 13,961.3 |
| 1990 | 83 | 3,612 | 827,242 | 15,115.3 |
| 1991 | 84 | 3,063 | 735,444 | 16,198.7 |
| 1992 | 114 | 4,439 | 1,067,216 | n.a. |
| Total | 1,695 | 82,317 | 14,404,764 | |

[a] Figures include both key tenants and normal tenants.
[b] Sales figures for all JSCA members.
*Source*: Compiled and adapted from JSCA (1993)

tenants within the membership create a significant overlap with these sectors, however.

Shopping centres in Japan are best discussed in two main groups. There are large-scale, general shopping centres which are usually focused on one or more large key tenant retailers, and speciality shopping centres which include both underground shopping malls and multi-storey shopping buildings. In either case, as they house both branches of multiple speciality store chains and local retailers, many are a further form of small-format retail organisation.

## General shopping centres

Large shopping centres are relatively rare because of the scarcity of suitable sites. There are a number of larger, multi-store shopping complexes, and in 1989 MITI indicated that it would like to encourage the development of more (MITI, 1989a). Major shopping and leisure complexes act as stimuli for regional development, and can involve large retail companies in co-operation with existing small local retailers.

Among the JSCA members, 1,064 centres had a single key tenant. By far the largest number of key tenants, 650, were general merchandise chain outlets. In addition, 264 member centres had more than one key tenant. Not surprisingly, only three members had two general merchandise outlets from competing chains in the same centre (JSCA, 1993: 6). These form the majority of JSCA members, but few were designed as shopping centres rather than as single large outlets with more than ten tenants.

The need for larger land area means that general shopping centres usually locate away from inner cities. Car parking facilities are more extensive at shopping centres than at most store types. The range of merchandise depends on the tenants at the centre, and many provide sports and leisure facilities in addition to retailing (MITI, 1989a: 237).

Some of the largest shopping centres are designed as 'retail towns'. One of the largest is MYCAL Honmoku in Yokohama. The MYCAL Group developed and operates the centre exclusively. It includes its own fashion building (see pages 160–3), a Saty superstore and numerous restaurants (Nichii, 1989; and see Chapter 7). Tsukashin in Hyogo Prefecture is another example (Seibu Saison Group, 1986). It has total sales space of 65,000 square metres, with a Seibu department store as the main outlet. The complex has 245 tenants, including a sports centre and a church (Seibu Saison Group, 1989: 237; 1988).

Saison Group also operates a joint complex at Hikarigaoka in Tokyo. Hikarigaoka includes both a Seibu department store and a Chujitsuya superstore, as well as numerous speciality stores. It was built in the middle of a large residential housing complex and is designed to meet the needs of local families. At weekends, the centre runs various events to entertain children and parents, and there is also a leisure club and cinema. With a large family market in the immediate vicinity, Hikarigaoka has relatively limited car parking space and is not built near to rail links. It does, however, have parking space for around 500 bicycles (Seibu Saison Group, 1989).

The largest single shopping centre in Japan in 1992 was Rarapōto in Chiba Prefecture with a total area of over 270,000 square metres and around 97,000 square metres of sales space. The key tenants are a large Daiei superstore and a Sogo department store, which together account for more than 50 per cent of the sales area. There are 345 tenants in total. Rarapōto is built on the Tokyo Bay waterfront, and relies on large car parking space (6,000 cars) to attract customers from a wide area. Weekend customer numbers usually exceed 150,000 people, with an average of 25,000 on weekdays (MITI, 1989a: 237).

One of the newest shopping developments is Harborland in central Kobe. It opened in the autumn of 1992, and has an unusual design. The local Kobe city government co-operated in the development of the site in order to spread shopping facilities out of the city centre. Harborland includes both Seibu and Hankyu department stores, a fashion building (see below), the largest outlet of the Daiei general merchandise store chain and about 200 speciality stores. Daiei also opened Japan's first wholesale club in the complex. Harborland uses an innovative mixture of underground and overground design, and includes a separate complex of speciality stores designed as a series of red-brick buildings along narrow pedestrian streets.

Other cities and companies would like to open similar large complexes, but most companies are wary of the continuing decline in consumer spending. For example, Harborland, one of the most innovative designs and one of the newest big shopping centres, is suffering from low customer flow through most of the complex even at weekends. The only part that is highly successful is Daiei's wholesale club, again indicating the shift towards the popularity of lower-price retailing.

## Speciality shopping centres

There are two types of speciality shopping centres in Japan and both exist mainly because of land scarcity. One type extends underground, and the other several storeys above ground.

There are extensive underground shopping facilities in all of the largest cities, including Tokyo, Nagoya, Osaka, Sapporo and Kyoto. Nagoya in particular is famous for two large underground areas, one in the station area and one in the city centre.

For the consumer, there is little difference between underground malls and speciality shopping centres. Each is self-contained, but the malls often link with public transport nodes and large department stores within city centres. Customer flow is high as many people pass through the malls to avoid both cold in winter and heat in summer, and to gain access to subways. The central Nagoya underground mall, called Central Park, serves just these purposes. It includes 241 restaurants and speciality stores in one and a half kilometres of underground walkways.

The cost and specialist design needs of underground centres mean that they are only built where absolutely necessary. Cities which have a subway system can develop these centres relatively easily, and most have done so. Where underground is not an option, multi-storey shopping buildings are popular, and have become one of the most characteristic parts of Japanese retailing.

These shopping buildings are the most common single form of shopping centre in Japan. They are called 'fashion buildings', and they are everywhere. As speciality shopping centres, fashion buildings represent another form of small retail organisation. They mix the traditional organisation of small stores into street associations with the popularity of speciality stores into a single retail facility.

As their name suggests, most fashion buildings have a strong merchandise bias towards fashion apparel. Most have no large, key tenants, and house only small-format speciality apparel, accessories and variety outlets. Only 367 of the JSCA's members had no key tenant in 1992, but this was the second largest category after those based on general merchandise stores (JSCA, 1993: 6). While the latter are general merchandise stores first and 'shopping centres' second, fashion buildings are designed and developed purely as shopping centres.

Fashion buildings are multi-storey structures, usually with at least four floors. Most locate in city centres, often close to department stores, and this means they need little parking space as customers can reach them on public transport.

By varying their tenant mix, some buildings are more down-market, with less famous-brand tenants, for example Joinus in Yokohama, but others represent the most exclusive retailing, like the Fuji TV Building in central Nagoya.

Fashion buildings are commonly found above or next to main railway stations. Yokohama station has five fashion buildings built above or immediately adjacent to the station itself, and there are similar examples in medium and small cities such as Mito, Omiya, Matsue and Morioka. Developing fashion buildings above railway stations is a popular form of regional development. All the big Tokyo stations have some kind of shopping development over or around them, and most include fashion buildings.

The layout of fashion buildings is similar to that of department stores, rising from food floors, through fashion goods, to variety goods and finally restaurants at the top. Tenants are speciality chain stores and local retailers.

As already noted, manufacturers sell different fashion brands through differentiated outlets, and a single manufacturer may operate several outlets within a fashion building, either directly or by franchise. The second largest group of tenants are variety retailers selling toys, accessories, stationery, records and tapes, posters and general merchandise. Many buildings include at least one bookseller, and some have services such as opticians, booking offices, fortune telling and hairdressing. Newer fashion buildings also take health clubs, saunas, culture centres and even hotels as tenants.

Tenant restaurants are located on the top floors. Most fashion buildings offer a mixture of foods, including both Japanese and Western food. Larger fashion buildings, like department stores, also house a number of speciality food stores in the basement.

The majority of fashion buildings are single operations, but the original fashion building design came from the Saison Group. The company now operates a chain of fashion buildings under the name Parco. Other companies have developed their own chains, including 109 (Tokyu Group), Forus (Jusco Group), Moars (Odakyu Group) and Vivre (MYCAL Group). Parco and Vivre include some of the largest fashion buildings in Japan, and dominate this retail format (see Table 5.5).

Fashion building operators take care to target their mix of tenants.

*Table 5.5* Leading fashion building outlets by sales, 1992

| Ranking for all retail stores | Store | Prefecture | Sales (¥ million) | % change 92/91 |
|---|---|---|---|---|
| 1  | 71  | Nagoya Parco | Aichi | 36,525 | 1.2 |
| 2  | 72  | Ikebukuro Parco | Tokyo | 36,460 | −5.6 |
| 3  | 109 | Sapporo Parco | Hokkaido | 27,475 | −2.9 |
| 4  | 111 | Shibuya Parco | Tokyo | 26,639 | −12.6 |
| 5  | 116 | Chofu Parco | Tokyo | 25,921 | −1.6 |
| 6  | 136 | Yokohama Moars | Kanagawa | 22,261 | n.a. |
| 7  | 154 | Chiba Parco | Chiba | 20,144 | −12.9 |
| 8  | 184 | Kawasaki Moars | Kanagawa | 17,481 | n.a. |
| 9  | 189 | MYCAL Honmoku | Kanagawa | 16,846 | −2.6 |
| 10 | 194 | Tsudanuma Parco | Chiba | 16,578 | −8.8 |
| 11 | 197 | Shin-Tokorozawa Parco | Saitama | 16,412 | −2.7 |
| 12 | 208 | Tenjin Vivre | Fukuoka | 15,728 | 2.3 |
| 13 | 221 | Atsugi Vivre | Kanagawa | 14,764 | n.a. |
| 14 | 248 | Yokohama Vivre | Kanagawa | 14,067 | −1.3 |
| 15 | 249 | Kichijoji Parco | Tokyo | 13,944 | −8.6 |

*Source*: Nikkei Ryūtsū Shinbun (1992: 424; 1993g: 388)

The majority of fashion buildings cater for young customers, but individual buildings target fairly narrow age ranges.

The fashion buildings in Shibuya in Tokyo offer the best example. In one small area there are three 109 buildings, three Parco buildings and Seibu Seed. These are in addition to three department stores, a large Seibu Loft, a Tokyu Hands outlet and three Marui buildings in the same area. Marui stores resemble fashion buildings in design, with lots of small, single-brand corners, but operate like a department store.

In Shibuya, each building, including Marui's stores, differentiates the type of merchandise it stocks and the services it offers. For example, one Tokyu 109 fashion building targets students and young workers aged between 20 and 30, while another, a large building of nine floors, carries merchandise predominantly for the 13- to 20-year-old junior-high-school and high-school age groups. The three Parco buildings also each target slightly different clientele.

These Shibuya Parco stores were the first fashion buildings, opening in 1972 (Suzuki, 1984). They targeted young, fashionable consumers, and soon built a 'trendy' reputation. In the 1980s, Parco's Shibuya stores saw declining sales, as their original target customers grew older and moved on. The next generation of youngsters (see Chapter 2) saw Parco as old fashioned and too expensive (Sekine *et al.*, 1983).

The chain has since altered its strategy and tailored each of its buildings to local markets.

As Table 5.5 shows, the most successful Parco fashion building is in Nagoya. The store has a total area of 73,200 square metres split between two buildings in the centre of Nagoya. It houses 340 tenant stores in 44,000 square metres of sales space (Shimizu, 1989). It has eleven floors six for retail tenants, two restaurant floors, and a hotel and sports club, including a swimming pool, in the top three. The annex has a further six retail floors, a planetarium and a night club. Sales exceeded ¥36,500 million in 1992 (see Table 5.5). It was the seventy-first largest retail outlet by sales, and one of only two fashion buildings among the leading stores to achieve sales growth in 1992–3.

Stores like Nagoya Parco represent a direction for future shopping centre development. They combine the prestige of a department store with the flexibility and familiarity of a fashion building. Large retail groups can employ their knowledge of other formats, and their strength in general distribution. As tenants, smaller stores, including small independent stores, also find these buildings attractive new locations. Most fashion buildings include a number of local retailers in their tenant mix, and consumers like to find local companies in the store. In the chains of fashion buildings that Saison and MYCAL operate, only the best local retailers are suitable, but those developed by local authorities offer a means to support small retailing within a large-format retail building.

## CONCLUSION

This chapter has ranged across a wide selection of retail formats, with small-store retailing as the unifying theme. Small retailing is far from dead in Japan. While small independent stores are in decline, they are being replaced by new shops, often not much bigger. Rather there is a shift from independent retailing to multiple corporate chains. Convenience store chains employ franchising, which should leave the original retailer with a degree of independence, but even franchisors keep tight control on member stores, and expect the same loyalty from franchisees as they would from employees.

The small store is still important for the consumer. Small stores are popular. Even in the largest cities where there are many larger-format stores, chains of convenience stores and speciality stores have moved in to take the customer's attention. In addition, many shopping centres are simply a means to bring together a number of smaller stores into a single retail building.

In the past, it was too easy for observers of Japanese retailing to see the mass of independent shops and little else. While there are more small, independent shops in Japan than in any other advanced country, it is the large chains, the retail corporations, that rule the retail industry, whether they operate large-format stores or small ones. As in the West, the future of retailing in Japan, whether small format or large format, is in the hands of the largest companies.

In the following chapters I consider the other end of the scale: the department stores and the general merchandise store groups that together make up the largest retail corporations in Japan.

# Chapter 6

# Department stores

## Traditional large-format retailing

The traditional aspects of retailing in Japan are not restricted to the small-store sector. While the role and importance of department stores have declined in many Western retail systems, they continue to play a prominent role in Japan. This role is largely due to their traditional position within Japanese society, and the high level of respect they receive both from consumers and from other members of the industry.

On the other hand, the 'traditional' aspects of department store retailing extend to their relationships with suppliers and their store management systems. These are no longer appropriate in most situations, and since 1991 the department store sector as a whole has experienced a sudden and marked downturn in fortune.

Department stores include some of the largest retail companies, offering high quality, wide assortment and, usually, high prices. The best-selling stores are all department stores, and these boast very high daily takings and customer flow. The largest and most prestigious are located in Tokyo, but most cities have their own local department stores.

On the other hand, there are significant differences in the range of merchandise and management ability between large companies based in Tokyo, Osaka or Nagoya and those in regional cities. In many cities, department stores are the most prominent retail outlets in their own areas, but as superstore chains expand, offering equally large, but cheaper and better presented stores, the position of local department stores is more and more tenuous.

This chapter takes a broad look at the various types of department stores in Japan and their current and possible future position.

## DEPARTMENT STORE DEFINITIONS IN JAPAN

### Japanese terms for department stores

There are two Japanese terms for department store in general use. The most basic, and probably the most common, is *depāto*. As with many words in modern Japanese, it is taken directly from English, and the majority of people would equally understand the full English term 'department store'.

The original Japanese word for a department store is *hyakkaten*, the literal translation of which is 'hundred goods store'. The final character, *ten*, means 'shop', while *hyaku* means 'hundred', and *ka* 'good' or 'treasure'. Okada (1988: 10–12) notes that a large store with a lot of merchandise is the essence of a typical department store.

### More formal definitions and characteristics

As in the West, Japanese department stores are usually managed on a departmental basis, with each department being responsible for a different type of merchandise or service. This allows specialisation by merchandise within particular departments, and provides an interesting shopping environment for customers. It also can cause problems with management coordination. Manufacturers and wholesalers commonly operate concessions within department stores, further enhancing the differences between departments. But most definitions do not consider store operation, preferring to concentrate mainly on store size.

In the Census of Commerce, MITI includes department stores with other general merchandise stores in Industrial Classification Number 5311 (MITI, 1992b: 638). Under this definition, general merchandise stores (GMS) sell a wide range of goods, including food, apparel and other merchandise, with no less than 10 per cent and no more than 70 per cent of sales arising from any one type. In addition, they must employ more than fifty people full-time.

To differentiate more clearly by format, the Census further differentiates department stores as not using self-service, as opposed to general merchandise superstores which do (see Chapter 7). MITI includes further definitions of store formats based on the 1979 Large Store Law Type 1 store categories of 1,500 square metres or greater and 3,000 square metres or greater in the largest cities (MITI, 1992b: 6).

This is a broad definition and it causes a few anomalies. For example, in the census one general merchandise store employs over fifty people, but has less than 20 square metres of sales space. But the Census provides the best source of general data and allows comparison with other broadly defined retail categories.

The Japan Department Store Association uses a similar definition to distinguish member stores. This is also based on store sizes laid down in the 1979 amendment to the Large Store Law (Japan Department Stores Association, 1988: II). In 1989, the Association had 110 members representing 253 stores (Japan Department Stores Association, 1990).

The 1991 Census recorded 455 department stores (see Table 6.1). All but twenty-nine of these were Type 1 stores under the Large Store Law (see Chapter 4). Together they had sales of over ¥11.4 billion, 8 per cent of total retail sales in 1991. Overall, department stores accounted for 6 per cent of total retail space, 3 per cent of all full-time retail employees and only 0.03 per cent of all outlets. They were the largest stores, however, averaging over 15,000 square metres and ¥25,000 million in sales for every outlet.

Despite problems with formal definitions, department stores in Japan have at least two other common characteristics. They offer a very high level of personal service and a very wide range of merchandise (Okada, 1988: 123–4). Both aspects are clearly visible in any major department store. Using Census data, in 1991 the average department store outlet employed over 455 people full-time, more than three times any other format. In addition to services, the largest stores stock merchandise that runs into hundreds of thousands of items, and sell everything from food to pets (Okada, 1988: 11–12). Both service and merchandise range are what consumers expect from department stores and these are discussed in more detail below.

## TYPES OF BUSINESSES OPERATING DEPARTMENT STORES

In addition to the physical products and services, consumers see department stores as conferring prestige and added value on purchases. This puts them at the top of the retail hierarchy in terms of the respect they receive. But there is also a hierarchy among department stores themselves. Each department store holds a particular position in a ranking of prestige shared by consumers and other retail companies.

Table 6.1 Main retail formats, basic statistics 1991

| Type of store | Sales per store (¥ million) | Sales per employee (¥ million) | Sales per square metre (¥ million) | Space per store (sq m) | Employees per store | Space per employee (sq m) |
|---|---|---|---|---|---|---|
| Department stores | 25,085.77 | 55.07 | 1.67 | 15,020 | 455.5 | 32.97 |
| General superstores | 5,267.64 | 37.07 | 0.89 | 5,922 | 142.1 | 41.67 |
| Other GMS | 313.01 | 32.92 | 0.79 | 395 | 9.5 | 41.58 |
| Speciality superstores | 1,122.38 | 30.66 | 1.03 | 1,091 | 36.6 | 29.80 |
| Convenience stores | 166.91 | 19.65 | 1.24 | 135 | 8.5 | 15.87 |
| Other superstores | 143.26 | 23.93 | 1.07 | 134 | 6.0 | 22.32 |
| Speciality stores | 64.60 | 16.94 | 1.49 | 43 | 3.8 | 11.35 |
| General retailers | 66.87 | 18.95 | 1.13 | 59 | 3.5 | 16.79 |
| Other retailers | 121.20 | 21.31 | 1.47 | 83 | 5.7 | 14.51 |
| Average over all retailing | 88.38 | 20.28 | 1.28 | 69 | 4.4 | 15.84 |

Source: Compiled from MITI (1992a)

The key measures that determine this position, in addition to consumer perceptions, are the store's history and location. This ranking relates directly to the importance of tradition for department stores, and it has endured even through changes and modernisation within other sectors of the industry.

Speaking generally, there are two kinds of department store company: old ones and new ones. Older companies have histories that stretch back to the nineteenth century or before. They are the most prestigious and highest-class retailers of all. The majority of department store companies have long histories, and some of the largest companies fit into this category, but the majority are small, regional companies with only one or two stores.

The newer department store companies were founded after the First World War. Most of them began as private railroad companies. There are fewer of these companies than traditional department stores, but all are now relatively large. Historical and locational differences are related. Older stores are invariably located in city centre areas, while newer stores have taken a more flexible strategy, and locate where they can access the highest flow of customers. As railroad operators most of these are located at rail terminals.

**The retail samurai: traditional department stores**

Traditional department store companies are the oldest existing retail institutions in Japan, and operate the most prestigious and respected stores. They were founded in the era of the samurai, the famous Japanese class of warriors that ruled the country from the sixteenth to the nineteenth centuries. In the same way that samurai were at the top of a strict social hierarchy, when modern consumers buy gifts, especially gifts given under social obligation (see Chapter 2), a traditional department store is preferable.

There are a lot of these companies. The top stores in Tokyo and Osaka are all on the level of Harrods in London or Bloomingdales of New York, that is to say, at the very top end of the retail market. In terms of prices and the range of goods and services they stock, they are perhaps even higher.

Physically, the traditional department stores are distinguished largely by their location rather than just their age. They are the city centre stores. In terms of business success, there are major differences between companies that have stores in central Tokyo and Osaka and those with outlets in the regions only.

Regional department stores are usually small, local companies and most have only one or two outlets. All the same, these are often the largest retailers in their own local markets. Consumers in the area hold their local department store in high regard, but people from other parts of Japan may have never heard of it.

While such small, local department store companies are now rare in many Western countries, they are found in almost every small city in Japan. Of the main 116 department store companies operating in 1992 (Nihon Keizai Shinbun, 1992), excluding terminal department stores (see below) and direct affiliates of larger traditional department stores, sixty-seven were regional department stores.

Many regional stores do not live up to the standards of their counterparts in larger urban areas. With relatively limited management structures and distribution facilities, many struggle to compete against the national chains of general merchandise superstores. In the 1980s, the Large Store Law served to insulate many regional department stores against these competitive pressures, but they will face stiffer competition in the 1990s as the law is relaxed.

On the other hand, those traditional department stores with their main outlets in large urban areas like Tokyo, Osaka and Nagoya are a different matter again. These are the largest, the most prestigious and the oldest retail companies.

Only a handful of traditional companies operate stores in these areas. The largest are:

- Mitsukoshi
- Takashimaya
- Daimaru
- Isetan
- Matsuzakaya
- Sogo
- Matsuya.

All seven companies have very large stores in the centre of Tokyo, and each has a history stretching back over one hundred years. Mitsukoshi, Isetan and Matsuya are based in Tokyo, Takashimaya, Daimaru and Sogo in Osaka, and Matsuzakaya in Nagoya. Excluding Matsuzakaya, Sogo and Daimaru, four companies have their largest and most impressive stores in Tokyo, no matter where they originate from.

As with many aspects of Japanese society, a department store's prestige and status come with age. All traditional department stores originate from very old retail companies. Most began business as small, specialist clothing retailers selling mainly kimonos, the traditional Japanese dress. Some actually began as kimono discounters.

Table 6.2 shows when some of the oldest companies were founded and when they converted their businesses into department stores. The Mitsukoshi department store business was founded in 1904, Matsuzakaya in 1910, Matsuya and Takashimaya in 1919, Daimaru in 1920 and Isetan in 1930 (Nihon Keizai Shinbun, 1992), but all of these companies were involved in retailing for many years previously. Mitsukoshi was founded originally in 1673 by the same founder of the Mitsui Group, Kori Mitsui. The company began life as the Echigoya kimono shop in Nihonbashi in central Tokyo. This is still the home of the Mitsukoshi headquarters and main store. Tokyu also originated as a small clothing outlet in 1662. The other Tokyo department stores, Isetan and Matsuya, were founded in the late nineteenth century. The big Osaka companies began life in the early 1800s, except for Daimaru which was founded in 1717.

The very oldest department store companies are, however, in Nagoya. The Nagoya area was the centre of power for two of the main feudal warlords of the fifteenth century, Nobunaga and Tokugawa. Matsuzakaya is the oldest surviving large retail company in Japan, originating in Nagoya in 1611 as the Ito-Gofukuya kimono shop. Today, neighbouring the Matsuzakaya headquarters store in the city centre is Maruei, a local Nagoya department store, which was originally founded only four years later in 1615.

The long histories of these stores give them a level of prestige that other large retail companies cannot match. There are a few speciality stores, especially those selling traditional products, which can trace histories that rival the traditional department stores, but these are much smaller companies and have much more limited markets. A few of the other major retailers have histories stretching back sixty years or more. Superstore chain Ito-Yokado was originally founded in 1920, for example, and some new department store companies were founded before the Second World War, but while these compete directly with their older rivals, they do not have the same social standing.

Unlike the regional department stores, some of the largest urban companies now operate chains across the country. Mitsukoshi, the largest, had fourteen directly operated outlets in 1992. In addition, the company also had three regional subsidiaries, and twenty-three stores overseas.

Table 6.2 Leading department store companies founded pre-1900

| Company | Home city | Original business | Year original business founded | Year department store business founded | Years from founding to department store |
|---|---|---|---|---|---|
| Matsuzakaya | Nagoya | Kimono retailer | 1611 | 1910 | 299 |
| Maruei | Nagoya | Kimono retailer | 1615 | 1943 | 328 |
| Tokyu | Tokyo | Kimono retailer | 1662 | 1919 | 257 |
| Mitsukoshi | Tokyo | Kimono retailer | 1673 | 1904 | 231 |
| Saikaya | Kawasaki | Wholesaler | 1716 | 1950 | 234 |
| Daimaru | Osaka | Kimono retailer | 1717 | 1920 | 203 |
| Yamagataya | Kagoshima | Kimono retailer | 1751 | 1917 | 166 |
| Iwataya | Fukuoka | Kimono retailer | 1754 | 1935 | 181 |
| Fujisaki | Sendai | Cotton dealer | 1819 | 1912 | 93 |
| Tenmaya | Okayama | Kimono retailer | 1829 | 1918 | 89 |
| Sogo | Osaka | Kimono retailer | 1830 | 1919 | 89 |
| Takashimaya | Osaka | Kimono retailer | 1831 | 1919 | 88 |
| Matsuya | Tokyo | Kimono retailer | 1869 | 1919 | 50 |
| Marui Imai | Sapporo | Kimono retailer | 1872 | 1919 | 47 |
| Isetan | Tokyo | Kimono retailer | 1886 | 1930 | 44 |

Source: Nihon Keizai Shinbun (1992: 1–124)

Sogo is a special case. The Sogo department store company has only three directly operated stores, but there are another twenty-six Sogo stores across the country. Each of these operates as a separate independent company. In this way, the management structure at each store is simple and has independence to make decisions concerning its own local market. The group as a whole bears some resemblance to a *keiretsu* or franchise chain, however, with central guidance and control always operating to some degree.

Most of the largest companies have semi-independent stores in the same way as Sogo and Mitsukoshi. Several are also leaders of national buying organisations. In addition to affiliated companies and subsidiaries, most independent regional department store companies also participate in at least one of these organisations.

Table 6.3 shows the names and the main member stores in each organisation. Five buying groups are led by one of the traditional department store companies, and one is led by one of the new companies, Seibu, as described in the next section. The activities of each organisation stretch to department store companies nationwide, although there is some concentration in the Tokyo and Osaka areas. There is also some overlap between the organisations, with a number of companies being members of more than one.

The purpose of the organisations is to allow member stores flexibility in their merchandising strategies, providing greater combined buying power and wider ranging sources for goods. The organisations also provide financial and consultancy functions. The operation of member stores remains autonomous, with the companies that organise the buying associations being little more than the largest and most powerful firm involved. They do not exercise control over the activities of other members in the way that occurs in *keiretsu* or franchise chains, for example. But they do provide advice and close co-operation when requested to do so.

Compared with the new superstores, most department store companies have been rather slow in developing new strategies and adopting modern retail techniques (see *Shūkan Daiyamondo*, 1987a, 1987b, 1989b, 1989e). The older, more traditional companies have been the slowest of all. Only the very largest companies, which have better developed management systems, were able to react quickly to the economic downturn at the beginning of the 1990s, and even these with limited success.

For example, the introduction of the Consumption Tax in April 1989 exposed the outdated information systems of some companies.

*Table 6.3* The six main department-store-organised buying associations

| Organising company | Organisation name | No. of member stores[c] | Main member stores |
|---|---|---|---|
| 1 Mitsukoshi | Mitsukoshi Buying Group | 51 | 13 Mitsukoshi stores and affiliates, Kintetsu, Maruhiro, Izutsuya, Tsuruya |
| 2 Daimaru | Daimaru Buying Group | 40 | 7 Daimarus and affiliates, Daimaru Peacock, Jujiya, Tokiwa, Yamagataya |
| 3 Isetan | ADO[a] | 31 | 6 Isetan stores, Matsuya, Marui-Imai, Fujisaki, Maeitetsu, Tenmaya, Iwataya |
| 4 Seibu | JMA[b] | 22 | 16 Seibu-stores and affiliates, Hanshin, Yamagataya, Matsukiya |
| 5 Takashimaya | Hi-Land Group | 21 | 6 Takashimaya stores and affiliates, Keio, Maruei, Yamagen, Tsuruya |
| 6 Matsuzakaya | Matsuzakaya Buying Group | 8 | 9 Matsuzakaya stores and affiliates, Kawatoku, Fukuoka Tamaya |

[a] All Nippon Department Stores Development Organisation.
[b] Japan Department Stores Management Association.
[c] Excluding organising stores.
*Sources*: Dodwell Marketing Consultants (1991: 193–226); Okada (1988: 174–9)

A number of regional stores found it necessary to buy integrated POS terminals for the first time in order to cope with the added paperwork needed for the new tax. Prior to this, they had relied on non-integrated, and in the case of some regional companies virtually non-automated, systems, with each cash register operating as a single computer (Hoshino, 1989; Nikkei Ryūtsū Shinbun, 1989c: 31–4).

More recently, with an expansion of high-quality retailing in other formats, smaller regional department stores have become the targets of takeovers and mergers. A number have been absorbed by one of the larger department store groups, or into the group headed by a superstore chain company.

All department stores now face even greater problems. The 1990s have brought a shift in consumer values away from high-price, high-prestige products and towards cheaper goods with greater physical value. This may be largely temporary, but it has opened the eyes of many consumers to the fact that other general merchandise retailers are selling the same products as traditional department stores, only cheaper. This will continue to hurt older, smaller companies as they simply cannot cut their costs sufficiently to compete. It is the newer and the larger companies that stand a better chance of survival and are changing their way of business to do so. In the department store sector, new companies are quite different from traditional firms.

## New department store companies

Not all department store companies have a long history. In the twentieth century, a new generation of department stores emerged from within large private railway companies. They first became involved with retailing as early as the 1920s. These companies moved into retailing on the strength of their considerable holdings of land. In addition, by linking department stores into their own rail networks, they could maintain an almost guaranteed customer flow.

The majority of these new, non-traditional department stores are built within or above railway terminals. In extreme cases, for example the Seibu Ikebukuro store in Tokyo, the ticket barrier opens directly into the store. Consequently, these retailers are frequently called terminal department stores (*tāminaru depāto*).

A few very successful companies, notably Seibu and Tokyu,[1] now operate separate, powerful retail organisations in addition to their transport businesses, but these are the exceptions. The other major terminal department stores are Odakyu, Keio and Tobu in Tokyo,

Sotetsu in Yokohama, Meitetsu in Nagoya, and Kintetsu, Hanshin, Hankyu and Sanyo all in the Kansai area.[2] These companies still rely heavily on customer traffic generated through key rail nodes.

The terminal department stores pursued a far more aggressive policy of store expansion than most of their older rivals. Many railroad company retail divisions are also involved in supermarket or superstore retailing in addition to their department stores. Based around their own transportation networks, several, including Seibu, Sotetsu and Meitetsu, have developed complete residential housing areas, including comprehensive retail facilities (Honma, 1989). Key examples include the Seibu Hikarigaoka complex along Seibu rail lines to the west of Tokyo, and developments by Meitetsu in Ichinomiya and other cities to the north of Nagoya.

Within these groupings, there is a great deal of variation in the degree of coherence between their retail and other operations. In some, for example Meitetsu and Sotetsu, the various functions of real estate, transportation and retailing are closely amalgamated. In others, notably Seibu and Tokyu, the strength of the retail operation is such that it is now independent of the transport company although co-operation is still profitable to both.

The Seibu Department Stores company is the core of the Saison Group, the third largest retail conglomerate (see Chapter 7). Today, however, Seibu retailing is totally separate from Seibu Tetsudō, the rail and leisure company. Having been built by a single founder, the two groups were split between his two sons (Aso, 1985: 210–23; *Economist*, 1988e; 1988f; Larke and Arima, 1992).

This does not make the department store division within the group a special case compared to other railroad-based companies. The cohesion of the original group means that many stores are still located near to Seibu rail lines. The main department store branches are nearly all terminal stores, but the number of Seibu department stores that are built away from rail nodes is probably greater than for other companies. The newer superstore operations within the same group are different, however, and operate as a separate business.

There are only ten terminal department store companies. Taking the large number of regional stores into account, traditional department stores outnumber terminal department stores overall. Of the 455 department stores in Japan in 1991, only around seventy were operated by companies that were, or were originally, railroad companies. In the Tokyo and Osaka areas alone, however, terminal stores match the older stores by number of outlets.

Beginning with these department stores, many retail companies began to base their stores around or at major rail terminals. In the same way that major suburban road intersections are popular locations in the West, almost every city rail terminal in Japan also doubles as a shopping area. Terminals are favourite locations for both department stores and fashion buildings (see Chapter 5). Recently superstore companies also prefer locations close to railway stations, especially in the suburbs of the larger urban areas. This is all due to the pioneering expansion of the newer department store companies.

## THE LEADING DEPARTMENT STORE COMPANIES IN THE 1990s

### The leading companies by sales

Table 6.4 shows the largest fifteen department store companies by sales volume for 1992–3. The second column of the table gives the overall company ranking for all retail companies. Mitsukoshi, the largest department store company, was the fifth largest retailer overall. The sixth and eighth largest companies were also department stores, Seibu and Takashimaya.

Together the top fifteen department store companies accounted for 5 per cent of total retail sales from the top 500 companies in the 1993 *Nikkei* survey. Within the top 500 overall, department stores accounted for 26.5 per cent of sales. No one company has more than a single percentage point share of the retail market. In addition, regional department stores accounted for only 7.5 per cent, with 19 per cent from the largest, urban companies. The share of department store sales fell consistently in the 1980s (see Chapter 5), as more new retail formats emerged and grew more quickly than the department store sector.

Mitsukoshi regained its traditional spot at the top of the department store rankings in 1992, after Seibu had been the largest company for most of the 1980s. Arguably, Mitsukoshi is the most widely famous and the most prestigious department store in Japan. The company's main stores are in central Tokyo, but there are Mitsukoshi stores in several regional cities. Nagoya Mitsukoshi is a large affiliate which operates several stores in the Chubu region.

Seibu dropped to second place in 1992. It is still the leading 'new' department store company, but the company's parent group, Saison Group, suffered considerable financial pressure after a number of

Table 6.4 Leading department store companies by sales, 1992–3

| Overall retail rank No. | rank | Company | Business region | Sales (¥ million) | % change 93/92 | Operating profits (¥ million) | % change 93/92 | % pre-tax operating margin | Store nos |
|---|---|---|---|---|---|---|---|---|---|
| 1 | 5 | Mitsukoshi | Tokyo | 842,372 | -3.9 | -2,157 | -119.6 | -0.3 | 14 |
| 2 | 6 | Seibu Department Stores | Tokyo/Osaka | 808,074 | -11.9 | n.a. | n.a. | n.a. | 17 |
| 3 | 8 | Takashimaya | Tokyo/Osaka | 788,462 | -6.5 | 4,926 | -63.1 | 0.6 | 10 |
| 4 | 9 | Daimaru | Kansai area | 569,799 | -6.3 | 4,658 | -23.2 | 0.8 | 7 |
| 5 | 12 | Matsuzakaya | Nagoya | 491,367 | -2.1 | 3,775 | -62.3 | 0.8 | 10 |
| 6 | 13 | Isetan | Tokyo | 442,895 | -5.4 | 5,030 | -64.3 | 1.1 | 6 |
| 7 | 16 | Tokyu Department Stores | Tokyo | 378,841 | -7.7 | 6,703 | -27.3 | 1.8 | 6 |
| 8 | 18 | Hankyu Department Stores | Osaka | 344,729 | -2.9 | 6,607 | -42.0 | 1.9 | 8 |
| 9 | 22 | Kintetsu Department Stores | Kansai area | 284,142 | -1.8 | 62 | -94.4 | 0.0 | 9 |
| 10 | 24 | Sogo | Tokyo/Osaka | 280,039 | -9.8 | 3,819 | -47.4 | 1.4 | 3 |
| 11 | 27 | Yokohama Takashimaya | Yokohama | 269,489 | -5.1 | 5,811 | -37.2 | 2.2 | 3 |
| 12 | 28 | Odakyu Department Stores | Tokyo | 235,241 | 13.1 | n.a. | n.a. | 1.0 | 2 |
| 13 | 34 | Tobu Department Stores[a] | Tokyo | 188,686 | 4.7 | n.a. | n.a. | 0.7 | 2 |
| 14 | 38 | Yokohama Sogo | Yokohama | 167,000 | -3.0 | n.a. | n.a. | n.a. | 1 |
| 15 | 46 | Keio Department Stores | Tokyo | 146,801 | -3.2 | 712 | -54.7 | 0.5 | 2 |

[a] Tobu Department Stores changed its accounting period; sales figures for eleven months only.
Source: Compiled from Nihon Keizai Shinbun (1992); Nikkei Ryūtsū Shinbun (1993d: 236)

expensive takeovers in the late 1980s and early 1990s. The situation was not helped by poor consumer spending after 1991. Almost 44 per cent of Seibu's sales arise from the company's main flagship store in Ikebukuro. This store had the highest sales of any single outlet in Japan up to 1992, but the reopening of the Tobu department store only 100 metres away after major refurbishment further hurt the store's sales.

The decline in sales for Seibu was simply the worst case in a general trend among the leading companies. Only two companies, Odakyu and Seibu's rival Tobu, saw sales increase on the year, and every company saw very large falls in profits. The leading company, Mitsukoshi, actually suffered a significant loss on the year to cover the cost of store refurbishment and other improvements. Kintetsu and Keio also recorded significantly low profits. As a result, profit margins in the department store industry, which were never good, were even lower in 1992. The highest operating profit margin among the top fifteen was 2.2 per cent by Yokohama Takashimaya. Most companies were lucky to break a 1 per cent margin, and none of the top five did.

**Department store sales declining in the 1990s**

For all of the top companies, 1993 was the second year in succession that profits have fallen, and with sales also falling, it is an indication of a dangerous and ongoing trend. Companies are finding it more and more difficult to attract customers, and many are having to offer lower prices by cutting margins.

A new land tax also hit the larger and older stores that own their own sites in the centre of Tokyo in 1991. This all occurred at a time when consumers were feeling a bit foolish about their behaviour in the 1980s when they would buy expensive items from department stores simply because of the price tag. Mitsukoshi and others had already instigated large investment plans, including major store refurbishment and, in some cases, the first new stores for many years. Mitsukoshi invested ¥52,000 million in 1991, a company record for a single year (Dodwell Marketing Consultants, 1991). This included extensive renewal of several stores and the opening of a new annex to the large Shinjuku store.

The fall in consumer demand also encouraged some department stores to review their management systems. Reliance on traditional distribution systems, especially giving considerable autonomy to suppliers, means that cost performance at department stores is poor. This is no longer acceptable for many companies, especially now that consumers no longer accept what manufacturers insist they should be buying.

A significant proportion of department store sales arises from concessions which are staffed and operated by suppliers. Even when the department store sells merchandise itself, in many cases the goods are on consignment, that is sale or return, conditions. For this privilege, stores accept less control over merchandise mix and pricing. In order to offer a better balanced selection of goods and services, companies are having to take more direct control of merchandise selection, display and especially pricing. They are also introducing more of their own brands and designs. While this will help the more skilful companies in the long run, it means they will incur greater costs.

The evidence is in the dreadful profit results for 1992, with department stores being unable to make immediate cost adjustments to compensate for a bad year. Both Takashimaya and Mitsukoshi have restructured their management systems over the past two years, both with the basic aim of reducing the number of middle management levels. This reduces costs and allows the fewer remaining managers to take a broader view of store operations. Mitsukoshi now uses a system of floor rather than department managers, which allows flexibility in changing the merchandise type and volume across the whole floor rather than just a small section. All the top companies are looking for similar ways to cut costs and improve efficiency, while at the same time maintaining the high level of service which consumers expect.

## The largest stores in Japan

As individual shops, department stores are the largest and have the highest sales per outlet. In the Nikkei Ryūtsū Shinbun (1993d: 357–76) ranking of the highest-selling 1,000 retail stores in 1992–3, all of the top seventy stores were department stores. The top-selling superstore, Daiei's Tsudanuma branch, only ranked seventy-sixth. There were 253 department stores in the top 1,000 outlets, but, of the leading 150 stores, no fewer than 138 were department stores.

Table 6.5 gives the top-selling individual retail outlets in 1992–3. They are all department stores. The top store was the Mitsukoshi store in Nihonbashi. It had sales of almost ¥355,000 million in 1992,

*Table 6.5* Leading retail outlets by sales 1992–3

| Company | Store location | Sales (¥ million) | % change 92/91 | Total area (sq m) | Space change (sq m) |
|---|---|---|---|---|---|
| 1 Mitsukoshi[a] | Nihonbashi, Tokyo | 354,407 | -6.6 | 95,710 | +1,645 |
| 2 Seibu | Ikebukuro, Tokyo | 349,054 | -16.7 | 65,817 | +170 |
| 3 Takashimaya | Nihonbashi, Tokyo | 287,465 | -9.7 | 51,627 | +2,785 |
| 4 Isetan | Shinjuku, Tokyo | 284,304 | -7.0 | 61,814 | – |
| 5 Hankyu | Umeda, Osaka | 242,695 | -2.3 | 65,338 | +1,477 |
| 6 Takashimaya | Nanba, Osaka | 230,167 | -6.2 | 63,507 | +2,280 |
| 7 Yokohama Takashimaya | Yokohama | 218,118 | -5.0 | 71,425 | – |
| 8 Tokyu | Shibuya, Tokyo | 197,072 | -9.5 | 73,728 | +534 |
| 9 Odakyu | Shinjuku, Tokyo | 177,452 | -0.5 | 57,316 | – |
| 10 Matsuzakaya | Nagoya | 167,731 | -1.9 | 75,958 | – |
| 11 Yokohama Sogo | Yokohama | 167,000 | -3.0 | 68,413 | – |
| 12 Daimaru | Shinsaibashi, Osaka | 161,727 | -9.4 | 37,490 | – |
| 13 Kintetsu | Abeno, Osaka | 152,762 | -0.9 | 58,600 | – |
| 14 Tobu | Ikebukuro, Tokyo | 148,482 | 14.4 | 82,963 | +38,700 |
| 15 Sogo | Kobe | 132,392 | -9.0 | 48,962 | – |

[a] Mitsukoshi Nihonbashi operates several stores included in figures.

*Source*: Nikkei Ryūtsū Shinbun (1993d: 357)

a drop of 6 per cent. This is still some ¥971 million a day. As mentioned above, Seibu's Ikebukuro store was the leading store up to 1991, when it had sales of over ¥1,100 million a day.

The top four stores are all department stores located in the centre of Tokyo. The number three store, Takashimaya's leading Tokyo branch, is only 200 metres away from the main Mitsukoshi store in Nihonbashi. Between the two, also in Nihonbashi, there is also the third largest store in Tokyu's chain, but this store was only fifty-second in the ranking, with sales of ¥51,278 million.

There are three more stores in Tokyo among the leading fifteen, including the Tobu store mentioned earlier. This was the only store among the leading fifteen that recorded sales growth on the year. The refurbishment of the store, which was completed late in 1991, added almost 39,000 square metres to its total floor space to make it the largest single-building retail store in Japan. This investment, which was an expensive move for a second-tier department store company, has been rewarded with much improved sales. The refurbishment also shifted the store more up-market, and it accommodates a large number of large, high-rent tenants which helped to fund some of the development.

Overall, the same survey showed declines in department store sales in all of the main urban areas. Whereas the larger companies in these areas are stronger than their regional counterparts, the business environment is much more competitive in Tokyo, Osaka and Nagoya. There were small percentage increases in sales of between 0.3 and 0.9 per cent in the regions of Tohoku, Chugoku and Kyushu. Department stores in Kanto and Kinki saw sales drop by 6.7 per cent and 5.3 per cent respectively in the more difficult market conditions there (Nikkei Ryūtsū Shinbun, 1993d: 378–9).

## Department store sales

Figure 6.1 shows month-on-month sales figures for the five leading department store outlets between June 1990 and June 1993. The seasonal differences in sales are clearly visible. The main season for all general merchandise retailers, including both department stores and general merchandise superstore chains, is December. This corresponds with the main social gift-giving season as well as New Year and the annually increasing Christmas market. Both department store outlets and GMS chains derive 10–12 per cent of their annual

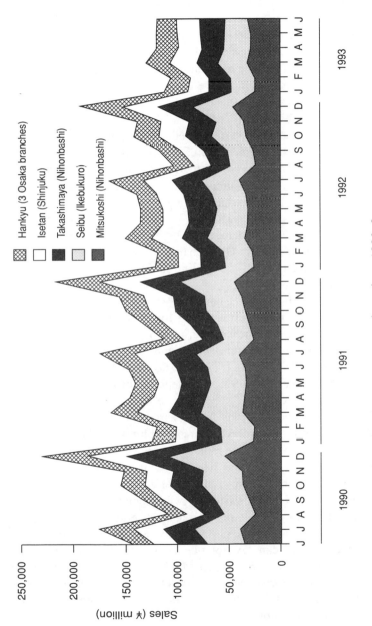

*Figure 6.1* Monthly sales of leading department store branches, 1990–3
*Source*: Nikkei Ryūtsū Shinbun (1988; 1989c; 1990b; 1991; 1992; 1993d)

income from this single month. GMS chains actually do better because they sell a wider range of merchandise at this time, particularly food for the festive seasons. Department store sales are boosted because of gift buying.

The second largest season is in July, which adds a further 8–10 per cent of annual income depending on the company. This gives about a fifth of total income from these two months alone. July is the second big gift season, but, unlike in December, there are no major festivals. The sales peak in this month is almost solely as a result of gift purchases. Consequently, while GMS chains' sales also increase somewhat, the department stores benefit much more.

In the 1980s the department stores dominated both the December and the July markets because of their importance for gift buying. In the early 1990s, as consumers turn away from the high prices in many department stores, general merchandise chain stores are gaining ground in these seasons. Figure 6.2 shows the monthly year-on-year percentage change for both the leading five department stores and the top five GMS chains. There is a clear downward trend for both sectors, but the decline in department store sales is far more marked.

More importantly, up to the end of 1991, the rate of sales increase in the two key gift months was higher for the GMS chains than for the department stores. Furthermore, moving into 1992, department store sales went into constant decline, and fell at a higher rate than the GMS chains. In the July *o-chūgen* season in 1993, GMS chains improved their sales over 1992, while department store sales declined even faster.

There are two explanations for this trend. First, consumers are sending fewer gifts regardless of social obligation. They prefer to hold onto what cash they have rather than give gifts that may or may not bring future favours and benefits. Consequently, department store sales are notably down in July and December.

Second, consumers are switching what spending they do make, even on gifts, more and more to cheaper retailers including the general merchandise chains. GMS chains can offer everything that a department store can, except the name and the prestige. Now consumers are much more concerned with price, and, as suggested earlier, many are surprised at themselves for paying such high prices in the 1980s. Today, GMS chains are not cheap, but they are cheaper than the department stores.

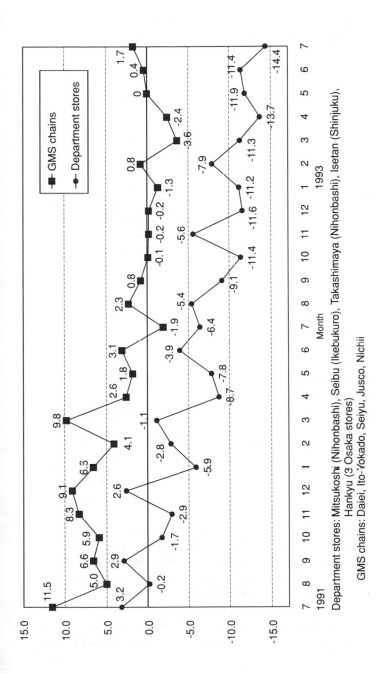

*Figure 6.2* Year-on-year percentage monthly changes in sales for leading five department stores and leading five GMS chains, July 1991 to June 1993

Department stores: Mitsukoshi (Nihonbashi), Seibu (Ikebukuro), Takashimaya (Nihonbashi), Isetan (Shinjuku), Hankyu (3 Osaka stores)

GMS chains: Daiei, Ito-Yokado, Seiyu, Jusco, Nichii

*Source*: Nikkei Ryūtsū Shinbun (1992; 1993d)

## DEPARTMENT STORE EXPANSION AND CHANGES

Japanese retailing has come full circle. In the 1960s and 1970s, the large superstore chains grew on the basis of 'pile-it-high, sell-it-cheap' strategies. Such a development proved a serious threat to the high price strategies in department stores, and some of the older stores suffered substantial sales losses.

In the 1980s, as consumers became ever more affluent, they were keen to supplement a lack of space in their homes through exciting, conspicuous consumption. The department stores came back to prominence, realising that consumers were willing, even eager, to buy luxury items at high prices (*Economist*, 1989e; Nikkei Ryūtsū Shinbun, 1989b). In the early 1990s, the economic slowdown took sales away from department stores, and superstore chains increased their discount operations, swinging the situation back to that of the 1960s.

One consequential development of the department stores' success in the 1980s was the increasing number of niche speciality tenants opening within stores. Tenants selling famous brands extend the image of high quality, while handling their own concessions, and so presenting little added risk for the department store. Mitsukoshi, for example, has branches of Tiffany's (which Mitsukoshi partly owns) in most of its stores. Seibu operates the franchise for Benetton outlets all over Japan.

Another area where the traditional stores have proved to be relatively aggressive is in their international strategies, especially those involving direct imports and opening of branches overseas. There were well over fifty overseas branches of Japanese department stores in 1988, with many more buying offices (Okada, 1988: 180–1). It has been estimated that the London branch of Mitsukoshi takes 13 per cent of all Japanese tourist spending in Britain, and has a turnover of £24.5 million (*Economist*, 1989d). Mitsukoshi had the largest network, with over twenty overseas stores in sixteen countries in 1991.

All of the largest department store companies operate direct import systems (MITI, 1987a: 87–90; 1989a: 12–13; Yoshida, 1993a). Several companies operate development import schemes with countries in South-East Asia. These account for 3.8 per cent of all development imports to Japan (MITI, 1989a: 39).

Department stores have always offered a small number of high-quality private brands, especially in clothing. The number has increased in the 1990s as companies have tried to take an increasingly active role in choosing the merchandise that actually gets onto the shop floor, and not leaving everything to suppliers.

Until the late 1980s, the department stores relied on their high-prestige images to carry them along. Very few companies expanded in any way, and none matched the GMS chains in their aggressive store opening policies. The only exception was the Sogo chain which opened fourteen of its twenty-nine stores in the 1980s, and five more already in the 1990s to date.

Other department store companies were content to operate existing stores. They have been closely scrutinised since the second Department Store Law of 1956 (see Chapter 4), and restrictions on opening new outlets continued especially against these companies. Sogo avoided this partly by opening each outlet as a semi-independent affiliate.

Mitsukoshi's annex to its Shinjuku store was the first large new department store in central Tokyo or Osaka since the 1970s. With the relaxation of the Large Store Law in 1992, department store companies took advantage of the opportunity to expand existing outlets without the need to apply for approval. Table 6.5 for example shows that many of the leading department stores added to their sales space during the year.

Terminal department stores were little different to their traditional counterparts. Seibu, Tokyu and others are equally involved in building large chains of superstores and supermarkets, but only a few new department store outlets appeared. With the poor sales and profit results of 1992–3, this is unlikely to change in the immediate future.

Where department stores still have influence is in their prestigious image in the eyes of consumers. While improving their overall operating systems and management styles, the better companies will be careful not to lose this by lowering their standards of service and merchandise. This will not be easy to do, but necessary for companies who will survive.

## DEPARTMENT STORES AND JAPANESE CONSUMERS

Mitsukoshi, Takashimaya and the other traditional department stores are at the top of the retail hierarchy in terms of their status, but their share of the retail market is slowly declining (Nikkei Ryūtsū Shinbun, 1989c: 333). Department store outlets are larger and offer a wider range of goods and services than the GMS chains. For consumers, these are the three key distinguishing factors when shopping at a department store: the range of merchandise and customer services, and the prestigious image of the store that comes with them.

Department stores offer all kinds of merchandise, from convenience goods such as basic foods and vegetables, to luxury shopping items like uncut diamonds or imported Rolls Royce cars. Stores stock tens of thousands of lines and several hundred thousand items each. These are spread, typically, over eight or more floors, including one or more underground basement floors.

In addition to the physical merchandise, stores offer a full range of customer services. A top store employs between 500 and 5,000 people, as sales assistants, elevator operators, information desk personnel, store guides, interpreters, wash room attendants, wrapping specialists, floor walkers, porters and so on. As the following sections show, services are an important part of any department store's business.

### Free return of unwanted items

As much of the merchandise is held in department stores on a sale-or-return basis, and as suppliers allow stores flexible rights to return merchandise, customers also benefit by being free to return poor quality or merely undesired goods at will. Stores require a receipt, although in some cases, they will accept a product returned in the store's carrier bag or wrapping paper even if the receipt is lost (*Nikkei Trendy*, 1992b). The proportion of merchandise that department stores return to suppliers can exceed 10 per cent of total stocks in some cases (Nikkei Ryūtsū Shinbun, 1992: 36).

This is becoming more difficult, however. The Japan Fair Trade Commission introduced guidelines to reduce the practice of freely returning goods back up the distribution channel in 1991. Some stores, such as Takashimaya, acted on these guidelines in early 1992, instigating a system where the store took legal possession of some goods on delivery. But even this new system includes clauses to allow the store to return a certain proportion of merchandise without question.

### In-house credit cards and financial services

In a movement that began with the major department stores most large retail companies now offer some kind of in-house credit card. At present, using the department store's own credit card allows the holder a small discount, usually 5 per cent. Some stores are seriously considering doing away with this benefit in order to maintain profits.

Many companies also offer a wide range of financial services. These are most usually found in special service sections on the top floors. They include insurance, loans, stock broking, real estate transactions, gold bullion and precious metal exchange and dealing. Seibu department stores even suggests that customers do not need to bring money with them as they can borrow it at the store.

### Delivery of purchased goods

Many stores will provide free delivery of large items within a reasonable distance of the store. For a fee, delivery services are available to any part of Japan.

In gift-giving seasons, department stores are almost forced to provide nationwide delivery free of charge just to compete with each other and with the superstore companies (Yasumori, 1993). GMS chains can offer this service free because they have stores, each stocking similar merchandise, all across the country, and the distribution network to support them. Most customers expect not only delivery services to other parts of the country, but the delivery of all their chosen gifts both near and far. This is all part of the gift service.

### Gift services

As discussed in Chapter 2, department stores offer a full gift-choosing, purchasing, wrapping and delivery service both to individuals and to companies. They offer boxed gift sets of all kinds of products from socks to fresh salmon roe, and, for the customer who does not want to make the mistake of choosing the wrong products, gift vouchers up to the value of ¥100,000. More surprisingly, some stores even offer these vouchers as pre-paid cards, like telephone cards that are now available in many countries. These too have face values of many thousands of yen, making them expensive items to lose accidentally.

Superstores, with their nationwide distribution networks, cheap products and strong ambitions to gain a bigger part of this lucrative market, provide basically the same product range at this time of year. Department stores still maintain the edge, however, partly because of the image value of sending a gift wrapped in the paper of a top department store, but mostly because of the services that the store provides in choosing and coordinating gift-giving.

## Full wrapping services

Wrapping may seem connected with gift-giving, but all purchases made at department stores are wrapped and a marked paper carrier bag is also provided in addition to the wrapping on the product. In rainy weather, the same carrier bag will often be carefully covered with transparent plastic.

The value of buying from expensive department stores is conveyed in the store's individual wrapping paper. Most shops will wrap gifts on request, and in most cases this is free of charge. Department stores wrap automatically, without question. For a particular kind of gift, the store will include a small handwritten greetings slip. Both ornamental wrapping and Japanese calligraphy are necessary skills for many shop assistants.

Some stores began to experiment with reducing wrapping in the early 1990s in response to environmental concerns about wasting paper. Today, however, even the more cost-conscious superstore chains have done away with such ideas because consumers simply will not accept products that are not wrapped. Even GMS chains provide free gift wrapping on request. Only in the most strictly cost-controlled discount chains is wrapping done away with altogether. For department stores, wrapping purchases in their own distinctive papers is a major part of their business, because it makes purchasing from a department store that much more prestigious. Visitors from overseas are often appalled by the amount of wasted paper involved, but neither department stores nor consumers are likely to change this situation in the near future.

## Cultural services and events

Department stores provide a range of cultural, entertainment and professional services including community centres, evening classes, in-store cinemas and concert halls, ticket booking offices, travel agents, dry cleaning and many others. The new Mitsukoshi annex in Shinjuku has an art gallery on its top floor which is linked to the Metropolitan Museum of Art in New York. Seibu maintains a separate film production company within its overall retail group called Cine Saison, and also runs several theatres. For special sales promotions, top department stores often co-operate closely with the more active foreign embassies to run regular exhibitions of imported merchandise.

Table 6.6 provides an illustration of the range of other services available at department stores. The Saison Group, the owners of Seibu Department Stores, produced this list for promotional purposes, but the list of services is not untypical. Seibu have been especially keen to present stores that sell anything the customer could possibly dream of, and the services to go with the merchandise.

*Table 6.6* Services provided by top department stores

| Food | | Education | |
|---|---|---|---|
| **Food** | Food delivery | **Education** | Culture schools |
| | Made-to-order lunch | | Correspondence |
| | boxes | | courses |
| | Catering | | Private tutors |
| | Safekeeping of wine | | Nursery school |
| | | | Word processing |
| **Apparel** | Garment alterations | | Educational goods |
| | Storage/cleaning | | rental |
| | Garage sales | | Health consultancy |
| | Made to order | | |
| | | **Leisure** | Ticket sales and |
| **Housing** | Renovation | | reservations |
| | Maintenance | | Party arrangements |
| | Cleaning | | Musician dispatch |
| | Security systems | | Home photo service |
| | Housing | | Event production |
| | Furniture storage | | Travel agency |
| | | | Leisure goods rental |
| **Home affairs** | Roundsmen | | Wrapping service |
| | Buying agent | | Pet beauty salon |
| | Removals service | | |
| | Household items | **Information** | Presentation media |
| | rental | | rental |
| | Handyman | | Catalogue sales |
| | Home nursing | | EFTPOS |
| | | | Computerised dating |
| **Financial** | Credit | | service |
| | Loans | | Computer consulting |
| | Insurance | | |
| | Mortgages | **Business** | Lunch box catering |
| | Securities | | Lease of OA |
| | | | equipment |
| | | | Lease of office |
| **International** | Overseas mail order | | supplies |
| | Overseas real estate | | Computer translation |
| | sales | | Investment consulting |
| | International credit | | Temporary secretary |
| | card | | service |

*Key*: ETFPOS: Electronic Funds Transfer at Point of Sale, OA: Office Automation.
*Source*: Fukuda (1988: 43)

They dubbed this, 'the total life concept' (Aso, 1985: 210–12; Seibu Saison Group, 1989), and, to varying degrees, it is now a strategy employed by most major department stores (MITI, 1989a: 270–1).

### Personal customer accounts: the ultimate in prestige

Finally, one factor that well illustrates the social status of department stores is the personal account for privileged customers. In addition to their normal daily business, department stores provide large bulk purchasing services for corporate customers, and special accounts for privileged personal customers. Again, these are especially important during the twice-yearly formal gift-giving seasons, when both high-status individuals and companies buy a lot of gifts. Small and medium companies often use department stores when they make bulk purchases of stationery, uniforms and office fittings for their businesses. These large purchases are handled by a department found in all department stores called the *gaishō* department. This is an important, traditional part of department store retailing and is little known outside Japan.

Since their origins as high-class kimono stores a hundred years ago, department stores have provided valued customers with personal store accounts. The original *gaishō* salesmen would take cloth samples for kimonos to the homes of rich customers (Takaoka and Koyama 1970: 86–7). The *gaishō* business expanded to include the whole range of merchandise available through the store, and anything the store can order separately.

Before the Second World War, competition between the then maturing department store businesses reached a peak. Tokyo stores sent their *gaishō* salesmen all over the country, competing with local retailers as well as with each other.

From these origins, *gaishō*, literally meaning 'out-sales', departments today offer a range of services to individual and corporate customers who use the store regularly. It is also a popular means of purchase among organisations such as small companies, local government offices and schools. Many large prestigious high schools have contracts with particular department stores to supply their uniforms on an exclusive basis through the same stores.

Store accounts held by individuals are less important, and are generally limited to long-standing family customers, many of them also linked to small family businesses. Most major department stores are willing to visit individual homes to sell particularly high-value goods such as kimonos, precious stones and metals, paintings and furniture. Many stores have a list of particularly wealthy customers to whom they will make regular visits in order to make sales, and in order to maintain the personal contact with the family.

*Gaishō* departments organise promotional events as part of their business. One example is 'special invitation exhibition sales' or *tenji sokubai kai* (Takaoka and Koyama 1970: 86–7). These invitation-only promotions are frequently held in major hotels, with kimonos, jewellery, antiques and paintings being popular items for display. Department stores invite appropriately wealthy *gaishō* account holders to each event.

Occasionally, *gaishō* departments are also hired to find, secure and furnish new apartment buildings or company offices for wealthy families, or on behalf of companies needing to relocate executive managers.

For corporate customers, *gaishō* provide an easy means to make bulk or high-value purchases. In addition, department stores are large enough to provide a high degree of reliability. Modern superstores could offer similar services, but they lack the status and traditional trustworthiness of the department stores.

Overall, the *gaishō* department accounts for up to 30 per cent of a store's sales. As the main customers are businesses, however, fluctuations in the economic climate affects *gaishō* sales heavily (Okada, 1988: 125). In the 1990s, stores have had to put particular effort into these departments to maintain sales volumes, but often with little success as customers no longer feel a need to pay for the high image and prestige of using them (Ohashi, 1989).

In addition, long-term relationships with some customers are not necessarily advantageous. On the basis of trust, the majority of sales are made on credit, and the stores often have to take the burden of interest. Many clients also expect discounts as a matter of course. Where a bulk purchase is involved, this is not a problem, but many stores find themselves providing discounts even for minor *gaishō* transactions (Okada, 1988: 125). This does not mean the store makes a loss, but it does reduce profit margins.

## THE FUTURE OF DEPARTMENT STORES

Department store companies remain a major retail sector in Japan despite the decline of similar stores in the West. Japan is the only advanced nation where department stores still continue to flourish.

This is largely due to the liking that consumers have for high-status products, and their demand for high reliability, trustworthiness and, it must be said, a high degree of pampering. In these ways, other retail sectors have been unable to provide similar services on an economic basis. Most recently, however, some department store companies have been unable to provide the same services economically and make a profit.

Low profits among even the top companies indicate that department stores are losing their position. In their business operation, they tend too much towards conservatism. While it is still the most important retail sector in terms of social status, it is also the oldest sector, both historically and in terms of business methods. Some observers have begun to consider not just the decline of department store retailing in Japan, but even its extinction over the coming decade (Fields, 1993a; Fukui, 1993; Imoto, 1993; Sakaida and Tanaka, 1993).

This opinion is perhaps a little too severe, but department stores will suffer greatly unless there is a second major consumer spending boom in the mid-1990s. Even then, consumers have now realised that goods sold by the general merchandise store chains are the same as those in the department stores, only cheaper.

The largest and the most prestigious stores continue to provide something that other retailers cannot: status. This is an important factor in Japanese society, and will always be in demand. If they can improve and modernise their management systems, stores that can truly supply prestige and status will survive.

Smaller department stores, that is the regional companies who find themselves competing directly with major superstore chain companies in regional cities, will find business increasingly difficult. Some will move away from high-set-price merchandise, and begin to resemble superstores in their merchandise and service mix. Others will simply merge with larger retail companies. Many will disappear altogether. It is likely that these stores will be replaced by new, larger, more up-market superstores. Some may even be converted from old regional department stores into high-grade supermarkets, using the same physical store, simply with different management.

Whatever the details, the department store business will undergo considerable change up to the year 2000 and beyond.

# Chapter 7

# Conglomerate retail groups

## The new samurai

Department stores are not the only large retail formats in Japan, and they are no longer the largest companies either. They have been surpassed by a new breed of retail company. More accurately they are not companies so much as groups of many different companies. Retailing forms the central core of each group, but their activities now extend across other types of business also. They are retail conglomerates. The Japanese often refer to them as 'conglo-merchants' (Nakata, 1988).

These groups are very large indeed. In previous chapters, the names of these companies have already appeared. The top three also operate the leading convenience store chains, and some also have chains of speciality stores and even department stores. At the core of all the largest groups is a chain of general merchandise stores (GMS), often called superstores or general merchandise outlets, and these are the main business, usually with the highest single revenues and profits within the whole conglomerate.

These companies now run the biggest chains of both general merchandise outlets and supermarkets in Japan. But, compared to department stores, their main rivals in terms of size, they are relatively new to Japan, mostly originating after the Second World War. In that short time, they have grown to dominate the retail market. In the early 1990s, even the corporate retail industry remains highly fragmented, but concentration is increasing among these groups.

This chapter looks at the conglo-merchants and their importance in the retail market both now and in the future. Whereas in many ways department stores in Japan are unique to the local culture, the superstores and supermarkets that are at the heart of these conglo-merchant groups are quite similar to those in the West. The only major differences are merchandise mix and management style. As the leading retail companies, however, they are the focus of retail developments and change. It is these companies that are moving away from the more traditional methods, ideas and techniques described in previous chapters.

## SUPERSTORES AND SUPERMARKETS: SUPER STORES?

First, consider the core businesses within these groups. These are multiple chains of general merchandise outlets and supermarkets. Taken alone, the largest GMS chains are the single biggest retail companies in Japan, and have been since the early 1970s. In terms of operation, GMS chains are similar to large retail chains in the West, but, as with any retail format, some cultural differences do exist.

As with department stores and shopping centres, these companies come together in their own professional association, called the Japan Chain Store Association. Membership is made up of the largest multiple chains in retailing, including GMS, supermarket and speciality chains. Members must have at least eleven outlets, and annual sales exceeding ¥1,000 million. All the department stores in the top 500 retailers qualify by sales, but only two, Mitsukoshi and Seibu, have enough outlets in their main groups. Consequently, 'chain stores' and 'department stores' are differentiated in Japan.

Formally, the main difference between supermarket chains and GMS chains is their merchandise mix. Supermarkets sell mostly food, deriving more than 70 per cent of income from this merchandise sector alone, while GMS chains, as their name suggests sell a more general range of products, with less than 70 per cent, but more than 10 per cent, from all of foods, apparel and household goods (Tajima, 1980: 63–4).

Consumers have got around these formal definitions, however. To them both supermarkets and general merchandise outlets, or superstores, are simply *sūpā*. This word, a simple contraction of 'supermarket' or 'superstore', is so common that it has found its way back into the Census of Commerce.

As noted in Chapter 6, the Census differentiates department stores and large general merchandise outlets solely on the basis of whether they use personal sales or self-service techniques. Even in the Census, self-service general merchandise outlets are called *sōgō sūpā* or 'general superstores'. The Census recorded 1,549 GMS outlets in

1991, with sales per company of ¥5,268 million (MITI, 1992b: 66–7). Most of these outlets are members of the same GMS chains that are the key businesses within the conglomerate retail groups.

In addition, however, the same groups and other companies operate a number of other types of so-called *sūpā*. In addition to food supermarkets (food *sūpā*), as defined above, the Census identifies apparel and household goods *sūpās* as well. These were defined in Chapter 3, Table 3.13. They differ from speciality stores in that sales only exceed 70 per cent from one product type, while speciality stores must exceed 90 per cent, and by size. Speciality food, apparel and household *sūpās* must have more than 500 square metres of sales space, meaning they qualify as at least a Type 2 store under the 1979 Large Store Law. There were 7,130 speciality *sūpās* in Japan in 1991, each averaging sales of ¥1,122 million a year (MITI, 1991a: 230; 1992a: 67).

The type of large general merchandise stores that make up the biggest retail chains in Japan within retail conglomerates are usually large superstore-type outlets. To continue with the Japanese classifications just a little further, the nearest term for these is *ryōhanten*, or literally 'mass sales store'. But as superstores and supermarkets are so much more numerous than department stores, and as there are various speciality categories of *sūpās* too, the term *ryōhanten* is not as commonly used as the phonetic abbreviation from English. Japanese have none of the French qualms about their language becoming swamped with English, and will quickly 'Japan-ify' any useful term or phrase.

## THE LARGEST RETAIL COMPANIES IN JAPAN

The largest retail groups operate a wide range of retail formats, with GMS chains at their core. In the latter half of the 1980s, to avoid the costs involved with traversing the Large Store Law, these groups opened more small-format chains, including convenience stores and speciality stores. In the 1990s, with continuing moves to deregulate the opening of large stores, the same companies are leading the rush to open new, larger outlets, increasing the number of submissions for new store approval (see Chapter 5).

GMS chains are the main large retail format, but the structure of the superstore sector is similar to that for department stores. That is, there are a small number of national or semi-national chains run by the largest companies, and numerous smaller companies operating in more limited geographical areas. From the point of view of the consumer, advances in the quality of GMS buildings and merchandise mean that the only real difference between department stores and GMS outlets is the use of self-service in the latter. Increasingly, the newest, largest GMS outlets resemble department stores in terms of merchandise range and price levels. Management efficiency and performance results are considerably better for GMS.

Figure 7.1 shows the sales figures for the largest ten retail conglomerates. The diagram shows sales figures for both the core chains and any consolidated sales figures for the core subsidiaries as a whole. Two groups have sales exceeding ¥2.5 billion. Only three more have sales over ¥1 billion, and only two more over ¥500,000 billion. Considering the core chains of general merchandise stores alone, only the top six chains achieved sales over ¥500,000 million in 1991–2.

These six largest companies are considerably bigger than any other retail companies. Only two department stores, Mitsukoshi and Takashimaya, can match them in terms of group sales. Even this is an incomplete picture, however. Consolidated sales include only companies which are directly controlled by the main concern, and not other group members operating semi-independently. Uneed Daiei, Maruetsu and Chujitsuya are all partly owned by Daiei, although each is large enough to appear separately within the largest twenty chains. Including the non-directly owned subsidiary companies in the figures would make the general merchandise chain groups even larger.

Table 7.1 lists the leading fifteen chain store companies. These are all GMS chains and supermarkets. There is also some overlap between companies, with the four parts of the Daiei Group mentioned above all appearing in the list. Several companies are part of other groups, including Tokyu Stores, part of Tokyu Group.

In terms of sales values, Daiei, the number one GMS chain, is a long way ahead of the other companies. On the other hand, Ito-Yokado is by far the most profitable retail company. With the exception of Ito-Yokado, however, profit margins are very low indeed. A pre-tax profit margin of 3 per cent or more is very high. The reason for low profits is the high cost structure even among chain store companies, although the situation is slightly different for each individual group.

In general terms the high costs incurred by superstores and supermarkets are due to a number of factors. Most stores provide a

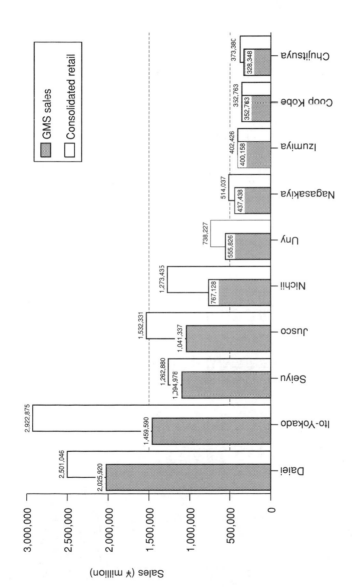

*Figure 7.1* GMS chains and consolidated group sales for leading ten retail conglomerates, 1991–2
*Source*: Compiled from Nihon Keizai Shinbun (1992)

Table 7.1 Leading general merchandise chains by sales, 1992–3

| Sales ranking over all retail companies | Company | Format | Sales (¥ million) | % change 93/92 | Operating profit (¥ million) | % change 93/92 | Operating profit margin % | Store nos | Store no. change |
|---|---|---|---|---|---|---|---|---|---|
| 1 | Daiei[a] | GMS | 2,015,230 | −0.5 | 24,044 | −12.7 | 1.2 | 225 | +10 |
| 2 | Ito–Yokado[b] | GMS | 1,511,553 | 3.6 | 97,508 | 0.4 | 6.5 | 143 | – |
| 3 | Seiyu[c] | GMS | 1,103,778 | 0.8 | 12,838 | −19.9 | 1.2 | 204 | +1 |
| 4 | Jusco | GMS | 1,005,664 | −3.4 | 27,535 | −6.9 | 2.7 | 168 | +1 |
| 5 | Nichii | GMS | 789,462 | 2.9 | 24,074 | −17.4 | 3.0 | 150 | −2 |
| 6 | Uny | GMS | 569,799 | 2.5 | 12,048 | −30.8 | 2.1 | 119 | 0 |
| 7 | Nagasakiya | GMS | 414,563 | −5.2 | −539 | −113.1 | −0.1 | 374 | −33 |
| 8 | Izumiya | GMS | 400,844 | 0.2 | 12,199 | −19.3 | 3.0 | 78 | 0 |
| 9 | Coop Kobe | Co-op | 351,707 | −0.3 | 6,751 | −27.1 | 1.9 | 149 | +1 |
| 10 | Chujitsuya[a] | GMS | 321,911 | −2.0 | 375 | −92.6 | 0.1 | 73 | +1 |
| 11 | Maruetsu[a] | SM | 321,045 | −0.1 | 6,180 | −24.9 | 1.9 | 172 | −3 |
| 12 | Uneed Daiei[a] | GMS | 298,149 | −2.0 | 1,642 | −23.9 | 0.6 | 66 | +5 |
| 13 | Kotobukiya | GMS | 281,347 | 0.2 | 1,563 | −33.1 | 0.6 | 122 | 0 |
| 14 | Tokyu Store[d] | SM | 275,691 | 0.5 | 4,876 | −8.7 | 1.8 | 85 | 0 |
| 15 | Heiwado | GMS | 208,987 | 6.2 | 8,098 | 6.8 | 3.9 | 65 | +1 |

[a] = Daiei Group.
[b] = Ito–Yokado Group.
[c] = Saison Group.
[d] = Tokyu Group.
Key: GMS = General merchandise store, SM = supermarket, Co-op = co-operative society.
Sources: Compiled from Nihon Keizai Shinbun (1992); Nikkei Ryūtsū Shinbun (1992: 270; 1993d: 236)

large range of services such as free delivery and wrapping services. These are not as comprehensive as those offered by department stores, but they are still expensive. Labour costs are high, and stores employ a relatively large number of people. Physical distribution is expensive. Even the largest companies maintain a mixed system including both their own distribution facilities and direct delivery from suppliers. Ito-Yokado moved more quickly than the other main chains to rationalise distribution and information systems and have reaped the benefits in terms of higher profits.

Daiei, Ito-Yokado, Seiyu, Jusco, Nichii and Uny, the six largest groups, have several similar features. First, they are large, highly diversified groups, and include a wide mixture of businesses. Second, they have the largest geographical spread of stores, and include some of the largest chains in terms of store numbers. Third, all are relatively new businesses, most beginning their chain store operations at various times in the 1950s. Finally, each of the largest groups is led by a single charismatic individual who has been largely responsible for the development of the company. Each of the top six groups is briefly introduced below to illustrate these differences.

In addition, these retail groups are likely to increase their domination of some retail sectors throughout the 1990s. Whereas a handful of department stores achieve turnover almost as high as the chain stores, any single department store group is considerably more limited in its store network and mix of retail formats. The largest general merchandise chains are by far the most important retailers in the 1990s. With around one hundred companies in each major group, these are true conglomerates.

The leading six groups are introduced in order of turnover for 1991.

## Daiei Group

Daiei was founded in 1957 by Isao Nakauchi, the current president and chief executive. It is by far the largest retail group in Japan. In terms of retail sales alone, the second and third largest groups, Ito-Yokado and Saison (which includes both Seibu and Seiyu), are close, but the overall sales of Daiei including both retail and non-retail concerns are considerably larger than those of any other retail conglomerate. In 1992, overall group sales at Daiei were ¥5.1 billion, arising from 182 companies (*Gekkan Keiei Juku*, 1992: 116).

Figure 7.2 illustrates the range of businesses within the company. In addition to retailing, which accounted for about ¥3 billion of total group sales, other major concerns include Daiei Finance, which operates the Daiei credit card and other consumer finance products, Ichiken, a land development company, Oriental Hotels and Fukuoka Daiei Hawks, a leading professional baseball team. The other big groups have a similar large array of companies.

Over recent years the group has expanded into new areas, primarily mass media, publishing and leisure. The crowning glory of this strategy is the opening of a huge new sports complex called the Fukuoka Twin Dome, the home of the Daiei Hawks.

Daiei has long maintained a strategy of company acquisition, largely at the instigation of chief executive Nakauchi. The most striking of these in 1992 was the acquisition of a 35 per cent stake in the Recruit publishing and media company. Other acquisitions in 1992 included the Sun TV station in Kobe, and controlling interests in two major retailers, Uneed Daiei in the southern island of Kyushu where Daiei is otherwise weak, and Chujitsuya, a large Tokyo-based GMS chain.

Retail interests in Daiei extend across the full range of retail formats with the Daiei GMS chain at the centre. This alone achieved sales of over ¥2 billion in 1991, the first single retail company to break the ¥2 billion mark. The other major parts to the Daiei retail business are the Daiei convenience store system, and Printemps department stores.

The Daiei convenience system, as mentioned in Chapter 5, includes two chains, Lawson Japan and Sun Chain stores. Sun Chain is another acquisition, entering the group in 1990. The Lawson name is licensed from the American chain of the same name. This is the second largest chain of convenience stores in the country, and the most profitable part of Daiei's retail business.

The Printemps name is also used under licence, this time from the Parisian department store. Daiei maintains five of these more up-market stores in prime retail locations. The largest are in Ginza in Tokyo and in Namba in Osaka. Unlike the more traditional Japanese department stores, Printemps is operated more like a fashion building (see Chapter 5), with numerous small boutiques and merchandise corners. Food is restricted to packaged gift confectionery in most outlets, and the main product lines are fashion apparel.

In total, the group operates over 10,000 outlets in numerous formats. Average sales for a single day in 1992 exceeded ¥9.72

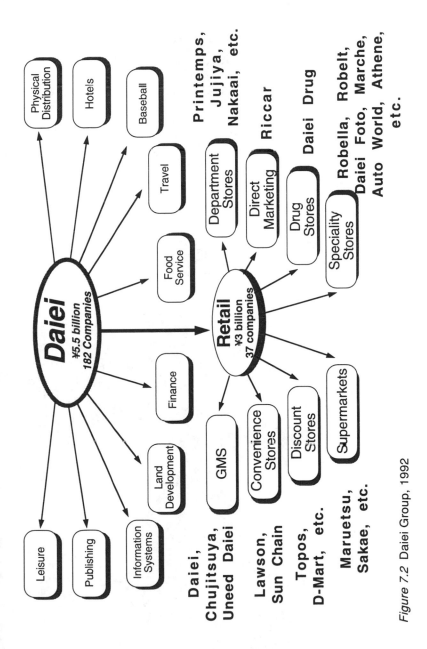

*Figure 7.2* Daiei Group, 1992

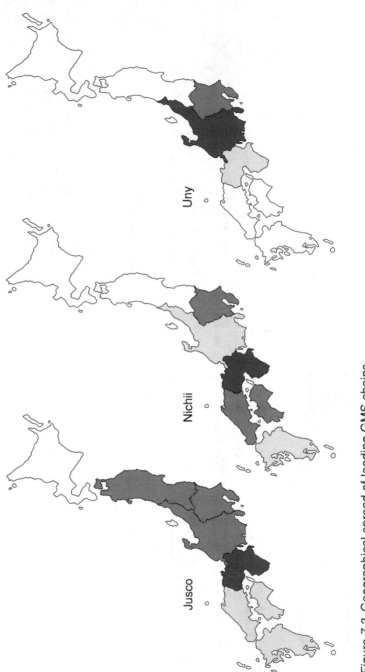

*Figure 7.3* Geographical spread of leading GMS chains
*Sources*: Compiled from Nihon Keizai Shinbun (1992)

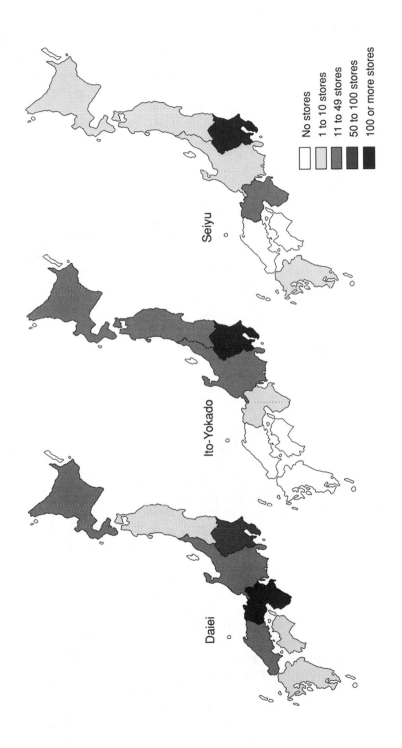

Seiyu

Ito-Yokado

Daiei

No stores
1 to 10 stores
11 to 49 stores
50 to 100 stores
100 or more stores

million from over 4 million customers. Daiei also operates a number of family restaurant chains including franchises for Victoria Station and Big Boy steak restaurants and for Wendy's hamburgers.

The GMS chain at the core of the group had 215 outlets at the end of 1992. Compared to the other main chains, Daiei stores have a wider geographical spread throughout Japan (see Figure 7.3). In 1992, Daiei superstores were located in thirty-five of the forty-seven prefectures. In addition, subsidiary companies spread the chain even further. Only Jusco and Nichii can claim a similarly nationwide network of stores, and this is only due to a number of separately operated regional subsidiaries. No other single chain is so widespread.

This allows Daiei to offer various unique services to its customers. Merchandise is bought through the central office in Tokyo, allowing considerable standardisation throughout the chain, and giving the company considerable buying power.

All the major chains have offered a small number of retail brands since the 1970s. In the early 1990s, as consumers began to take a greater interest in price over brand, Daiei began to offer a new range of own brands, deliberately aimed to be cheaper, and called 'savings' (Nikkei Ryūtsū Shinbun, 1993a). Daiei 100 per cent fruit orange juice sold for ¥188 a litre in 1992, compared to ¥300 or more for most national brands. The Daiei convenience system also introduced their own cheaper brands of milk and canned coffee.

While the superstores are not traditionally strong for gift sales, end-of-year sales of gifts in 1992 actually rose for the GMS chains, while sales at department stores, although higher, declined on the 1991 figure. Daiei, with a standardised line of gift items and a nationwide network of stores, offered free nationwide delivery of gifts, with very little cost burden on the company, something only Seiyu and Jusco can properly match. Orders for gifts to be delivered to another part of the country are simply passed on to the nearest Daiei outlet (Yasumori, 1993).

Isao Nakauchi is now over 70 years old. He is expected to retire some time in the mid-1990s. His eldest son, Jun Nakauchi, will take over. This perpetuates Daiei as a family business, even though it is the largest retail company in Japan.

At the beginning of the 1990s, however, Daiei had huge interest-bearing debts totalling some ¥500,000 million. The interest on this alone accounted for some 70 per cent of pre-tax profits, making it the one reason Daiei does not make the profits boasted by Ito-Yokado. In 1992, Daiei announced a five-year plan to cut the debt by two thirds and increase net profit margin to 3 per cent, twice the level in 1992. Isao Nakauchi, has said he wishes to reduce this burden prior to passing the company on to his successor (Gekkan Keiei Juku, 1992).

## Ito-Yokado Group

The Ito-Yokado Group has a longer history than the other major superstore chains, originating as a small family shop in 1920. The chain store company was founded in 1958. As at Daiei, development of the Ito-Yokado Group was largely driven by a single man, Masatoshi Ito. Unlike at Daiei, however, Masatoshi Ito stepped down in 1992, with a non-family member, Toshifumi Suzuki, becoming president. The founder retired following a scandal within the company. His son, Yasuhisa Ito, waits in the wings as a board member, and his father is said to still have considerable influence on the decision-making process (Nikkei Ryūtsū Shinbun, 1993d).

The core GMS chain in the Ito-Yokado Group has the second highest sales for a single retail company, over ¥1.5 billion in 1992–3. While this was significantly lower than sales at Daiei, the Ito-Yokado chain was by far the most profitable retailer in Japan, achieving net profits before tax of over ¥97,000 million in the same year. This was almost four times the figure for Daiei. The company has achieved this largely through better management cost control and long-term business strategy (Ishihara, 1989).

Both Ito-Yokado and Daiei outlets average around 7,500 square metres of sales space per store, with Ito-Yokado stores being slightly larger than those of Daiei. The geographical spread of Ito-Yokado stores is, however, far more limited. Ito-Yokado does have stores all the way to Hokkaido in the north, but of the 142 stores in the chain in 1992, only sixteen were located south of the Kanto area (see Figure 7.3). There were only two stores in the Kansai area, a major market for Daiei, Jusco and Nichii.

Total group sales in 1992–3 exceeded ¥5.5 billion. The group is less diverse than Daiei or Saison (see below) in terms of the non-retail business it operates, although it does include a full range of retail formats. Table 7.2 shows the main companies within the Ito-Yokado retail group.

The Ito-Yokado Group owns the leading Seven-Eleven Japan convenience store chain. After its parent, the Seven-Eleven chain is the second most profitable retailer overall, with profits exceeding

*Table 7.2* Ito-Yokado Group, 1992

| | |
|---|---|
| Group sales | ¥5.5 billion |
| Companies | 88 |
| GMS chains | Ito-Yokado, Marudai, Maruki Tobshima |
| Supermarket chain | York Benimaru, Sanei |
| Department stores | Robinsons Japan, York Matsuzakaya |
| Convenience stores | Seven-Eleven Japan |
| Discount store | Daikuma |
| Main speciality stores | Merian, Steppes |
| Mail order | Shop America Japan |
| Restaurants | Denny's Japan, Famil |
| Food production | Aiwai Foods, Nihon Nosuishu |
| Real estate | Urawa Building |
| Finance | Union Lease |

*Sources*: Maruki (1992); Nihon Keizai Shinbun (1992)

¥85,000 million in 1992–3. In 1991, Ito-Yokado bought just under 70 per cent of the American Southland Corporation, effectively taking control of the Seven-Eleven convenience store operation worldwide. Seven-Eleven Japan is now working hard to restructure their new US chain, introducing some of the techniques that were successful in Japan.

Other major chains in the Ito-Yokado Group include York Matsuzakaya and Robinsons department stores. The name of the latter is licensed from the California retailer of the same name.

Ito-Yokado also operates York Benimaru, York Mart and Sanei supermarkets, several speciality store chains and a discount chain called Daikuma. The company holds the licence for Denny's family restaurants in Japan, in addition to operating several other restaurants and fast food chains.

Although still somewhat smaller than Daiei, no part of the Ito-Yokado Group is unsuccessful. The profit record of the company is unrivalled. Within this, the Seven-Eleven Japan chain of convenience stores has been the most strikingly successful of all. This success is based on the effective use of complete information systems and an almost ruthless pursuit of distribution efficiency.

The company claims to have been the first retailer in the world to use POS systems to gather marketing information for merchandising purposes. This is now standard in all the leading convenience stores. The system was first introduced in 1982, and has undergone various updating of both hardware and software. In 1990, expert systems were introduced for store merchandising control, and the whole chain was linked to an ISDN (Integrated Service Digital Network: see Chapter 5) in 1992 (Ito-Yokado, 1992).

In terms of distribution efficiency, Ito-Yokado was the first company to introduce a system of jointly operated distribution centres. These distribution centres are built on land owned by Ito-Yokado suppliers and are jointly operated by the same suppliers who deliver to Ito-Yokado stores collectively. In some cases, competing suppliers are required to use the same centre to supply similar products.

Uno *et al.* (1988: 235–8) provide an example of this system. In the mid-1980s, Ito-Yokado stores in Tokyo were supplied by no less than ninety separate makers and wholesalers of undergarments. Each handled distribution to Ito-Yokado outlets in their own area. The company chose just five of these to act as the main suppliers. The remaining eighty-five were required to supply Ho-Yokado through these five wholesaler businesses, reducing the total number of deliveries to each store.

This is just one example of the aggressive way in which Ito-Yokado moved to rationalise its distribution and management systems. Today, all the big companies exercise the same power. Ito-Yokado was the first to demand positive improvements in distribution and force their implementation.

## Saison Group

The Saison Group operates two of the largest five retail companies. The first, and the main part of the group as a whole, is the Seiyu chain of GMS outlets. The Seiyu Group exists as a separate entity within the Saison Group as a whole. The second major part of the Saison Group is the Seibu Department Stores company which was mentioned in Chapter 6.

In 1992, Saison Group included 197 companies (Maruki, 1992: 20). This is by far the most diverse of all the large conglo-merchants (Table 7.3). In addition to GMS, department store, convenience store, fashion building and speciality store chains, all of which are individually among the largest retail chains by sales, Saison Group has a wide range of service companies, including the Intercontinental chain of hotels, and even a helicopter sales and servicing company.

In 1989 Saison Group was, for a single year, the largest retail grouping in terms of overall turnover. It was in the same year that the group acquired the Intercontinental Hotel chain at, it is said, too

*Table 7.3* Saison Group, 1992

| | |
|---|---|
| Group sales | ¥4.4 billion |
| Companies | 193 |
| GMS chains | Seiyu |
| Department stores | Seibu Department Stores |
| Convenience stores | Family Mart |
| Main speciality stores | Parco buildings Mujirushi Ryōhin |
| Mail order | Ozawa Shokai |
| Food production | Seiyo Food Systems |
| Real estate | Seiyo Development |
| Finance | Credit Saison, Saison Insurance, Seibu Auto Lease |
| Others | Intercontinental Hotels, Asahi Engineering, Asahi Senyo, Cine Saison |

*Sources*: Maruki (1992); Nihon Keizai Shinbun (1992)

high a price and one too far beyond the group's resources at the time. Like Daiei in many ways, Saison grew rapidly by acquisition as well as through the establishment of new, innovative businesses. In this case, however, expansion was too rapid, and too thinly spread over various businesses for the good of the company. Consequently, in 1992, the ranking of the Saison Group by sales value had fallen to third place behind Daiei and Ito-Yokado.

Once again, like Daiei and Ito-Yokado, the Saison Group is the result of the leadership of a single highly charismatic individual, Seiji Tsutsumi. The company originated prior to the Second World War as a private suburban railway in Tokyo. In 1949, it established Seibu Department Stores. On his death, the founder, Seiji Tsutsumi's father, split the group between his two sons, giving the railway and a large chunk of the leisure business to the younger and, it was said, more ambitious Yoshiaki Tsutsumi, and the retail business, then the poorer half of the company, to Seiji Tsutsumi (*Economist*, 1988f; Larke and Arima, 1992).

Seiji Tsutsumi was educated at the highly prestigious Tokyo University and is something of an intellectual. He has published his own poetry, and widely promoted the arts in Japan. Saison Group is heavily involved in sponsoring and promoting various forms of art, much more so than the other retailer groups. Saison includes its own film production company, Cine Saison, that has links with Robert Redford's Sundance Institute. The group also operates eighteen movie theatres and several drama theatres. Ticket Saison is the second largest booking office and play guide service, selling over 6.5 million tickets in 1992.

The Tsutsumi brothers are not, however, the best of friends (see *Economist*, 1988f). This led to considerable rivalry between the two groups and this is largely responsible for Seiji Tsutsumi's desire to build the Saison Group ever larger.

One way in which he did this was through new, innovative and unusual retail concepts. On the other hand, new ideas have been too common in some ways, with some projects proving more aesthetic than profitable. Seiyu is the only company among the leading five which has a worse profit record than Daiei.

Seiji Tsutsumi stood down as president in 1990 as results became increasingly worse, with the burden of paying for Intercontinental Hotels, the last major acquisition by the group to date, clearly to blame. The current president, Seiichi Mizuno, is part of the Tsutsumi family by marriage.

While Saison Group may not be known for outstanding profit making, some of the group's retail innovations have been very successful. The Parco chain of fashion buildings (see Chapter 5) has been copied by Jusco, Nichii and hundreds of independent retail developers.

The Loft chain of craft, amusement and variety department stores has also been successful, selling a wide range of gimmicks and toys to young people. Loft stores are typical of the Saison Group, with their distinctive black and yellow colour schemes, dark ceilings full of silver air conditioning vents and thousands of small, amusing or unusual merchandise items. The largest outlets are located on prime sites in Shibuya in Tokyo and in Umeda in Osaka, with others due to open in other cities in the near future. These stores are very popular with younger consumers who like to spend hours browsing. Loft also offers a number of artistic services such as printing, photographic services and specialised wrapping services.

Mujirushi Ryōhin is a speciality store chain selling a wide range of generic brand goods in simple brown packaging and on plain wooden shelving. The name means 'no brand, good merchandise'. When it was introduced in 1980, the concept of generic goods was so unusual in brand-conscious Japan that this range of 'non-branded' goods became a high-class brand in their own right. Today both Jusco and Daiei carry similar lines. In 1992, the chain, which operates in the Seiyu part of Saison Group, opened stores in the UK under the name Muji.

The core of the Saison Group is similar to the other large retailers. The three core chains are Seibu Department Stores, the second largest department store chain in Japan, Seiyu superstores, the third largest GMS chain, and Family Mart convenience stores, the third largest convenience store chain.

Family Mart has all the characteristics of other convenience store chains, including high growth rates. Along with its rivals operated by the other big groups, Family Mart is gradually securing a major foothold in the convenience store market overall (see Chapter 5).

After Daiei, the Seiyu chain has the most widespread network of stores. Seiyu outlets are a lot smaller on average than those operated by either Daiei or Ito-Yokado, averaging only around 4,500 square metres of sales space per store. Within the Seiyu chain, some of the larger stores also use the name Seibu in order to create a higher, department store image. In typical Saison Group style, Seiyu is one of the few companies to experiment with exterior store design. While the vast majority of other chains stick firmly to a simple, square box design for their stores, some Seiyu stores are designed to resemble ships and aeroplanes.

The group is currently undergoing a general consolidation in order to weed out and slim down less profitable ventures. The best Seiyu stores and Seibu department stores are being further improved. The Seiyu store in Kasugai, Aichi Prefecture, which was the number one selling chain store outlet in Japan in 1989, is one example. This store is one of those which uses the Seibu name (*Gekiryū*, 1988). It has added numerous leisure facilities such as a cinema and a lot of tenant speciality stores. The aim is to build on the existing popularity of the store. The more unusual and successful chains of Loft variety stores and Parco fashion buildings are also being expanded into new areas of the country.

## Aeon Group

The Aeon Group manages the Jusco chain of retail stores. Jusco is unique among the leading chains in that the company has grown through a long series of mergers between separate regional supermarket and superstore chains to form a single national operation. In 1992, the core Jusco chain had 168 outlets spread widely throughout Japan, but with a smaller number in the Tokyo area compared to the three larger companies. In addition, Aeon Group includes a further fourteen regional chains operating in more limited areas. There is

*Table 7.4* Aeon Group, 1992

| | |
|---|---|
| Group sales | ¥26 billion |
| Companies | 157 |
| GMS chains | Jusco, Shinshu Jusco, Isejin Jusco, Ogiya Jusco, Tochigi Jusco, Hokuriku Jusco, Sanyo Jusco, Jusco Okuwa, etc. |
| Supermarket chain | Wellmart, Aomori Wellmart, Kakudai Wellmart, Apple, Joy Mart, Mie Wellmart, etc. |
| Department stores | Bon Belta Isejin, Bon Belta Ueo, Tachibana Hyakkaten, Bon Belta |
| Convenience stores | Mini-Stop |
| Discount store | Big Bahn |
| Main speciality stores | Forus buildings, Cox, Ability Japan, Talbots Japan, Book Bahn, Blue Grass, MyLord Shoes, Nishiki, Laura Ashley, Body Shop, etc. |
| Restaurants | Gourmet Doru, Jack, Red Lobster, Chimney, etc. |
| Others | Jusco Hong Kong Java Jusco, Siam Jusco, Talbots USA, etc. |

*Sources*: Maruki (1992); Nihon Keizai Shinbun (1992)

some overlap in the areas covered by stores managed directly by Jusco and those managed by regional subsidiaries.

The Aeon Group is more concentrated on retailing than the other groups. Aeon included 157 companies in 1992, including real estate and land development, credit services, restaurants and catering, and leisure services, but these are more integrated into the retail business than is the case with Daiei, Ito-Yokado or Saison (Table 7.4).

All parts of the Aeon Group retail operation are strong in terms of sales, profits and growth in store numbers. Retailing, again, extends across the full range of formats. Jusco GMS chains were undergoing a major image improvement programme at the beginning of the 1990s. Growth through mergers has left some parts of the group with older, smaller stores. The central chain is now concentrating on larger, more up-market outlets, and the company has even changed its corporate colours and logo, using a mark similar to that used by a modern department store.

Supermarkets within the group are separate again from GMS chains, operating largely under the name Wellmart. Like the Jusco GMS outlets, Wellmart is split into a number of separate regional operations. Aeon also operates several department stores under the name Bon Belta, but newer GMS developments, like the 100,000 square metre shopping centre at Noa in Ibaragi Prefecture, are, if anything, even more up-market.

Aeon also has a convenience store chain called Mini-Stop. Mini-Stop is the only convenience store chain operated by one of the leading groups that is not in the top ten for its format ranking. The chain is growing, but is still well behind those operated by four of the top six groups. Mini-Stop convenience stores often include a small fast-food section with tables and seats in addition to the normal selection of convenience store merchandise.

There are two unique aspects to the retail business of the Aeon Group that set it apart from the other major companies. One is the number of successful brand speciality store chains within the group. The company has developed several carefully targeted speciality fashion store chains that can operate independently of the Jusco chain. The largest of these are Cox and Blue Grass fashion stores. Both chains carry men's and women's fashion apparel, with Blue Grass aimed at a younger clientele. These chains operate free-standing outlets, and as tenants within various fashion buildings. Aeon has a small number of its own fashion buildings called Forus in Sendai, Himeji and Akita that are similar to the Parco buildings run by Saison.

A second unique aspect of the Aeon Group is the strong international links developed by the company. Aeon is the head Japanese franchisee for Laura Ashley fashion stores, Body Shop cosmetics shops and Red Lobster restaurants. Each of these chains was introduced into Japan by Aeon, and each is very successful in the Japanese market. Laura Ashley expanded rapidly following the first links between the British company and Jusco in 1986. Now the chain includes a number of prime, free-standing locations throughout Japan, and numerous tenant stores in leading department stores such as Mitsukoshi or Hankyu, to make a total chain of over forty stores. In 1989, Aeon acquired 50 per cent of Laura Ashley USA and 15 per cent of the UK head operation.

Aeon became head franchisee for Body Shop in 1990. In 1992, the chain was expanding rapidly, following on the experience of Laura Ashley. In December 1992, the chain had seven outlets all in and around Tokyo. The first of these opened in the main fashion district of Aoyama, and had the highest sales of any Body Shop store anywhere in the world. Unlike the Ito-Yokado operation of Seven-Eleven, for example, Body Shop and Laura Ashley operations have not been 'Japanified' in any way.[1] Both the stores and the merchandise are similar if not identical to those found elsewhere in the world.

The international operations of Aeon Group are not confined to Japan. In 1988, the group acquired The Talbots, a women's clothing store based in the north-east USA. Jusco also operates a number of superstore outlets across South-East Asia including stores in Thailand, Hong Kong and Malaysia.

Today, Aeon Group is such a mixture of amalgamated companies that, compared to Daiei, Ito-Yokado and Saison, an individual leader is less prominent. The group originated in 1969 through a merger of three companies wishing to form a buying group. The heads of two of these are today the chairman and chief executive, Tatsuya Okada, and the president, Hidenori Futagi. These two men have been responsible for the success of Aeon. The ability of these two leaders to build the group through careful and considerate amalgamation with other chains, and their ability to spot success in new international ventures, suggests a special kind of retail understanding. They have avoided the temptation to greatly diversify out of retailing. Consequently, while a little smaller than some, the Aeon Group has a firm business base.

## MYCAL Group

MYCAL (pronounced 'my-kal') stands for 'Young minded, casual amenity lifestyle'.[2] MYCAL Group is the amalgamated name for the group of companies led by the Nichii GMS chain.

Nichii is largely a Kansai-based company, with seventy-two of the 150 stores in the main chain being located in the prefectures of Osaka, Kyoto, Hyogo and Nara. The group was originally formed in 1963 by the amalgamation of three clothing chains. As with the Jusco chain, the current chairman of Nichii was the founder of one of these original companies. The company entered the GMS business in 1967. Like Aeon Group, Nichii merged with a number of retail, wholesaler and manufacturing companies during the early 1970s, and had become the fifth largest GMS chain by the beginning of the 1980s, a position it has since held. Table 7.5 shows the member companies within the Nichii/MYCAL Group.

It was at this point that Nichii decided it was better to differentiate the group from other similar chains. In 1982, a new strategy was instigated, beginning by changing the name of the group from Nichii to MYCAL. This long-term restructuring policy aims to greatly

*Table 7.5* Nichii/MYCAL Group, 1992

| | |
|---|---|
| Group sales | ¥2 billion |
| Companies | 97 |
| GMS chains | Nichii, Hokkaido Nichii, Tohoku Nichii, Niigata Nichii, etc. |
| Supermarket chain | Saty, Yonago Nichii, etc. |
| Department stores | Dac City |
| Main speciality stores | Vivre buildings, Elleme, McLord, Sporsium, etc. |
| Restaurants | Calos, Cohms, Arby's Japan, Gourmet Road, etc. |
| Resorts | Risonare, etc. |
| Finance | Nichii Credit Service, Nichii Financial Services, NIA, etc. |
| Others | Play and Service, Nichii International, Nichii Enterprise, USA Nichii, etc. |

*Sources*: Maruki (1992); Nihon Keizai Shinbun (1992)

upgrade the Nichii chain away from basic, low-price GMS outlets, to mid-price fashionable stores. Cheaper outlets continue to operate under the Nichii name, relying very much on 'pile it high, sell it cheap'. Many of these are now old and have received little invest-ment for refurbishment in recent years, but the newer stores are very different.

Nichii/MYCAL is one of the few groups to have actively closed stores during the 1980s. In 1986, the main GMS chain included 166 outlets. By 1991, this had been reduced to 149. In 1992, Nichii closed a further twelve stores group-wide but added three more to the GMS chain. Overall, in 1992, the GMS company operated 152 outlets, with a total of 283 outlets in the group as a whole (Nichii, 1992).

As with the Jusco GMS chain, the MYCAL Group includes several regional companies that operate superstores and other outlets in different parts of the country. If these are included the Nichii chain has a coverage that stretches beyond its home base of Kansai, but still not as much as the other major groups. Nichii has only a very small number of stores in the Tokyo area, for example.

The second major aspect of the strategy to upgrade the group was to introduce new, higher-quality stores among the main Nichii general merchandise outlets. This is another reason why existing Nichii stores have not been refurbished, with the company preferring to move to totally different designs.

The first of these were Vivre fashion buildings, the second largest chain of these speciality shopping centres after Saison's Parco. The first Vivre outlet opened in 1982 in Fukuoka, with the second store opening in the main Harajuku fashion district in Tokyo the following year. By 1992, there were fifteen outlets across Japan. The Vivre store in Sendai had the highest turnover within the MYCAL Group, with sales exceeding ¥24,000 million in 1991 (Nichii, 1992), although this was later overtaken by larger developments.

The second new chain introduced by the group were Saty[3] superstores. These tend to be smaller than most Japanese GMS outlets, averaging between only 4,000 and 5,000 square metres. The main merchandise lines are food and basic clothing items, giving the stores the feel of a large, fashionable supermarket. Emphasis is placed on merchandise quality rather than on low prices. The company likes to refer to these stores as 'suburban lifestyle department stores'.

One of the striking features of the Saty stores is the large range of foods. As in all supermarkets, fish is a very important part of the merchandise mix. Saty stores are unusual in that almost all outlets have huge fish tanks – fifty to eighty tonne aquariums. Stores carry up to forty varieties of live fish and twenty varieties of live shellfish. Assistants, bedecked in rubber boots and aprons, net the customers' choice of swimming dinner. The largest fish sales floor in a Saty store is over 420 square metres.

In 1992, there were sixteen Saty outlets. These will be how most Nichii stores look in the future, although larger formats are still being opened under the original Nichii name (Nichii, 1992). In 1992, Vivre and Saty outlets accounted for 25 per cent of total sales within the main GMS chain. The company plans to increase this proportion to around 80 per cent over the 1990s.

The MYCAL Group, like the first three groups described above, is highly diversified. It includes two major health and fitness club chains called XAX and People, insurance services, travel, consumer finance, leasing and wholesaling businesses. The other major section of the company is, however, that dealing with land development.

In 1989 Nichii opened the MYCAL Honmoku shopping centre to the south of Yokohama city centre. This is a massive shopping development covering 38,000 square metres of land in the middle of a nine square kilometre suburban housing and leisure development. Total floor space within the complex is over 121,000 square metres, of which just under 50,000 square metres is sales space. The complex has ten buildings and is the pride of the MYCAL Group. It includes a Saty store, a fashion building, numerous restaurants and a wide array of leisure facilities. In the first year, Honmoku received over 15 million visitors, and in 1992 it had the highest turnover in the group, with sales of ¥16,800 million (Nikkei Ryūtsū Shinbun, 1993d: 388).

The Honmoku shopping centre is six kilometres south of central Yokohama, and a ten-to-fifteen-minute bus ride from the nearest station. Although the complex has space for 2,500 cars, the location of the centre away from rail transport is a major limitation. Indeed, projected sales for the first year were over ¥26,000 million (*Hanbai Kakushin*, 1989), but after three years of operation it had not achieved this figure. Nevertheless, Nichii plans to build similar complexes in other parts of the country during the 1990s (Ito, 1989; Kimura, 1989; Nichii, 1992).

## Uny Group

Uny is not quite in the same league as the top five groups, but it is far larger than the next nearest rival, Nagasakiya. It is also the only group that comes close to the other five in terms of diversity.

Uny, pronounced 'you knee',[4] has a history dating back to 1911 when the father of its long-standing chairman and the driving force behind the group, Toshio Nishikawa, opened a small clothing store in Aichi Prefecture. The group came into being in 1969 with the amalgamation of several small clothing chains. The name 'Uny' is said to be derived from the English words 'unique', 'united', 'universal', 'unity' and 'unify' (Uny, 1992: 6). Today the group is still concentrated predominantly in Aichi Prefecture and the prefectures surrounding there, with Kanagawa Prefecture just south of Tokyo being the group's second stronghold. The Uny group had overall sales of some ¥770,000 million in 1992–3, and, including all formats, a total of over 2,100 stores. Over half of these were accounted for by the fastest growing of the leading convenience store chains, Circle K Japan.

In all, Uny outlets are spread over only fifteen prefectures. Including department stores, it is the largest company that is not based in either Osaka or Tokyo. All of the leading ten retail companies have their headquarters in one of these two cities.[5] Uny is based in Nagoya, as is the next biggest retail company, Matsuzakaya department stores. Uny was also the only large chain to operate stores in the central Japan Sea prefectures of Fukui and Ishikawa in the early 1990s, although other chains were set to move into these areas.

Within the Uny Group there are the usual range of retail formats. The core chain is a basic GMS chain using the name Uny. This was diversified in the mid-1980s and now includes more up-market suburban outlets that have the name Apita, and larger shopping centre outlets called Sun Terrace.

While Uny general merchandise outlets are especially strong in the company's home prefecture, recent growth has largely been in convenience store and speciality store retailing. Circle K Japan was established in 1984, with the name being licensed from the American convenience store chain of the same name. Uny entered the convenience store market relatively late, but, by 1991, sales at Circle K were growing by over 30 per cent a year, making it the fastest growing chain among the top ten companies.

Uny operates a number of speciality chains. The largest is the Sagami chain of specialist kimono boutiques. This chain is spread nationwide and has 302 outlets. Other chains are smaller and largely confined to prefectures in central Japan, namely Aichi, Gifu and Shizuoka, but with a small number in Kanagawa. The largest of the speciality store chains are the Morie and the Paremo ladies' fashion stores, which together have some 200 outlets, and the Akari and Rough Ox men's fashion stores with some 100 outlets.[6]

In 1993, after falling sales, the long-term chairman of the Uny Group stood down. The new chairman, not a family man, is looking to push Uny up with the larger chains. Already, he has announced the scrapping of the fashionable but expensively designed Apita format of variety department stores, and has taken steps to cut administrative costs in the group as well.

## PRESENT AND FUTURE TRENDS IN GENERAL MERCHANDISE RETAILING

In the 1980s, the Large Store Law was the main reason for a relatively slow rate of growth in the number of superstore outlets overall. Even so, the number of large stores did increase, slowly, but steadily.

Table 7.6 shows the leading GMS outlets across the country. No outlet has sales that can rival the department stores (see Table 6.5). They sell cheaper merchandise and have less revenue from services or sales on account, both of which account for a significant proportion of department store revenue. Within the leading twenty

Table 7.6 Leading individual general merchandise and supermarket outlets, 1992–3

| Sales ranking over all retail stores | Company | Store | Prefecture | Sales (¥ million) | % change 93/92 | Sales space (sq m) |
|---|---|---|---|---|---|---|
| 1 | 76 | Daiei | Tsudanuma | Chiba | 34,214 | -0.3 | 27,413 |
| 2 | 130 | Ito-Yokado | Tsudanuma | Chiba | 23,483 | -1.3 | 17,176 |
| 3 | 135 | Uneed Daiei | Shopper's Daiei | Fukuoka | 22,281 | -5.5 | 21,136 |
| 4 | 145 | Toyota Coop | Toyota | Aichi | 21,217 | -2.4 | 12,068 |
| 5 | 150 | Daiei | Himonya | Tokyo | 20,541 | -3.3 | 14,009 |
| 6 | 152 | Daiei | Sendai | Miyagi | 20,402 | -2.9 | 11,800 |
| 7 | 160 | Fuji | Fuji Grand Hiroshima | Hiroshima | 19,247 | n.a. | 13,070 |
| 8 | 161 | Ito-Yokado | Funabashi | Chiba | 19,235 | -1.6 | 17,391 |
| 9 | 165 | Daiei | Niigata | Niigata | 18,801 | -1.5 | 16,369 |
| 10 | 169 | Fuji | Fuji Grand Matsuyama | Ehime | 18,403 | 4.2 | 12,701 |
| 11 | 175 | Seiyu | Oizumi | Tokyo | 17,946 | n.a. | 16,871 |
| 12 | 178 | Daimaru Peacock | Senri Chuo | Osaka | 17,811 | -1.4 | 8,311 |
| 13 | 179 | Seiyu | Koteyubi | Saitama | 17,780 | -2.4 | 15,000 |
| 14 | 182 | Uneed Daiei | Daiei Kagoshima | Kagoshima | 17,668 | -3.1 | 13,051 |
| 15 | 187 | Ito-Yokado | Espa Akijima | Tokyo | 17,113 | 3.2 | 14,090 |
| 16 | 202 | Ito-Yokado | Atsugi | Kanagawa | 15,991 | -4.0 | 12,155 |
| 17 | 203 | Nichii | Ebina | Kanagawa | 15,988 | -0.3 | 13,467 |
| 18 | 209 | Daiei | Shin-Matsudo | Chiba | 15,626 | -3.9 | 10,000 |
| 19 | 210 | Uny | Ichinomiya | Aichi | 15,585 | 3.0 | 12,714 |
| 20 | 211 | Seiyu | Hibarigaoka | Tokyo | 15,554 | -2.6 | 12,650 |

Source: Nikkei Ryūtsū Shinbun (1993d: 358–61)

outlets, three of the top companies, Daiei, Ito-Yokado and Seiyu, have several stores.

By the 1990s, most urban shoppers had at least one superstore within a reasonable distance of their home. In Japan, a reasonable distance means within a short walk or bicycle ride. In the late 1980s and early 1990s, in an effort to open even larger stores or shopping centres, some of the major chains began to build outlets designed to attract greater numbers of car-borne customers. Such examples include Nichii's MYCAL Honmoku complex and the Daiei-operated Hyper Mart store in Futami, Hyogo Prefecture, which has parking for over 1,500 cars. The poor road system in most of Japan, however, means that a commercial area within a thirty-minute car ride is equivalent to only a few kilometres' distance. As yet, few families are willing to drive tens of kilometres to do their weekly shopping.

In all the larger cities, superstores are confined to the suburbs, with central shopping districts being dominated by department stores. There are very few exceptions to this rule. Daiei has stores in the centre of Yokohama, Nagoya and Kobe, the second, fourth and fifth largest cities, but these are the only examples. There are no other superstores within walking distance of such large city centres. There are no superstores in the centre of Tokyo, although Seiyu does have one or two smaller stores within the Yamanote circular line that rings the heart of the capital.

All the big chains do have outlets in the middle of smaller, regional cities. In every medium and small city there is one large outlet. Most towns have a local department store, but, in cities that applied the Large Store Law less stringently during the 1980s, and where the local market offered sufficient potential, superstores moved in. These compete directly with the department stores in the city centre.

Where local department stores are relatively weak, large superstores (GMS) have been able to capture large shares of the local retail market. In some cases, a superstore has replaced local department stores as the dominant retailer. Even as members of one of the large department store buying organisations, the department stores are limited by their supposed role as relatively high-price, high-image retailers. From within conglomerate groups, the GMS chains, on the other hand, have the buying power of nationwide chains, and the flexibility to adjust the mix and price of the merchandise for the area. The Large Store Law was extended in 1982 in an attempt to combat precisely this strength of the large chain stores (see Chapter 4)

As with some local department stores, most existing individual large superstore outlets have also gained from the Large Store Law. The majority of general merchandise outlets have relatively undisputed markets, with no equal competitors within the same sales area. Without being directly involved, large stores were able to influence the approval process for new large outlets planned in their own areas by instigating the help of local small retailers who, in any case, are none too happy about a second large store in their area.

Frequently, compared to the case in many Western companies, large superstore outlets have a significant degree of independence from central management control. The size and market area of most superstores allow scope for the development of individual store character. Significant differences between different geographical areas of Japan, not least in terms of climate, actually make this a necessity. Each prefecture has its own agricultural speciality produce and reputation for quality. Superstores make sure they carry a sufficient volume of local produce, although naturally the larger chains also offer their customers a variety of fresh foods from across the country. Customers expect this kind of familiar feel to their stores.

Towards the end of the 1980s, some suggested that the superstore sector of retailing was on the point of stagnation (Akamatsu, 1989; Honma, 1989; Mori et al., 1989). Restrictive legislation on store openings and the high cost of buying or renting suitable new sites made the opening of new stores difficult and costly. Competition, while never fierce within the superstore sector itself, was not increasing. Where direct competition did exist, stores differentiate their merchandise assortments, service offering and store characteristics rather than compete on price.

In the early 1990s, two factors led to changes in this situation. One was the relaxation of the Large Store Law as detailed in Chapter 4, and the other was the slowing of the economy which forced retailers to turn to low prices as a means to attract customers. Modern superstores have a depth of merchandise and are of a size which clearly rival department stores. Until the economic downturn of the early 1990s, the majority of companies were moving away from high-volume, low-price retailing, and looking to build larger profit margins. With the coming of a relatively slower economy, consumers became more price conscious.

Daiei and Ito-Yokado, the two largest retailers, are beginning to expand discount chains with ever more aggressive price-cutting strategies. These discount outlets are, however, carefully distinguished from other parts of the overall group so as not to damage the image the core chains have established. The main discount chain operated by Ito-Yokado is called Daikuma, and is based in Kanagawa Prefecture and southern Tokyo. Daiei operates three large store discount formats under the store names Topos, D-Mart and Hyper Mart. These outlets frequently offer identical merchandise to that available in normal Daiei stores, except that the price is lower.

The new, larger suburban superstores provide as much car parking space as possible within the limits of the store site. Car parking either surrounds the store or is located on the roof. There are fewer large stores in and around the Tokyo and Osaka areas because of the scarcity and cost of land and congested road systems. In general, larger outlets are located on the very outskirts of these major conurbations because the largest groups prefer to provide as much car parking as possible.

The level of competition between superstores themselves and between superstores and other retail formats will intensify throughout the 1990s. Competition amongst GMS chains will increase with the relaxation of the Large Store Law, allowing a relatively rapid expansion of large outlets. In the face of such competition, many aspects of present-day Japanese distribution could be lost permanently, including a large number of independent wholesalers and retailers and many weaker department stores.

An incident in 1989 within the chain store sector suggests one possible scenario for the 1990s. With the aim of controlling prime land, the chairman of the Shuwa Real Estate Company, Shigeru Kobayashi, built up large shareholdings in several major retail companies. These included Chujitsuya, Maruetsu and Inageya, all second-level superstore and supermarket chains, and in the Isetan and Matsuzakaya department store companies. At their peak, Shuwa's total retail holdings were valued at ¥150,000 million (Allen, 1989; Suzuki, 1990).

The company already had a major and co-operative shareholding in Life Corporation, the thirty-sixth largest retail company in 1992. Kobayashi then began the double takeover of Chujitsuya and Inageya, claiming to want to combine the three companies into what would have been the seventh largest retail operation in Japan (*Ekonomisuto*, 1989; Fields, 1989b: Ito and Ozawa, 1989; *Shūkan Tōyō Keizai*, 1989a; 1989b; Suzuki, 1990).

Chujitsuya and Inageya together fought the takeover bitterly, resorting to illegal swapping of shares between themselves in an attempt to dilute the Shuwa holding (*Shūkan Daiyamondo*, 1989c: 1989d; *Shūkan Tōyō Keizai*, 1989a; 1989b). In the end, their opposition proved successful. Shuwa, suffering from poor conditions in the real-estate market, ran out of funds, and was forced to back off.

In October 1989, at the end of this corporate scuffle, a curious turn of events brought the intervention of the Daiei Group chairman, Isao Nakauchi, as a rescuer for Shuwa (*Shūkan Daiyamondo*, 1989d). Shuwa sold off shares in Life Stores for a profit of ¥200,000 million (Suzuki, 1990), while Daiei provided mortgage funds or bought many of the shares held by Shuwa in the other chains, effectively taking control of the Chujitsuya operation.

In early 1993, as Daiei began moves to reduce its debt burden, calling in the loans made to Shuwa, the realtor began looking to sell off his remaining shareholdings. To the surprise of many, Ito-Yokado moved to buy Shuwa's large holding of shares in the prestigious Isetan department store. Isetan voiced considerable opposition to becoming part of the number two retail group, and the deal did not succeed. Shuwa still owns significant numbers of shares in some of the country's leading retail companies, and this will continue to cause concern to those companies in the future.

As the gap between the very top conglomerate retailers, especially the leading five, and other, smaller chain stores grows, this kind of acquisition activity is a possible way in which the biggest groups will try to further expand their market shares. Similarly, medium and small chains may try to protect themselves through merger with others similar to themselves.

Several leading groups, and Daiei in particular, have a history of collecting companies to build and diversify their groupings. It is probable that similar takeovers will occur in the near future. This is one of the few options available to retailers who wish to expand rapidly. It is also a way in which the larger companies can gain access to the rapidly diminishing number of good retail sites.

Some small and medium sized chains have welcomed friendly takeovers or mergers in the face of a worsening local business climate or a hostile takeover attempt. This is how Aeon Group and, to a lesser extent, MYCAL Group grew during the 1970s. In 1992, for example, Aeon Group took the large Keiyo chain of DIY outlets under its wing. Further mergers will certainly occur.

The Shuwa affair makes an important point. The chairman of Shuwa has been quoted as wanting to 'shake up' Japanese retailing before he retires. Suzuki noted that, as with big businesses the world over, 'personal relationships sometimes loom larger than balance sheets and egos can be a factor as decisive as floor space' (Suzuki, 1990: 29).

Both inside and outside the retail sector, the vast majority of companies in Japan remain under the control of a particular family, no matter how big the companies become. The sons of retail company chairmen are conspicuous on the boards of Daiei, Ito-Yokado and Uny, surrounded as they are by largely sexagenarian and septuagenarian co-directors. In the early 1990s, the founders of first generation of chain stores have been reaching retirement age. Demands for the deregulation of retailing, along with the presence of men like Shuwa's Kobayashi, could well push the industry into a period of radical change (Allen, 1989).

The Large Store Law is unlikely to be abolished completely in the near future. In the economic climate of the 1990s, however, the Law will be altered to allow rapid growth in large retail outlets. With or without the law, there are many who want to see rapid concentration in the retail industry similar to that seen in many Western nations. No matter what the government decides, this could well occur in the near future.

Retailing will change greatly during the 1990s. On the whole, department stores are most likely to decline, small stores will disappear more rapidly, and the speciality store and convenience store sectors will reach saturation point. The economic climate in the early 1990s has been a barrier, but the one sector to benefit on a large scale will be the conglomerate retail groups, built around their general merchandise chains, and with their widely diversified businesses and flexible management skills. While these companies will not begin to take a significant share of the retail market overnight, slowly but surely they will become clearly identified as the leaders of the retail industry both now and in the future.

# Chapter 8

# Japanese retailing in the 1990s and beyond

This book has provided a wide ranging but detailed description of the distribution system in Japan as it really is. It gives a large volume of statistical data, and provides detailed descriptions of all the main retail sectors that play a significant role in the system in the 1990s. There are other aspects that could have been mentioned in brief, but all the major points – the control of channels by manufacturers, the large independent sectors in both the wholesale and retail industries, the unusual business customs and all the main retail sectors (independents, speciality stores, convenience stores, department stores and general merchandise groups) – have been covered.

The one overriding conclusion is that Japanese retailing can be described and understood. The volume of data and information available on the subject is truly vast. Although most of it is in Japanese, this should not be a barrier to any genuine scholar of Japanese distribution, and especially not to prospective business-people looking to enter the market, no matter what their nationality.

There are other points relating to the contents of the book, however, with which we can conclude overall. Chief among them is that the distribution system is now at the beginning of major changes that will alter the way both companies and consumers view retailing and distribution. Most of these have been mentioned and outlined in the preceding discussion, but the most important are reiterated in this final chapter.

## CHANGES IN CONSUMER BEHAVIOUR

Japanese consumers are affluent, and seemingly rather naive. In the 1980s, as the economy boomed, they paid high prices for luxury branded items and expensive new services. At the time, for example, it was far more expensive for Japanese tourists to visit Europe than it was for Europeans to visit Japan, but in addition, it was only a little cheaper to travel within Japan when the costs of train fares and hotels were taken into account.

In the 1980s, many ordinary consumers made a lot of money – largely through the rise in land prices and in the value of stocks and shares. Land prices, as shown in Chapter 2, rose rapidly in the 1980s on the back of widespread speculation. Many landowners made quick and substantial profits from this situation. Real-estate agents have a monopoly on information relating to land and rents and were able to push prices up. This was supported by banks who provided generous loans for people and companies to purchase land, further increasing the demand for land, and consequently its price (Hasegawa, 1987; Yamaichi Securities, 1990). Japanese families all dream of owning their own house. Most young families begin by renting, or possibly buying a flat. Wives squirrelled away their husband's earnings for that house in the suburbs, but, by the 1990s, an affordable house was two hours from the city centre.

Looking back, retailers and other companies saw their opportunity and took it. Why mark up an item 50 per cent when it will still sell with a mark-up of 100 per cent or even more? This philosophy was never voiced, but it is one that almost all discerning businesses adhered to. Consumers got used to the prices. After all, when the most basic food is six times the price in any other country, consumers are less likely to expect other items to be cheaper.

Yet the experiences of foreign travel, and frequent media concern with high prices in Japan, began to have an effect, and this is still going on. In addition, although some companies try to keep it quiet, it is common for goods exported from Japan to actually cost less in London or New York than they do in Tokyo. There is a growing, but so far suppressed, feeling of distrust among consumers towards some companies for this reason (Sano, 1993; Toshida, 1989).

In the early 1990s the economic recession that was biting in Europe and the USA began to trickle back into Japan. A fall in the sales of exports and other international effects was soon felt by workers, and the consumer market began to slow down quite markedly from the summer of 1991.

Since then wages and incomes have not fallen overall, but the rise in 1992 was almost a full percentage point lower than in 1991 (Asahi Shinbunsha, 1993b: 101). Workers who received a substantial proportion of their incomes from bonuses saw these bonuses reduced as company earnings fell back. Consumers became increasingly cautious about their spending, more careful about what to buy and when, postponing a new car, and not bothering with expensive luxuries (Fukunaga, 1993a; Nihon Keizai Shinbun, 1993a).

Compared to the West, the Japanese economy is still doing well. There has been only a small rise in unemployment, and, as noted in Chapter 2, the 1993 crop of students could all expect to find work of some kind. The slow-down in consumer spending has been the worst since the oil shock of the early 1970s, however, and consumer goods companies and most retailers have seen their sales fall, and, as they look to reduce prices by cutting back margins, experiencing even greater falls in profits.

At a time when consumers were willing to pay almost any price for something they wanted, some retailers used high gross margins to carry them along. Now, these companies are suffering the most. They are finding that they must not only cut their prices, but also improve their overall marketing offering and efficiency in order to continue to attract customers.

Other retailers, mainly the more progressive and innovative companies over the years, along with one or two newcomers, have seen new opportunities in the price-conscious consumer market. Discounting is a new retail strategy for most companies, although this was the most common format among the larger chains up to the early 1970s. Now it is making a comeback, and using modern cost-reduction techniques as well as some Japanese business ideas (see pages 234–6).

Japanese consumers are still as quality and style conscious as they ever were. When buying food, they still look for the cleanest, straightest cucumbers and the biggest, most rounded apples. They still want to own and carry Louis Vuitton luggage and wear Italian brand suits (Cendron, 1984; Maebara, 1993). Men still want fast cars, and women still want jewellery and their own houses. None of this will change. Where they buy various of these items will change, and how much they are willing to pay has already changed within the past two years. Consumers are more careful about where they buy, and larger retailers are supporting this trend by offering similar products in new low-price formats.

Other major changes will come with the demographic and social shifts described in Chapter 2. The junior baby-boom generation will be the one to watch especially. This is a large market, and most are just about to enter the work force for the first time. Normal social standards mean that most will still live at home, and be able to use all their new incomes for their own leisure, so they could provide just the boost that the Japanese economy needs. It will further drive the leisure services industry. The desire of these young people to enjoy themselves could possibly do more to bring down the average number of working hours a year than any government plan.

The parents of these young people, the senior baby-boom, must also not be forgotten. Because of their position in the workplace as senior and middle managers, these consumers are the most aware of, and the most professionally concerned about the economic downturn. They will be the most conservative and some of the slowest to regain their confidence when the economy picks up. But, encouraged by their children, they will return to the ways of dedicated consumers.

The senior baby boom will enter their fifth decade in the late 1990s. Many will begin to retire just after the turn of the century. Despite the common knowledge that Japan will soon be demographically the oldest society in the world, few companies are yet prepared to offer any significant proportion of goods designed for 50 and 60 year olds. In ten years' time there will be more scope for expansion and new marketing ideas to be aimed at these consumers because there is currently so little.

When this happens, depending on the economic climate of the time, they could well offer a whole new market for more relaxed leisure activities. These will vary from new forms of adult education and cultural activities, to physical fitness centres with special over-50 programmes. The other significant beneficiary will be the travel industry as these wealthy middle-aged people go to places they never had time for during their working years.

Other general trends will also emerge, but the most significant will arise from these two large consumer groups. The other group that always needs to be watched from a marketing point of view are women. More and more women would like to have careers. Japan still lags far behind other advanced economies in this respect, wasting a valuable source of skills. Not only were female graduates forced to accept low level jobs, but the recession saw some companies quietly removing its excess of female part-time and, in the view of the companies, temporary workers. The situation may change in two ways: either a sudden, but unlikely backlash from women towards the way they are treated in society will bring them an equal footing in the workplace or, which is more likely the continuing decline in the standard of male graduates as many schools loosen their entrance requirements, taking on an ever more conveyor belt like system in order to attract greater student numbers from a shrinking pool.

As consumers, however, women will remain in charge. In the effort to get through school and to avoid standing out at work – not usually a good thing to do in Japan – men are becoming more and more introverted and insecure outside of their jobs. Women have a set lifestyle pattern in most cases, and even though this does not correspond with what women in the West would like, most Japanese women are well in control of their own lives, whereas men often are not. There is already an increase in the number of middle-aged and elderly couples who divorce after the man retires. Women, having been supported by their husbands for decades, cannot stand the same man, who with no interests but his work, idles around the house all day with nothing to do (Condon, 1985: 262–3).

More and more women wish to return to work after marriage, both in order to have extra money to buy the things they want for themselves and their families, and also to give themselves a measure of economic security.

## CHANGES IN DISTRIBUTION CHANNEL STRUCTURE AND BUSINESS PRACTICES

Most of the key trends in the distribution system are already visible and were outlined in Chapter 3. An increasing number of Western companies are now realising that it is worth making the extra effort in terms of research and learning in order to enter the Japanese market. Four British retailers – Laura Ashley, HMV, Body Shop and Virgin Megastores – for example, all have some of their most successful businesses in Japan. They have found that they gain over many Japanese companies by being different. There are a lot of stores in Japan, but the standard of design and the characteristic feel and atmosphere in stores from each of these companies make them stand out from the rather similar styles of most Japanese companies.

Toys'R'Us is an American example of the same thing (Kouyomdjian, 1993; Morishita and Otake, 1993). The expansion of the TRU chain in Japan is still continuing. The company uses larger outlets that come under the Large Store Law, and a single outlet can easily make more sales than all the small, fragmented toy shops combined within any area it enters. This causes problems with local retailers, but TRU stores are highly popular among consumers. They offer what consumers want: wide variety, lower prices and, as a concept, something new.

The opening of the market to these new companies represents also a shift in the business atmosphere within distribution channels. Corporate retailing is now the most important part of the market. Independent stores account for less than a third of total retail sales, and manufacturers are well aware that they must supply the larger chains in order for their products to reach the wider market. Manufacturers can no longer exclude retailers who do not co-operate by setting prices in the way manufacturers want.

Wholesalers are totally reliant on the other players within the distribution channel. As described in Chapter 3, they are now taking on more specialised roles, especially in terms of offering special physical distribution and storage services. Wholesalers also continue to find customers among smaller retailers, and the largest of them have been quicker to build up physical distribution, data processing and other skills than have many manufacturers and retailers. The more progressive and advanced these new systems become, the better chance wholesalers have to survive (Harada, 1987). At present the large number of wholesalers suggests a relatively stable position in the distribution system, but this will change quickly as more and more of the smallest retailers, their main customers, go out of business.

Small retailers will survive in large numbers compared to distribution systems in the West, but the total number will decline by hundreds of thousands of stores before the industry reaches a new equilibrium. Many Japanese want to be entrepreneurs, and Japanese consumers want a friendly local face to sell them their milk and their magazines. A lot of small stores will become franchisees in convenience store chains, and others will band together with local colleagues to create amalgamated shopping facilities.

A small number will find sources of supply and a way of selling specialised ranges of merchandise which will keep them in business on a small scale. Some shops have already done this, specialising in wine and sake, or in umbrellas, for example, and advising customers, being friendly and adding services such as repair or special orders all help (Fields, 1990b).

In the past, many have survived because the larger retail chains did not really offer much competition in terms of numbers or by price. Both aspects of the industry are changing. There are more and more larger stores. In 1991, there were only some 16,000 stores over 500 square metres in the whole of Japan. By the end of 1993, there were almost 20,000, and these larger formats will increase by up to 1,000 a year until the end of the century. This means more independent stores face the prospect of a big store opening in their areas.

Due to changes in consumer attitudes, the larger retailers are now also competing on price more than at any time since the 1960s. With lower costs, and wider ranges, they can now offer prices that pull customers from much further afield, affecting small stores over a wider area than ever before.

## CHANGES IN GOVERNMENT POLICY

One of the main spurs to the expansion of large stores is the relaxation in government restrictions. Again, this was covered in some detail in Chapter 4. The Large Store Law is not about to disappear, but, for the time being at least, retail companies have relative freedom to plan and open large-format stores. This they are doing with some enthusiasm. With the right economic climate towards the end of the century, the largest companies will increase the speed of opening even further.

Other aspects of legislation and policy changes will also affect the distribution industry. Many of these are being induced by pressure from abroad.

Japan has lifted the total ban on the import of foreign rice following the completion of the Uruguay round of GATT negotiations. But companies looking to pioneer this new trade still face very high import tariffs. These mean that imported rice for sale directly to consumers is as expensive as that produced domestically. Traditionally the two main arguments against rice imports have been that it will remove Japan's current food security in times of war, as rice is one of the few commodities in which Japan does have self-sufficiency, and that it will seriously harm the Japanese farming industry, putting many farmers out of business. Both arguments are true, but the question is whether either is still important in the present global economy.

The first argument is only valid if Japan expects to go to war. While there is always a danger of this and limited area conflicts are common at present, most of the largest industrial nations have a higher level of peace and understanding than at any time in the past. Most of them, such as the USA and UK, are now cutting back on defence spending – partly, it must be said, to pay for trade deficits with Japan. In Japan, on the other hand, defence spending was almost 14 per cent higher in 1993 than in 1990, and is increasing annually (Asahi Shinbunsha, 1993b: 65).

The second argument is also tenuous as some 60 per cent of Japanese farmers work their land only part-time, while holding other jobs with normal companies (*Economist*, 1988b; 1989c; 1990b). The government has supported farmers as a major political lobby, just like the small retail lobby, and farm land is protected by tax laws that discourage building. Many of the efficient, larger-scale, full-time rice farmers would survive a lifting of the import ban because their produce is of a high quality, and because consumers will always demand Japanese rice to some extent.

There are other arguments that are less important, but have greater influence on the consumer market (see Tadase, 1993; Nihon Keizai Shinbun 1990b). There is a lot of propaganda around which insists that imported rice, especially American rice, is unsafe because of the volume and type of pesticides used both in production and then in transporting it to Japan. Not being an expert on agriculture or a chemist, I cannot comment fairly, except to say that Californian rice does not seem to harm Americans.[1]

The largest retailers have been importing cooked rice in prepared dishes, for several years. It is still cheaper to make the dish overseas and import it than it is to use Japanese rice. Because of the high tariffs on imported rice, most consumers still insist on Japanese rice, but it is sure that more and more imported rice will be used in dishes like sushi, and in restaurants and other businesses where cost is more important than taste (do Rosario, 1992).

Other legislation is also affecting the retail market. The government's toughening of the anti-monopoly laws and of the Japan Fair Trade Commission continues, and will go on for a number of years before it reaches a level of control that is normal in Europe or the USA. Retailers are important influences, working against the restrictive practices and vertical restraints imposed by manufacturers. On the other hand, when a practice is to the advantage of a retailer, they may encourage it, for example insisting on high rebates or that the supplier take back unsold merchandise. But this works against the interest of other companies, especially the smaller stores who do not have the same power to demand such privileges, even though many of the same systems were originally a form of support for small stores.

Again, it is the large retail companies that are, in one way or another, forcing change in the industry.

## CHANGES IN MULTIPLE RETAILING STRATEGY

Even with 1.6 million retail outlets and 1.3 million retail businesses in Japan, it is no longer the small independent stores that lead the market. A relatively small number of large multiple-store chain companies are now the key players and the ones that lead changes in the industry and form the key trends.

This has been an underlying theme throughout the book. The largest retailers are generally most responsible for change. In the poor economic conditions of the early 1990s, these companies have seen both their sales and their profits fall away. They were also the quickest to respond.

Throughout the 1980s the largest companies built up wide ranging groups of retail chains in various formats and various merchandise sectors. They have also looked abroad and, while the rest of the industry was criticised for inefficiency and backwardness, realised that they could gain by importing efficient Western distribution techniques and ideas. All the large chains now have good distribution networks, with their own distribution centres and using their own individual systems. Some of these systems, especially the hardware needed to run them, are among of the most advanced in the world. They are also very good at scheduling solutions and at achieving a rapid, efficient flow of merchandise.

Much of the 1980s can be seen as the development stage of this process. Now in the 1990s, the successful companies are using what they have learnt and built to cut costs and gain competitive advantage over their rivals. In the case of Ito-Yokado, this feeds back to notably high profits compared to the rest of the industry. Daiei has used its own systems to set up the most extensive network of discount operations, including four different chains, and one wholesale warehouse club, by being able to cut gross margin, but still maintain overall profitability.

In other words, the industry is beginning to see the largest retailers take a lead and exert their own influence. In 1993, this also took the form of a sudden and dramatic increase in the number of retail brands appearing in the market. Large food chains had long offered their own brands of milk and juices, but the range now extends to batteries and video tapes and even video recorders, in addition to new food and household items.

Compared to Britain, for example, Japan still has a long way to go before retail brands can rival those of national manufacturers in terms of variety or overall volume, but they are already considerably cheaper in many cases, and the leading retailers have been careful to keep quality standards high. In some cases, manufacturers', brands are simply repackaged for the retailer, and will sell next to the original national brand in the store. Retailers buy on contract in large volumes and then use efficient, bulk distribution to reduce costs. They also have total control over their own pricing for these products and can still make profits while undercutting manufacturers.

In the 1990s, many concepts originating in the West will be introduced into the Japanese market via the largest groups. Retail brands are just one of these. Daiei's wholesale club, which charges ¥3,000 for a family membership, and had over 100,000 members before it even opened, is another. Based squarely on similar formats in the USA, the store is located in the Harborland shopping centre in Kobe, the home town of Daiei's chairman. Rather unoriginally, the club is even called 'Kou's' (Kōzu) which is the Chinese reading of the character for the chairman's first name – like Walmart's 'Sam's' wholesale club operation in the USA which is also named after the founder. Harborland is a fashionable, up-market shopping complex, including both Seibu and Hankyu department stores selling the usual mixture of high-price clothing brands, but has proved unpopular during the economic recession. Kou's is, however, a great success, with customers flooding through its doors while the pace in the department stores is rather too slow for the management's comfort.

This is a good indication of the future of Japanese corporate retailing, with companies looking around for new ideas and techniques, often importing them from the West. The successful ones will offer the consumer something new, and, at least in the near future, something cheap. Companies will look to dominate their own local markets as much as possible and seek differentiation on a national scale.

The same applies to the largest department store companies as well. Most will find it difficult to catch up with the big multiple chains because, although at the individual store level they have better performance results, they are too reliant on other companies within the channels to support their weaknesses. Only the largest, and those that can make rapid, effective changes to their management and store operations will survive in the long run.

## A FUTURE PICTURE OF RETAILING IN JAPAN

Japan is still a country of small stores. Towns and cities would not be complete without them. They offer the consumer a wide range of unique products in the same way that small local stores do in other countries. The best often make the items on their own premises, offering fresh *tōfu* (bean curd) or handmade pickles or cakes. Japanese consumers like them for their merchandise and their atmosphere. Hopefully, this will not change.

But, in the current climate, with a small number of large multiple chains now becoming increasingly powerful, this might be difficult. The Large Store Law was instigated to curb the expansion of these large chains and so protect smaller independent stores that cannot offer the same range of merchandise and cannot keep prices as low. As Chapter 4 described, the Law is now too controversial and un-popular among various parties to maintain in its old ambiguous form. Smaller stores are now disappearing because young people are finding jobs in large companies, and small retailing is being abandoned.

In many ways, much of the retail industry in Japan will gradually come to resemble systems in the West. This is inevitable. It means standardisation as a result of pursuing distribution efficiency and low costs. It means reducing merchandise variety and cutting back on services. For example, the former of these is already part of Daiei's strategy in introducing its own brands of fruit juices, at the same time removing other brands and other types of juice from the shelves completely.

If large retailers come to dominate the industry to the extent that they have in some Western countries, then the distribution system will become as open and as efficient as it is elsewhere. The current situation is so far away from the Western ideal, however, that this is unlikely. Small stores will continue to survive by adding their own small piece of variety to the system as a whole. This will keep the retail sector active and interesting. At the same time, large retailers will bring down costs in the industry and keep prices stable over a long period, giving consumers the best of both large and small worlds.

Japan was never a bad place for the consumer. Traditional and modern retailers in the system will work together to see that it only gets better.

# Notes

## 1 RETAILING IN JAPAN IN THE 1990S

1 The value of the Yen at the time of writing is approximately ¥110 to the US dollar and ¥170 to the British pound. This has little meaning however. The value of the Yen is appreciating steadily. Many non-Japanese believe it should be much more expensive. At the current rate an apple costs $1.13 or £0.73, a litre of milk $1.80 or £1.16 and buying a family size apartment less than $200,000 would be almost impossible in most parts of Japan. For these reasons the reader should compare values in Yen rather than make the conversion.

## 2 THE CONSUMER ENVIRONMENT IN JAPAN

1 Readers looking to read more about developments in this period and beyond, and to learn more about marketing in Japan, should refer to two excellent books by George Fields (1983; 1988a).
2 Numerous writers have discussed the group mentality of the Japanese. Japanese are as competitive as any race, but the existence of groups and the importance of group membership have been well noted. These groups may be family, friends, colleagues, classmates or people from the same geographical region. Equally, competition between groups, and even open hostility to members of other groups, is clearly apparent in Japanese society. These concepts are touched on elsewhere in the chapter, but readers should also refer to general discussions on Japanese society, for example Christopher (1983), Doi (1973), Kenrick (1990), Mouer and Sugimoto (1986), Nakane (1973), van Wolferen (1989), Vogel (1981), Woronoff (1981).
3 Many companies expect new employees to live either at home with their parents until they marry, or in a company dormitory. Men are given some leeway if they wish to find their own accommodation, but women are treated far less fairly (see pages 27–8). If they want to live away from home, but cannot find a proper job, many young people can still live by maintaining a number of part-time jobs. There are many ex-students living this way in Tokyo and Osaka.

4 Recently, recognising the unfairness and weakness of this system, some companies have begun to avoid asking job applicants which university they attended and place more emphasis on ability. This is still new, however, and such companies are still the exception. Sony, the leading electronics manufacturer renowned for creativity and innovation, announced in 1991 that it would no longer recruit graduates on the basis of the university they attended. This question was even removed from application forms. This was a major change and some other companies have introduced similar policies. In the Sony case, however, few applicants were surprised by the first question at the job interview: 'So, which university did you attend?'

5 With the senior baby-boom bulge there are now too many men of middle management age. To the horror of salarymen throughout Japan, companies have began to dismiss unnecessary employees. Even so, the reluctance to actually fire people is still evident. Some companies now pay employees to stay at home rather than dismiss them outright. This phenomenon is called *shanai shitsugyō*, or 'in-house unemployment' (Leadbeater, 1992; Lowry Miller, 1993; Nihon Keizai Shinbun, 1993c; TBT, 1993a, 1993b).

6 As I write, my own students have been looking for their first jobs. This was the first year for more than a decade that finding employment was not guaranteed. 1993 was the peak of the junior baby-boom, meaning more candidates, and the Japanese economy was facing its first recession since the early 1970s. But all the boys still found work without any problem. The girls, however, struggled, with most not even receiving a first interview. Companies are particularly reluctant to employ female graduates of four-year universities, because they are seen as having no more value than high-school or junior-college girls, but expect a larger salary. The situation is similar throughout Japan and will worsen in coming years (see Kashima, 1993).

7 Ironically, the emphasis on men in work and education has made many young males overprotected and psychologically weak. The Japanese call it *mazakon*, or 'mother complex'. In addition, the cost of failure to get into a good school or to get a good job is high. For both these reasons families now prefer to have girl children than boys.

8 A husband begging for extra pocket money because he has had a few too many beers is a common line in popular dramas. In my experience, many men build up a reserve of money in a separate bank account, sometimes kept secret from their wives. They do this by saving, by winning money at gambling or through various cash payments they receive.

9 The rest of the book describes the high level of service in the retail industry, but this is not emulated by Japanese banks, which are slow, and badly automated, open for short hours and levy high fees. ATM (automatic telling machines) are closed on holidays, after 7pm every night, and for most of the weekend. In response to this, most convenience stores allow utility and some other bills to be paid at their stores for as long as the store is open.

10 In Japan 49 per cent of all 'part-time' employees work for more than thirty-five hours a week. 'Part-time' work largely refers to fewer work

benefits and lower salary rather than less time (Ministry of Labour, 1989: 100–1). Most part-time positions are filled by either students or women.

11  There is at least one example of younger employees rising above their elders, however. Chapter 7 describes how the sons of the founders of the largest retail companies have quickly found their way into the boardroom.

12  Sushi is balls of vinegared rice topped with raw fish or something similar. The difficulty in preparation is getting the right consistency of rice. Tempura is shrimps, sweet potato and peppers, deep fried in a flour and milk batter.

13  The import of rice is currently a major political issue. Rice could only be imported if included in a pre-prepared dish. The Japanese government maintains large stockpiles of rice and buys a proportion of the rice harvest each year at fixed prices. This and the monopolistic grip of large agricultural co-operatives make the food market one of the most uncompetitive parts of the economy. Beginning with rice, all food is expensive compared to other merchandise and even more so compared to food in Western nations (*Focus Japan*, 1987b). Moreover, supermarket food often seems of poor quality compared to food available in the West. This is a result of poor distribution systems, small, inefficient farming and poor consumer education concerning nutrition. The Japanese consumer is convinced that good food quality is related to the outer appearance of the items alone.

14  I am not an educational psychologist, and perhaps some readers would disagree that rote memorisation is the best way to learn facts, but it is certainly the method of education employed in Japanese schools and cram schools. To understand this, one only has to study a little Japanese language. Japanese is a very simple language, in terms of both grammar and pronunciation. The only difficult part is the writing system. This is even more difficult than Chinese, on which it is based, because the reading of many of the 2,000 characters varies depending on context, whereas any character has only one reading in Chinese. The only way to master this system is the way the Japanese themselves use – rote memorisation.

15  The survey does not distinguish between low and high prices. Japanese observers avoid comment (Hoshino, 1990), but price competition is avoided by most retailers. In Japan, prices are high as a result of anti-competitive practices and legislation, as much as due to physical inefficiencies in distribution.

16  Some researchers suggest that frequent shopping justifies the fragmented nature of Japanese retailing as described in Chapter 3 (JCCI, 1989: 6; Mukoyama, 1990: 12).

17  Japan is a very mature country in terms of religion. Buddhists, Shintoists, Confucian values and a minority of Christians live happily side by side. Occasionally, new religions are marketed to the Japanese, and groups such as Mormons and the Unification Church have occasional success, but most Japanese feel little spiritual need over and above the three main types.

18  A famous illustration of the possibility of corruption through this system is the Recruit scandal where senior politicians received money and

shares to 'encourage' them to make particular decisions. Although scandalous in the size of the 'donations' changing hands, this is not an unusual practice in Japanese politics, and the embarrassment is now largely forgotten.

19 Adult's Day is 15 January. Young people who have reached the age of 20 in the previous year attend special ceremonies in celebration of becoming adults. Department stores take the opportunity to hire out formal kimonos to young women who have been busily growing their hair, the other prerequisite for wearing a kimono, for the past year in preparation.

20 7–5–3 Festival is on 15 November. Children aged 7, 5 and 3 are taken to shrines to pray for their future health and success. Despite its traditional air, Creighton (1988: 273–4) claims this to be a creation of the major retailers (cf. Valentine's Day). Originating in a small area of Tokyo, it has been expanded into a national event through promotion by retailers and shrines. It is a good occasion to buy gifts for children and as with Adult's Day, large department stores do a good business in formal dress hire for the kids.

21 Many companies now claim to ban employees from receiving gifts from clients and suppliers. Gifts are still given on a personal level, and may not exclude gifts to superiors within the same companies.

## 3 JAPANESE DISTRIBUTION

1 There has been a great deal of work, critical and otherwise, relating to problems within the distribution system. The volume increased in the late 1980s as the system became a more sensitive political issue. Key examples include ACTPN (1989), Batzer and Laumer (1989), Czinkota and Kotabe (1993), Czinkota and Woronoff (1986; 1991), Dawson (1984; 1985; 1989), Dodwell Marketing Consultants (1985; 1988; 1991), *Economist* (1981; 1987; 1988a), Elliot and Yoo (1980), Euromonitor (1989), Fields (1988a; 1988b; 1989a; 1990b), Glazer (1970), Goldman (1991; 1992), Gröke (1972), Hayashi (1980), JCCI (1989), Jones (1987), Katsumoto and Miyazaki (1984), Koyama (1984; 1985), Larke (1991; 1992a; 1992b), Larke and Dawson (1992), Lazer et al. (1985), McMilan (1984), Murata (1973), O'Donnell (1982), Ogawa (1984), Ross (1983), Scott-Plummer (1984), Shimaguchi (1977), Shimaguchi and Lazer (1979), Shimaguchi and Rosenberg (1979), Shioya (1989), Sletmo and Ibghy (1991), Tajima (1984; 1987; 1989), Takaoka (1984) and Tamura (1989).

2 There are numerous accounts of the success, failure and methods of overseas companies operating in Japan. A few include Nordika ski boots (Cohen, 1987), Levi jeans (Duin, 1990), Mercedes and BMW cars (Economist, 1988h), whisky (Economist, 1988i), pharmaceuticals (Economist, 1988j; 1988l), Filofax (Economist, 1988k), coffee (*Focus Japan*, 1983), dolls (*Focus Japan*, 1984), Baush Lomb contact lenses (*Focus Japan*, 1987a) and Laura Ashley (*Focus Japan*, 1990). There are also a number of publications which describe in general how foreign

companies have entered the Japanese market (Fuchi, 1989; Haynes, 1989; JCCI, 1989: 33–6; JETRO, 1982, 1983b; JETRO and MIPRO, 1985; Kakita, 1984; MIPRO, 1980, 1981, 1983b; MITI, 1983; Nakata, 1982; Udagawa, 1989).

3 The opening of the Japanese food market, especially the rice market, is discussed in Chapter 8. Also see do Rosario (1992) Hirose et al. (1993); Makihara, (1992) Osahi and Fujiyasu, (1993). People interested in this issue and in rice distribution in Japan should refer to Fukao and Akiba (1993).

4 Examples of popular interest in the LSL include *Asahi Shinbun* (1989; 1990c; 1990d; 1990e; 1990f; 1990g; 1990h), *Japan Times* (1990) and *Japan Times Weekly* (1990).

5 MITI carries out a Census of Commerce every three years. While there are some minor changes between surveys, the comparability of statistics between years is high and the data are very detailed. This is one of the best sources for statistical data on distribution in the world.

6 Trading companies handle the import and export of bulk quantities of goods of all kinds. Known as *sogo shōsha* in Japanese, they were responsible for more than 77 per cent of all imports into Japan in 1988. There is a considerable literature on the activities of the *sogo shōsha*. While they do play some part in the distribution of finished products to the retail industry, especially some famous branded items for which certain trading companies have exclusive import licences, they are no more important in the internal distribution system for finished goods than other wholesalers, having a far more significant role in the importing of bulk raw materials. The reader is referred to the following sources for further discussion of the Japanese trading companies: Dodwell Marketing Consultants (1988: 28–30), *Economist* (1988e) and McMilan (1984: 229–51) MIPRO (1983a).

7 All billions given in text refer to the British system, i.e. one million million.

8 Because of the difficulty of collecting accurate data on sales space and sales volume for such a large number of tiny, independent retail businesses, the Census of Commerce bases most of its statistics on the number of employees per outlet. This also emphasises the human element of retail businesses – so important in Japan. The Census includes any worker who was employed for eighteen or more days per month in both of May and June 1991 as a 'full-time' employee (MITI, 1992b: 11).

9 The Census shows that most of the stores omitted from the sales space statistics are in categories that employ few people, so it is likely that most were very small in physical size too.

10 Traditionally, a distribution keiretsu is headed by a manufacturer. The largest retail groups, however, are now so diverse that they often operate on the same principles of independent co-operation. Daiei, Jusco, Saison and Ito-Yokado all head groups of companies which work with the parent but are, to all outer appearances, independent (see Chapter 7). In addition, convenience store and other franchise chains are controlled to the same degree as some of the older electrical keiretsu.

11 See, for example, Czinkota and Woronoff (1986; 1991), Dentsu (1978),

Dodwell Marketing Consultants (1985; 1988; 1991), Kajiwara (1988), Maruyama *et al.* (1989), Mukoyama (1990), Shimaguchi (1977), Shimaguchi and Lazer (1979), Shimaguchi and Rosenberg (1979) and USITC (1990).

12  Consumers can buy some products such as electrical goods at below the manufacturer's recommended price, but these are relatively rare examples (Mishima, 1988a; 1988b; 1989; Yoshino, 1971: 119–20, 122–3). The electrical discount quarters of Tokyo and Osaka are mainly dumping grounds for out-of-date products from the major manufacturers. New products are channelled primarily through the manufacturer's keiretsu chains.

13  The large number of stores overall means that format classification cannot be too detailed, and definitions used in the Census are very broad. They are based on store size as measured by number of employees, rather than a more detailed comparison of sales space or store operation. These are, however, the only generally available definitions in use in Japan.

## 4  THE LARGE STORE LAW

1  In Japanese the LSL has at least three titles. Most formally the law is called the Law Relating to the Regulation of Retail Business Activity among Large-Scale Retail Stores [*Daikibo Kouri Tenpo ni okeru Kourigyō no jigyō Katsudō no Chōsei ni kansuru Hōritsu*] (Matsushita and Kawagoe 1980: 3). This title is abbreviated to *Daikibo Kouri Tenpo Hō*, or Large-Scale Retail Store Law. Most usually, however, the name is further abbreviated in all forms of literature to *Daitenhō*, or simply Large Store Law.

2  Readers interested in a more detailed discussion of this historical expansion should refer to Takaoka and Koyama (1970).

3  For more detail on the tightening of the LSL during the 1980s see Honma (1992), Kuraya (1981), Nihon Keizai Shinbun (1988: 240–3; 1990e: 29–62), Nikkei Ryūtsū Shinbun (1989a: 69–91), Omura and Ishii (1987), Otani, (1991) Saeki (1982), Seiki (1983), Shimizu (1980), *Shūkan Tōyō Keizai* (1981), Takeuchi (1983) and Tamura (1981).

4  Readers interested in a more detailed explanation of the workings of the LSL during the 1980s should refer to Larke and Dawson (1992).

5  In a far-sighted paper Dawson and Sato (1985) predicted this trend exactly.

6  Figures courtesy of Professor Akira Sogo, Senshu University, and chairman of Large Retail Store Deliberation Council.

7  Anecdote from Professor Yasuaki Suzuki, who is a member of the Tokyo regulatory committee for large retail stores.

## 5  TYPES OF SMALL-FORMAT RETAIL ORGANISATION IN JAPAN

1  There are numerous professional associations in Japan, many of which maintain a much higher profile than is usual in the West. There are also at least two associations of street associations.

2 Within the Census, 'commercial districts' are designated by three characteristics:

- generally, one *shōtengai* equals one commercial district
- in principle, a *shōtengai* is designated as being a member of the city or town's association of *shōtengai* is, or, if not a member, a street of stores of similar scale (that is a group of around thirty or more retail, restaurant or service outlets within a single area)
- multi-business buildings (such as station buildings or unplanned shopping buildings, or *yoriai hyakkaten*) are also counted as a single shopping area.

3 The 1991 Census statistics for 'locational and situational characteristics' were published in June 1993 and were unavailable at the time of writing.
4 The Consumption Tax (*Shōhizei*) is a sales tax introduced in 1989 against huge popular and political opposition. The tax rate is 3 per cent and is applied to almost all goods. Small retailers used this as an opportunity to increase prices in many cases, and most large retailers maintain the confusing policy of applying the tax only at the check-out, and not on the price tag. With the most basic denomination of bank note being ¥1,000, one interesting effect of the introduction of the tax was to provide a new life for ¥1 and ¥5 coins, both of which had become virtually unused over the years.
5 DIY home centres and discount store chains, which *Nikkei* records in the same survey, are omitted from the figures. Neither format specialises by type of merchandise or even by type of service. Discount stores are now an important and fast growing sector, but as the largest are operated within the major retail conglomerate groupings, Chapter 7 looks at them in detail.
6 Members of the JSCA should:

a. be developed as a multi-purpose retailing site
b. provide varied shopping facilities
c. provide additional community facilities and services
d. have an area larger than stipulated under the 1979 Large Store Law
e. have more than ten tenants in addition to the key tenant
f. use less than 30 per cent of the total area in the key tenant
g. have a tenant association and organise joint activities.

In addition, the JSCA provides the following definitions:

a. a developer is the person or organisation that is chiefly responsible for the centre's development
b. community facilities are facilities which make a major social contribution through the frequent supply of cheap or free services to the users of the shopping centre
c. a key tenant is a department store or other large retailer which has a major influence on the shopping centre's commercial area and type of target clientele (from JSCA, 1988; 1989).

## 6 DEPARTMENT STORES

1 Tokyu is an unusual case as the company claims that its department store division qualifies as a traditional store. The Tokyu Group likes to trace its origins back to 1662, to a small kimono store in Nihonbashi called Shirokiya, close to the present number two Tokyu store. By the early 1900s, Shirokiya had grown to department store proportions. The original department store was, however, founded in 1948 by the then Tokyo Kyōkō Railroad Company, and was called the Tōyoko Department Store. This department store then acquired the Shirokiya company in 1958. The group as a whole later took the name Tokyu in 1970 (Tokyu, 1992: 1). It is included as a terminal department store here because several of its outlets are located at or near the group's rail links.

2 The word or, more accurately, Chinese character *tetsu* actually means iron. The word for railroad is *tetsudō* or 'iron road'. This is why several of the terminal department store companies have the suffix *tetsu* on their names.

## 7 CONGLOMERATE RETAIL GROUPS

1 Although the Laura Ashley designs, merchandise and store designs have not been changed by Aeon, most Laura Ashley stores in Japan now sell mainly items that were produced in Japan from materials imported from the UK. This gives them a 'Made in Japan' label. In addition, the prices charged at Laura Ashley Japan are totally Japanese, being on average about three times the UK price for similar items.

2 The direct acronym was avoided so as not to be associated incorrectly with the YMCA.

3 'Saty' is another acronym. This time 'Satisfaction any time (for) yourself'.

4 Observers of Japanese retailing who are unfamiliar with the language should beware. Pronounced 'oo-knee' the group becomes 'sea urchin'.

5 Daiei is registered as having its headquarters in Hyogo Prefecture, home of the chief executive Isao Nakauchi, In fact, the company shifted its headquarters to Tokyo in the 1980s, and these are now based in Hamamatsu-cho.

6 Uny prefers to use Japanese katakana script for most of its store names and brands. This is unusual considering the Japanese consumer's love of romanised script on products. The 'Rough Ox' menswear stores are a case in point. Romanised directly from Japanese, the name is Rafokkusu, which at first I mistakenly thought was a Japanese version of 'La Fox'.

## 8 JAPANESE RETAILING IN THE 1990s AND BEYOND

1 As for the volume and type of pesticides used by Japanese farmers, I assume that, as production is largely small scale, and as it is often on land that is of poor quality, Japanese farmers also use a considerable volume of pesticides and artificial fertilizers. Despite the large number

of statistical publications available in Japan, I have never found statistics on this issue. Perhaps a reader could introduce me. Furthermore, as a personal anecdote, every year, several times before harvest, farmers around my home go around with loudspeakers warning us not to leave our homes overnight. They then spray the whole area – fields, cars, cats and unwary pedestrians – with pesticide. This is the downside of having rice farming in urban areas.

# Bibliography

Abegglen, James C. and George Stalk (1987) *Kaisha: The Japanese Company*, Tokyo, Tuttle Books.

*Across* (1988) Young women of character land [Kyarakutā no kuni no shojō-tachi] April: 12–51.

ACTPN (Advisory Committee for Trade Policy and Negotiations) (1989) *Analysis of the US–Japan Trade Problem*, Washington, DC, US Government Publishing Office.

Adachi, Katsuhiko, Takako Matsuo, Yuko Horiguchi, and Mariko Ito (1988) Birth of the parabola age of the ultra-new generation [Chō shinjinrui parabora eiji no tanjō], *Gekkan Adobataijingu*, July: 13-19.

Age of Tomorrow (1990) Gift-giving: communicating through presents, *Japan Update*, Winter: 3–7; reprinted from *Age of Tomorrow*, 110, 1989.

Akabane, Sachio (1986) The study of shōtengai [Shōtengai no kenkyū], *Shōkō Kinyū Shōkō Kumiai Chōkin*, 36(3), March: 3–16.

Akamatsu, Tomohiro (1989) Decline in strong brand enterprises ['Saikyō burando kigyō no shūraku], *Shūkan Tōyō Keizai*, 27 May: 10–21.

Allen, Mike (1989) Implications of the Shūwa charade, *BZW Japan*, September: 29–32.

Anzai, Tatsuya (1990) Will Toys'R'Us ignite another trade issue?, *Tokyo Business Today*, February: 58–9.

Aoki, Yukihiro (1983a) A consideration of consumers' in-store buying behaviour [Shōhisha no tenpo nai kōbai kōdō ni kansuru ikkōsatsu], *Nihon Māketingu Jānaru*, 3(3), March: 11–23.

Aoki, Yukihiro (1983b) Consumers' store choice behaviour and retailers' management strategy [Shōhisha no tenpo nai sentaku kōdō to kouri keiei senryaku], *Ryūtsū Seisaku*, 15, August, 56–62.

Aruta, Juntsuke (1988) The practicalities of many items in small quantities [Ta-hinshu shōryō-ka no jittai], *Nihon Māketingu Jānaru*, 8(2), 30: 18–24.

*Asahi Shinbun* (1989) Distribution reorganised on a clean sheet [Ryūtsū saigen kō shite hakushi ni], 22 November: 8.

*Asahi Shinbun* (1990a) Distribution industry is perplexed [Ryūtsū gyōkai ha tōkan] 23 February: 9.

*Asahi Shinbun* (1990b) Life Stores and the Large Store Law: unconstitutional, law suit brought [Raifu sutoa Daitenhō: kenpō to teiso], 31 March: 3.

*Asahi Shinbun* (1990c) Structural initiative intermediate announcement [Kōzō kyōgi no chūkan hōkoku], 6 April: 2–3.

*Asahi Shinbun* (1990d) US Toys'R'Us plans store in Chiba City [Bei Toizarasu Chiba-shi ni mo shutten keikaku], 10 May: 8.

*Asahi Shinbun* (1990e) Retail promotion: 30% of local authorities have independent regulations [Kouri ten no shinshutsu, jichitai no 30% ga dokuji kisei], 12 May: 3.

*Asahi Shinbun* (1990f) Deregulation of the Large Store Law starts today [Daitenhō kisei kanwa, kyō sutāto], 30 May: 3.

*Asahi Shinbun* (1990g) Editorial: for small and medium stores to survive [Shasetsu: chūshō mise ga ikinokoru ni ha], 31 May.

*Asahi Shinbun* (1990h) Store owners protest en masse [Shōten nushi no tumekake kōgi], 31 May: 23.

*Asahi Shinbun* (1991) At last a shortage of bar codes [Tōtō busoku bākōdo], 28 June.

Asahi Shinbunsha (1992) *The Japan Almanac 1993*, Tokyo.

Asahi Shinbunsha (1993a) *Population Power 1993 [Minryoku 1993]*, Tokyo.

Asahi Shinbunsha (1993b) *The Japan Almanac 1994*, Tokyo.

Asano, Ryosuke (1989) Networks raise efficiency of distribution information systems, *Business Japan*, October: 45–52.

Asano, Ryosuke (1993) Japan's distribution system information network, in Michael R. Czinkota and Masaaki Kotabe (eds), *The Japanese Distribution System*, Chicago and Cambridge, UK, Probus Publishing Company: 123–36.

Aso, Kunio (1985) *The Seibu Saison Group [Seibu Sezon Gurūpu]*, Tokyo, Nihon Jitsugyō Shuppansha.

Ato, Ekusa (1990) Little white lies, *Journal of Japanese Trade and Industry*, 9(2): 19.

Bandō, Mariko (1991) *Comparing Japanese Life with the World [Sekai no naka no Nihon no kurashi]*, Tokyo, Ministry of Finance.

Bandō, Mariko (1992) *The Japanese Women Data Bank [Nihon no josei dētā banku]*, Tokyo, Ministry of Finance.

Batzer, Erich and Loumer, Helmut (1989) *Marketing Strategies and Distribution Channels for Foreign Companies in Japan*, San Francisco and London, Westview Press.

Befu, Harumi (1986) Gift-giving in a modernizing Japan, in Takie Sugiyama Lebra and William P. Lebra (eds), *Japanese Culture and Behavior: Selected Readings*, Honolulu, University of Hawaii.

Byrne, John A. and Chuck Hawkins (1993) Executive pay: the party ain't over yet, *Business Week*, 26 April: 38–47.

Cendron, Bernard (1984) Changing dream: the Japanese and brand names, *Dentsu Japan Marketing/Advertising*, 2 (1): 43–7.

*Chain Store Age* (1992) Fighting the recession: strategies of the strong 'department stores' [Fukyō ni uchikatsu: tsuyoi 'hyakkaten' no senryaku kōzō], 15 November: 26–40.

*Chain Store Age* (1993) Aoyama Shōji: large scale store openings leave rivals behind [Aoyama Shōji: tairyō shutten de dokusō taisei katameru], 1 May: 45–7.

Christopher, Robert C. (1983) *The Japanese Mind*, London and Sydney, Pan Books.

Chūshō Kigyō Chō (1988a) *White Paper on Small and Medium Sized Companies [Chūshō kigyō hakusho]*, Tokyo, Ministry of Finance.

Chūshō Kigyō Chō (1988b) *The Shōtengai CI Manual [Shōtengai CI manyuaru]*, Tokyo, MITI Survey Committee.

Chūshō Kigyō Chō (1989) *Report of the 5th Basic Survey of Commercial Structure and Activity [Dai 5 kai shōgyō jittai kihon chōsa hōkokusho]*, (3 volumes) Tokyo, MITI.

Chūshō Kigyō Chō (1990) *White Paper on Small and Medium sized Companies [Chūshō kigyō hakusho]*, Tokyo, Ministry of Finance.

Chūshō Kigyō Chō (1992a) *Current Circumstances and Topics in the Wholesale Industry 1992: A New Role Expected in the New Era of Distribution [Heisei 4 nen oroshiurigyō no genjō to kadai: ryūtsū shin jidai ni kitai sareru aratana yakuwari]*, Tokyo, MITI.

Chūshō Kigyō Chō (1992b) *White Paper on Small and Medium Sized Companies [Chūshō kigyō hakusho]*, Tokyo, Ministry of Finance.

Clark, Rodney (1987) *The Japanese Company*, Tokyo, Tuttle.

Cohen, Luciano (1987) Success story: Nordica Japan Ltd, *Focus Japan*, 14(3), March: 8.

Condon, Jane (1985) *Half a Step Behind: Japanese Women in the 1980s*, New York, Dodd & Mead.

Creighton, Mildred R. (1988) *Sales, service and sanctity: an anthropological analysis of Japanese department stores*, unpublished PhD thesis, University of Washington.

Czinkota, Michael R. and Masaaki Kotabe (1993) *The Japanese Distribution System*, Chicago and Cambridge, UK, Probus Publishing Company.

Czinkota, Michael R. and Jon Woronoff (1986) *Japan's Market: The Distribution System*, New York, Praeger.

Czinkota, Michael R. and Jon Woronoff (1991) *Unlocking Japan's Markets: Seizing Marketing and Distribution Opportunities in Today's Japan*, Chicago, Probus Publishing Company.

Dawson, John A. (1984) *Distribution in Europe and Japan: Some Trends, Comparisons and Questions*, Institute for Retail Studies Working Paper, no 8408, Stirling University.

Dawson, John A. (1985) Change and continuity in Japanese retailing: trends creating a post-industrial retail structure, *Retail and Distribution Management*, March/April: 46–50.

Dawson, John A. (1989) *Japanese Retailing: Movement to the Post-Traditional Stage*, Institute for Retail Studies Working Paper, no 8901, Stirling University.

Dawson, John A. and Toshio Sato (1985) Controls over the Development of Large Stores in Japan, *Service Industries Journal*, 3(4): 136–45.

DEIJ (Distribution Economics Institute of Japan) (1988) *Statistical Abstract of Japanese Distribution*, Tokyo.

Dentsu Inc. (1978) *Marketing Opportunities in Japan*, London, McGraw-Hill.

Dentsu Sōken (1989) *'Mature Rich' Consumption ['Hōjuku' shōhi]*, Tokyo, Nikkei Mākedia.

Dodwell Marketing Consultants (1985) *Retail Distribution in Japan*, Tokyo.
Dodwell Marketing Consultants (1988) *Retail Distribution in Japan*, Tokyo.
Dodwell Marketing Consultants (1991) *Retail Distribution in Japan*, Tokyo.
Doi, Takeo, (1973) *The Anatomy of Dependence*, Tokyo, Kodansha International.
do Rosario, Louise (1992) Bow to the inevitable: Japan prepares to open its rice market, *Far Eastern Economic Review*, 10 December: 53.
Duin, Geoffrey E. (1990) Levi's won't fade in the Japanese market, *Tokyo Business Today*, April: 46.
*Economist, The* (1981) Japan: a nation of wholesalers, 19 September: 88–9.
*Economist, The* (1987) Business brief: why Japanese shoppers are lost in a maze, 31 January: 64–5.
*Economist, The* (1988a) The new Japan goes shopping, 13 August: 57–58.
*Economist, The* (1988b) Japanese agriculture: yesterday's farming, 20 August: 58–9.
*Economist, The* (1988c) Japan's Liberal Democratic Party: one party democracy, 24 September: 21–4.
*Economist, The*, (1988d) Japan's trading houses: the march of the middle men, 24 September: 89–90.
*Economist, The* (1988e) Grand Metropolitan: hooked on brands, 8 October: 71.
*Economist, The* (1988f) The Tsutsumi family: brotherly hate, 8 October: 71–2.
*Economist, The*, (1988g) Foreign business in Japan: drive on Fritz, 22 October: 81–2.
*Economist, The* (1988h) Foreign business in Japan: whisky vs 'whisky', 29 October: 68–9.
*Economist, The* (1988i) Japan's over the counter market, 29 October: 76–7.
*Economist, The* (1988j) Foreign business in Japan: Filofax, 12 November, 76–7.
*Economist, The* (1988k) Selling to Japan: a drug on the market, 10 December: 76.
*Economist, The* (1988l) When the mask has to drop, 17 December: 19–20.
*Economist, The* (1989a) America and Japan: bad sports, 25 February: 38.
*Economist, The* (1989b) America's trade policy: perestroika in reverse, 25 February: 68–70.
*Economist, The* (1989c) Japan: down on the farm, 25 March: 40.
*Economist, The* (1989d) Ginza, W1, 2 September: 32.
*Economist, The* (1989e) Japan's consumer boom: the pricey society, 9 September: 25–8.
*Economist, The* (1989f) Japanese anti-trust enforcement: up, Fido, up!, 16 September: 86.
*Economist, The* (1990a) Why can't little Taro think?, 21 April: 23–6.
*Economist, The* (1990b) Japan: the sun sets on rice, 21 April: 78.
*Economist, The* (1991a) Survey: Health Care, 6 July: 18–19
*Economist, The* (1991b) Used cars in Japan: young bangers, 21 December: 93–5.
*Economist, The* (1992) House prices: I own, I owe, so off to work I go, 26 December: 95–7.

*Economist, The* (1993) Japanese retailing: a kinder cut, 11 September: 82.

Efuji, Yasukichi (1982) International comparison of voluntary chains [Borantarii chēn no kokusei hikaku], *Ryūtsū Seisaku*, 9, January, 41–50 .

Ejiri, Hiroshi (1980) Are Japan's distribution channels really long? [Wa ga kuni no ryūtsū keiro ha hontō ni nagai ka], *Kikan Shōhi to Ryūtsū*, 4(4), Autumn: 72–9.

Ejiri, Hiroshi (1985) Can the returns system be reformed? [Henpin shisutemu ha kaikaku dekiru ka], *Ryūtsū Seisaku*, 21, May, 15–20.

Ejiri, Hiroshi (1988) *Distribution Keiretsu [Ryūtsū keiretsu-ka]*, Tokyo, Chūō Keizaisha.

*Ekonomisuto* (1989) Editorial: the reverse side of the Shūwa vs Chūjitsuya and Inageya dispute [Shasetsu: Shūwa vs Chūjitsuya, Inageya sōdō no uragawa], 1 August: 6–7.

Elliot, Clifford and Jang H. Yoo (1980) Innovations in the Japanese distribution system: are the barriers to entry being lifted?, *Arkon Business and Economic Review*, 11(1): 28–33.

EPA (Economic Planning Agency) (1986) *Distribution of Imported Goods and Trading Customs [Yunyū hin no ryūtsū oyobi shōkankō]*, Tokyo, Ministry of Finance.

EPA (Economic Planning Agency) (1992a) *The Plan to Become a Lifestyle Superpower in Five Years: Conditions and Problems for Progress to a Harmonious Society of Earth [Seikatsu taikoku 5 ka nen keikaku: chikyū shakai to kyōzon wo mezashite no suishinn jōkyō to kongo no kadai]*, Tokyo, Ministry of Finance.

EPA (Economic Planning Agency) (1992b) *Trends in Household Consumption [Kakei shōhi no dōkō]*, Tokyo, Ministry of Finance.

EPA (Economic Planning Agency) (1992c) *Household Consumption Trends 1992 [Heisei 4 nen kakei shohi no dōkō]*, Tokyo, Ministry of Finance.

EPA (Economic Planning Agency) (1993) *National Accounts Yearbook [Kokumin keizei keisen nenkan]*, Tokyo, Ministry of Finance.

Euromonitor (1989) *Consumer Japan*, London, October.

Eurostat (1992) *Basic Statistics of the Community – 29th edition*, Luxembourg, Office for Official Publications of the European Communities.

Fields, George (1983) *From Bonsais to Levi's*, London, Futura.

Fields, George (1988a) *The Japanese Market Culture*, Tokyo, Japan Times.

Fields, George (1988b) Changes in distribution can be promised, but are not so easy to come by, *Tokyo Business Today*, October: 21.

Fields, George (1989a) The Japanese distribution system: myths and realities, *Tokyo Business Today*, July: 57–9.

Fields, George (1989b) A Japanese 'outsider' causes another ripple in the already turbulent distribution pond, *Tokyo Business Today*, September: 27.

Fields, George (1990a) Unnecessary? Perhaps, but gift-giving continues to grow, *Tokyo Business Today*, March: 27.

Fields, George (1990b) Small stores can only survive by meeting consumer needs, *Tokyo Business Today*, August: 24.

Fields, George (1992) Great marketing concepts are not immutable, *Tokyo Business Today*, March: 35.

Fields, George (1993a) The sacred cows of Japanese retailing under challenge, *Tokyo Business Today*, May: 25.

Fields, George (1993b) More working women spurring chūshoku boom, *Tokyo Business Today*, June: 27.

Flath, David (1989) Vertical restraints in Japan, *Japan and the World Economy*, 1(1): 197–203.

*Focus Japan* (1983) Coffee binge, 10(4), April: 3.

*Focus Japan* (1984) Marketing technique: Cabbage Patch and Barbie dolls, 11(2), February: 4.

*Focus Japan* (1987a) Bausch and Lomb Japan, 14(8), August: 8.

*Focus Japan* (1987b) Japanscene: Japan's food prices higher than international standards, 14 (8), August

*Focus Japan* (1990) Oh to be in England: Laura Ashley Japan, 17(7), July: 8.

*Fortune* (1993) The billionaires, 28 June.

Fuchi, Keno (1989) Five ways of invading Japan [Itsutsu no patān de Nihon ni shintō], *Shūkan Tōyō Keizai*, 27 May: 61–4.

Fujigane, Yasuo and Peter Ennis (1990) Distribution keiretsu: electronics stores rebel, *Tokyo Business Today*, September: 35–6.

Fukao, Nobuo and Daisuke Akiba (1993) Spoiling rice [Mushibamareru kome], *Nikkei Business*, 1 November: 10–20.

Fukuda, Junko (1988) *New Developments in Retailing: The Onset of the Age of Information, Service and Internationalisation*, course for businessmen on the distribution system, marketing, and advertising in Japan, 5–10 September: 23–43.

Fukui, Jun (1993) Department Stores: conditions for survival [Hyakkaten ikinokori no jōken] *Shukan Tōyō keizai*, 13 February: 40–70.

Fukunaga, Hiroshi (1993a) Editorial: recession reforms Japanese lifestyles, *Tokyo Business Today*, March: 7.

Fukunaga, Hiroshi (1993b) Editorial: Japan is hell for working mothers, *Tokyo Business Today*, May: 5.

*Gekiryū* (1988) The day Seiyu will disappear as a supermarket [Seiyū ga sūpā to shite naku naru hi], November: 9–40.

*Gekkan Keiei Juku* (1992) Everything about Daiei Group in One Volume [Issatsu marugoto Daiei Gurūpu], special edition, 31 December.

Glazer, H. (1970) *Japan's Marketing Structure*, Bulletin 23, Tokyo, Sophia University Socioeconomic Institute.

Goldman, Arieh (1991) Japan's distribution system: institutional structure, internal political economy, and modernization, *Journal of Retailing* 67(2), Summer: 154–83

Goldman, Arieh (1992) Evaluating the performance of the Japanese distribution system, *Journal of Retailing* 68(1), Spring: 11–39.

Graven, Kathryn (1990) For Toys'R'Us Japan isn't child's play, *Wall Street Journal*, 7 February: B-1.

Green, Robert T. and Dana L. Alden (1988) Functional equivalence in cross-cultural consumer behavior: gift giving in Japan and the United States, *Psychology and Marketing*, 5(2), Summer: 155–68.

Gröke, Paul O. (1972) How Japanese department stores are meeting the challenge of a rapidly changing environment, *Journal of Retailing*, 48(3), Fall: 72–80.

Hanada, Tetsuya (1985) Kao's resale price maintenance [Kao seihin no saihanbai kakaku kōsoku jiken], *Kōsei Torihiki*, 420, October: 20–5.

*Hanbai Kakushin* (1989) Jusco's Noda Noa and Nichii's MYCAL Honmoku [Noda Noa to Maikaru Honmoku], 27(12), October: 101–2.

Harada, Hideo (1987) Possibilities for independent strategies in area wholesaling [Chiiki ton'ya ni okeru dokuji senryaku no kanōsei], *Ryūtsū Seisaku*, 28, March: 41–8.

Hasegawa, Tokunosuke (1987) The land price spiral: who is to blame?, *Japan Echo*, 14(4), November: 63–9.

Hatakeyama, Ryuichi (1989) 1988 Census of Commerce: red light in Aomori City as numbers of small stores fall by critical degrees [Shōwa 63 nen Shōgyō Tōkei Sokuhō: kenbu Aomori-shi ni aka shingō, shōten-sū no ōhaba genshō ni kiki-kan tuyomaru] *Shōgyōkai*, 70(6), June: 34–7.

Hayashi, Shuji (1980) The Japanese distribution system, *Journal of Enterprise Management*, 2(3): 263–75.

Haynes, Alison (1989) Big in Japan, *Retail Week*, 14 July: 10.

Higuchi, Ichiro, Fumi Kuwata and Shinji Tahara (1993) Wholesaling opens 'new physical distribution' [Oroshi ga hiraku 'shin butsuryū'] *Nikkei Business*, 7 June: 10–24.

Hirono, Renoa (1989) A summary of the 'Vision for Distribution in the 1990s' ['90 nendai ryūtsū bijon' no gaiyō], *Ryūtsū Seisaku*, 37, July: 4, 13.

Hirose, Yasuyuki, Yasushi Goto and Yuichiro Yamaken (1993) Opening the market to rice will change Japan [Kome kaihō ga Nihon wo kaeru], *Shūkan Tōyō Keizai*, 20 February: 10–20.

Holyoke, Larry (1993) What? Everyday bargains? This can't be Japan, *Business Week*, 6 September: 21–2.

Honma, Shigeki (1992) Deregulation of the Large Store Law and its influence on the regions [Daitenhō kanwa to chiiki he no eikyō] *Ryūtsū Dōkō*, February: 4–89.

Honma, Yasuhiro (1989) Remodelling from a distribution business to a developer business [Ryūtsū kara debcropā he tenshin], *Nikkei Business*, 17 July: 58–61.

Hoshino, Shigeru (1990) For quality-conscious Japanese consumers low prices also matter, *Tokyo Business Today*, September: 50–2.

Hoshino, Yoshinobu (1989) Building a quick response system for capital department stores [Shuto hyakkaten kuikku resuponsu shisutemu no kochiku wo] *Ryūtsū Nettowakingu*, March: 18–21.

Hulme, David C. (1993) Dialing for dollars: telemarketing takes off, *Tokyo Business Today*, March: 46–8.

Imai, Kenichi (1980) Distribution keiretsu and the anti-trust law policy [Ryūtsū keiretsu-ka to dokkinhō seisaku], *Jurisuto*, 716, 15 May: 32–6.

Imogawa, Tokutaro (1992) FTC: Still all bark, no bite, *Tokyo Buisness Daily*, August: 6.

Imoto, Shōgo (1993) Department stores depression [Hyakkaten fushin], *Nikkei Business*, June 5–12.

Ishihara, Tadako (1989) The business strategy that changed manual employees into merchants [Manyuaru shain wo shōin wo shōnin ni kaeta gyōkaku], *Gekiryū*, January: 10–55.

Ishihara, Takamasa (1985) Organising the shōtengai [Shōtengai no shoshikika], *Osaka City University Business Research*, 35(6), March: 1–19.

Ito, Masatoshi (1987) Product strategy for realising small lot many item merchandising [Ta-hishu shōryō-ka wo jitsugen saseta seihin senryaku], *Nihon Māketingu Jānaru*, 30: 46–51.

Ito, Takeo (1993) Aspects of shōtengais' facility building [Shōtengai no 'Machi zukuri' no sho taiyō] *Ryūtsū to Shisutemu*, 75, March: 18–30.

Ito, Tetsu (1989) Nichii: ambition hidden in the development business [Nichii: deberopā jigyō ni himeta yabō], *Shūkan Tōyō Keizai*, 1 April: 92–6.

Ito, Tetsu and Kiyoshi Ozawa (1989) Shūwa say, 'They will rebuild distribution' [Shūwa: 'Ryūtsū saihen kōsō'], *Shūkan Tōyō Keizai*, 5 August: 24–7.

Ito-Yokado (1992) *Company Report*, Tokyo.

Itozono, Tatsuo (1988) The Structure of Japanese Wholesale Distribution and current changes [Wa ga Kuni Oroshiuri Ryūtsū no Kōzō to sono henka], *Seinan Gakuin University Shōgaku Ronshu*, 34(4), March: 1–24.

Japan Department Stores Association [Nihon Hyakkaten Kyōkai] (1988) *Membership List [Kaiin meibo]*, Tokyo.

Japan Department Stores Association [Nihon Hyakkaten Kyōkai] (1990) *The 1988 Annual Statistical Summary of the Japan Chain Store Association [Nihon Hyakkaten Kyōkai tōkei nenpō shōwa 63 nen]*, March, Kōhō Chōsabu.

*Japan Times* (1990) Quicker store openings being reviewed, 28 March: 10.

*Japan Times Weekly* (1990) Prime Minister Kaifu walks tightrope on SII reform, 8 April: 23–9.

JCCI (Japan Chamber of Commerce and Industry) (1989) *Distribution System and Market Access in Japan*, Tokyo.

*JEJ (Japan Economic Journal)* (1990) Wanted: party boy for new-aged girl, 14 April: 11.

JETRO (Japan External Trade Organisation) (1982) *Now in Japan: Foreign companies in Japan* 33, Tokyo.

JETRO (Japan External Trade Organisation) (1983a) *How 62 Foreign Firms Successfully Market their Products in Japan*, Keys to Success Series, No. 6, March, Tokyo.

JETRO (Japan External Trade Organisation) (1983b) *Comprehensive economic measures*, paper presented to the Ministerial Conference for Economic Measures, Tokyo.

JETRO (Japan External Trade Organisation) (1987) *The Japanese Market: A Compendium for Information of the Prospective Exporter*, Tokyo.

JETRO (Japan External Trade Organisation) and MIPRO (Manufactured Imports Promotion Organisation) (1985) *Workshop Materials on Diversifying Import and Distribution Channels*, Fourth Workshop on Japan's Distribution Systems and Business Practices, 28 October, Tokyo.

JFTC (Japan Fair Trade Commission) [Kōsei Torihiki Iinkai] (1988) Survey of makers' recommended retail prices and the Fair Trade Commission's response [Mēkā kibō kouri kakaku ni kan suru chōsa to Kōsei Torihiki Iinkai taiō ni tsuite], *Kōsei Torihiki*, 452, June: 6–9.

JMA (Japanese Management Association) (1989) *Consumer Information [Seikatsusha Jōhō]*, Tokyo.

Johanssen, Johnny K. (1984) Japanese consumers: what foreign markets should know, *International Marketing Review*, 3(2), Summer: 37–43.

Jones, Randall S. (1987) The Japanese distribution system, *Journal of the American Chamber of Commerce in Japan*, December: 46–54.

JSCA (Japan Shopping Center Association) (1988) *Shopping Center Yearbook 1988 [Shoppingu sentia meikan '88]*, Tokyo.

JSCA (Japan Shopping Center Association) (1989) *Notes of the Association*, Tokyo.

JSCA (Japan Shopping Center Association) (1993) Shopping centers in Japan 1993 [Waga kuni shoppingu sentā no genjyō], Tokyo.

Kajiwara, Yoshio (1988) Receding control over distribution channel by manufacturers: marketing in Japan, Policy Research Project on Internationalisation of the Japanese Economy, Nagasaki University.

Kakita, Toshizumi (1984) Foreign capital enterprises operating in Japan's service industry, *Dentsu Japan Marketing/Advertising*, 11(1), January: 4–11.

Kaletsky, Anatole (1990) Japan devours an American totem, *Financial Times*, 27 March.

Kashima, Takashi (1993) Women find not-so-equal employment opportunities, *Nikkei Weekly*, 19 April.

Katsumoto, Muneo and Kazuo Miyazaki (1984) Overview of Japanese retailing, *International Trends in Retailing*, 1(2), Autumn: 3–13.

Kawade, Chihaya (1980) Treatment of distribution keiretsu under the antitrust law [Ryūtsū keiretsu-ka ni kan suru dokusen kinshi hō ue], *Keidanren Geppō*, 28(7), July: 43–5.

Kenrick, Douglas Moore (1990) *Where Communism Works: The Success of Competitive Communism in Japan*, Tokyo, Tuttle.

Kimura, Kazuhisa (1989) What's My-Cal Honmoku? [What's Maikaru Honmoku?], *Dime*, 15 June: 135–8.

Kirby, David (1984) Government policies towards the small retail business in Japan, *International Small Business Journal*, 2(4): 44–58.

Kishi, Shinji (1989) Supermarkets' bold moves towards organisation of retailing [Sūpā, kouri no soshikika he ogaki na kōdō wo], *Ryūtsū Nettowākingu*, March: 23–5.

Kitamatsu, Katsuro (1989) Icy welcome for MITI's retail law change, *JEJ (Japan Economic Journal)*, 21 October: 5.

Kobayashi, Itsuta (1988) Manufacturer's recommended retail pricing mechanisms and the anti-trust policy [Mēkā kibō kouri kakaku no kinō to dokusen kinshi seisaku], *Kōsei Torihiki*, 452, June: 10–18.

Kouyoumdjian, Virginia (1993) Foreign firms overcome obstacles, *Journal of Japanese Trade and Industry*, 5: 18–20.

Koyama, Shuzo (1984) The Japanese distribution system: complex and incomprehensible?, *Look Japan*, December.

Koyama, Shuzo (1985) The distribution structure in the Japanese market, *Management Japan*, 18(2), Autumn: 17–20.

Kunie, Hiroshi (1989) Shōtengai: joining retailers and wholesalers in cooperative networks [Shōtengai: kouri oroshiuri kyōdō nettowāku kōchiku he no kitai], *Ryūtsū Nettowākingu*, March: 28–30.

Kuraya, Shikishige (1981) The store opening plans of 840 stores frozen [Tōketsu sareta 840 tenpo no shutten keikaku], *Shūkan Tōyō Keizai*, 31 October: 39–41.

Kurosumi, Shashoku and Shohiro Omuko (1993) The day the gift market is taken by discount stores [DS ga gifuto wo ubau hi], *Nikkei Gifts*, March: 15–26.

Larke, Roy (1988) *A Consideration of Consumer Loyalty in Japan*, Institute for Retail Studies Working Paper No. 8801, Stirling University.

Larke, Roy (1990) *The Generation Gap Markets in Japan*, Institute for Retail Studies Working Paper No. 9003, Stirling University.

Larke, Roy (1991) Consumer perceptions of large retail stores in Japan, unpublished PhD thesis, Stirling University.

Larke, Roy (1992a) Japanese Distribution: An Appraisal with View to the Future, in *Proceedings of First International Federation of Scholarly Associations of Management (IFSAM) Conference*, Tokyo, 7 September: 51–6.

Larke, Roy (1992b) Japanese retailing: fascinating, but little understood, *International Journal of Retail and Distribution Management*, 20(1): 3–15.

Larke, Roy and Kenji Arima (1992) The Seiyu Ltd, in Adele Hast (ed.) *International Directory of Company Histories*, Detroit and London, St James Press: 187–9.

Larke, Roy and John A. Dawson (1992) Restrictions on the opening of new large retail stores in Japan, paper presented at the Institute of British Geographers Conference, Swansea, 8 January.

Larke, Roy and Kota Nagashima (1992) Takashimaya Co. Ltd, in Adele Hast (ed.) *International Directory of Company Histories*, Detroit and London, St James Press: 193–6.

Lazer, William, Shoji Murata and Hiroshi Kosaka (1985) Japanese marketing: towards a better understanding, *Journal of Marketing*, 49 (Spring): 69–81.

Leadbeater, Charles (1992) Sayonara to job security, *Financial Times*, 20 October.

Local Authorities Ministry (1993) *Nationwide Population, Household Numbers and Population Movement Tables 1993 [Zenkoku jinkō, setaisu hyō, jinkō dōtai hyō Heisei 5 nen]*, Tokyo, Kokudo Chiri Kyōkai.

Lowry Miller, Karen (1993) Land of the rising jobless, *Business Week*, 11 January: 16–17.

McMilan, C.J. (1984) *The Japanese Industrial System*, Berlin and New York, de Gruyter.

Maebara, Toshiyuki (1993) Tired of thrift? Luxury brands begin to sell [Setsuyaku tsukare? Kōkyū burando hin ga urehajimeta], *Shūkan Daiyamondo*, 22 May: 36–7.

Makihara, Kumiko (1992) The import of rice, *Time*, 14 December: 28–9.

March, Robert M. (1990) *The Honourable Customer: Marketing and Selling to the Japanese in the 1990s*, London, Pitman.

Maruetsu Headquarters Secretariat and Hiroko Misawa (1992) *The True Face of Modern Food Lifestyles [Gendai shoku seikatsu no sogao]*, Tokyo, Seibundō Shinkōsha.

Maruki, Tōru (1992) *A Quick Reference Map of the Distribution Industry [Ryūtsū gyōkai haya wakari mappu]*, Tokyo, Kō Shobō.

Maruyama, Magoroh (1985) The new logic of Japan's young generations, *Technological Forecasting and Social Change*, 28: 351–64.

Maruyama, Masayoshi (1989) Distribution: calling it a non-tariff barrier is a mistake [Ryūtsū: hi-kanzei shōheki ron ha ayamari da], *Shūkan Tōyō Keizai*, special edition, 16 June: 38–45.

Maruyama, Masayoshi, Yoko Togawa, Kyohei Sakai, Nobuo Sakamoto and Masaharu Arakawa (1989) *Distribution System and Business Practices in Japan*, paper presented at EPA International Symposium Structural Problems in the Japanese and World Economy, Economic Planning Agency, 12–13 October, Tokyo.

Matsushita, Mitsuo and Kenji Kawagoe (1980) *Compendium of Laws and Regulations Relating to Distribution [Ryūtsū kankei kihon hō kishū]*, Tokyo, Yūhaikaku Shinsho.

Matsuzaka, Takeshi (1993a) Garment maker tests no-return system, *Nikkei Weekly*, 8 March: 8.

Matsuzaka, Takeshi (1993b) FTC challenges cosmetics price structure: Shiseido offices raided in investigation of possible anti-monopoly law violation, *Nikkei Weekly*, 27 September: 10.

Matsuzaka, Takeshi (1993c) Shiseido ruling: one for the discounters: court tells cosmetics firm it cannot pressure retailers to sell products at suggested price, *Nikkei Weekly*, 4 October: 10.

Ministry of Education (1991) *Basic Survey of Schools [Gakkō kihon chōsa hōkoku sho]*, Tokyo, Ministry of Finance.

Ministry of Education (1992) *Survey of Student Lifestyles [Gaukusei seikatsu chōsa]*, Tokyo, Ministry of Finance.

Ministry of Health and Welfare (1991) *Future Projections of Japanese Population [Nihon no shōrai suikei jinkō]*, Tokyo, Health and Welfare Statistics Association.

Ministry of Justice (1991) *Immigration Control Statistics Yearbook [Shutsunyūkoku kanri tōkei nenpō]*, Tokyo, Ministry of Finance.

Ministry of Labour (1989) *White Paper on Labour [Rōdō hakusho]*, Tokyo, Ministry of Finance.

Ministry of Labour (1991) *White Paper on Labour [Rōdō hakusho]*, Tokyo, Ministry of Finance.

Ministry of Labour (1992) *White Paper on Labour [Rōdō hakusho]*, Tokyo, Ministry of Finance.

Ministry of Transport (1991) *Outline of Transport Economics Statistics [Unyu keizai tōkei yōran]*, Tokyo.

MIPRO (Manufactured Import Promotion Organisation) (1980) The import and distribution of consumer goods, *Penetrating the Japanese Market*, 1, July.

MIPRO (Manufactured Import Promotion Organisation) (1981) Product marketability and business practices, *Penetrating the Japanese Market*, 2, January.

MIPRO (Manufactured Import Promotion Organisation) (1983a) A note on Japanese general trading companies, *MIPRO Mission to Europe*, special note.

MIPRO (Manufactured Imports Promotion Organisation) (1983b) *An Analysis of and Recommendations Regarding the Japanese Distribution System and Business Practices* (summary of Japanese report), 16 June, Tokyo.

Mishima, Mari (1988a) A distribution revolution begins, *Economic Eye*, September: 12–16.

Mishima, Mari (1988b) Will the high yen bring about price destruction? [Endaka ha 'kakaku higai' wo hiki-okosu ka], *Ekonomisuto*, 31 May: 50–7.

Mishima, Mari (1989) The realities of the 'price revolution' as seen in the Western liquor and electrical products [Yō-zake, kaden ni miru 'kakaku kakumei' no genjitsu], *Ekonomisuto*, 28 March: 57–60.

MITI (Ministry of International Trade and Industry) (1983) *Japanese Market Is Open to the World*, special report, November.

MITI (Ministry of International Trade and Industry) (1984) *The Census of Commerce for 1982 [Shōgyō tōkei hyō: Shōwa 57 nenban]*, Tokyo, Ministry of Finance.

MITI (Ministry of International Trade and Industry) (1986) *The Census of Commerce for 1985 [Shōgyō tōkei hyō: Shōwa 60 nenban]*, Tokyo, Ministry of Finance.

MITI (Ministry of International Trade and Industry) (1987a) *Building Excellence in the Distribution System [Yutakasa no kōchiku ryūtsū sangyō]*, Tokyo, MITI Survey Committee.

MITI (Ministry of International Trade and Industry) (1987b) *Large Scale Retail Store Listing [Daikibo kouri tenpo yōran]*, Tokyo, MITI Survey Committee.

MITI (Ministry of International Trade and Industry) (1988) *Trade and Industry White Paper [Tsūshō hakusho]*, Tokyo, Ministry of Finance.

MITI (Ministry of International Trade and Industry) (1989a) *Vision for Distribution in the 90s [90 nendai no ryūtsū bijon]*, Tokyo, Ministry of Finance.

MITI (Ministry of International Trade and Industry) (1989b) *The Census of Commerce for 1988 [Shōgyō tōkei hyō: Shōwa 63 nenban]*, Tokyo, Ministry of Finance.

MITI (Ministry of International Trade and Industry) (1990a) *1988 Census of Commerce: Statistics on Distribution Channels [Shōwa 63 nen shōgyō tōkei: ryūtsū keiro betsu tōkei hen]*, Tokyo, MITI Survey Commitee.

MITI (Ministry of International Trade and Industry) (1990b) *The Final Report of the US–Japan Structural Impediments Initiative Discussions: A Scenario for the New US–Japan Era [Nichibei Kōzō Mondai Kyōgi Saishū Hōkoku: Nichibei Shin-jidai Shinario]*, Tokyo, MITI Survey Committee.

MITI (Ministry of International Trade and Industry) (1991a) *Commerce in Japan [Wa ga kuni no shōgyō]*, Tokyo, MITI Survey Commitee.

MITI (Ministry of International Trade and Industry) (1991b) *Explanation of the Extraordinary Law for the Development of Commercial Facilities [Tokutei shōgyō shūseki seibi hō no kaisetsu]* Tokyo, MITI Survey Committee.

MITI (Ministry of International Trade and Industry) (1992a) *The Census of Commerce: Advanced Report [Shōgyō tōkei sokuhō]*, Tokyo, MITI Survey Committee.

MITI (Ministry of International Trade and Industry) (1992b) *1991 Census of Commerce Volume 1 [Heisei 3 nen shōgyō tōkei hyō dai 1 maki: sangyō hen (sōkatsu hyō)]*, Tokyo, Ministry of Finance.

Miwa, Yoshiro (1992) *Japanese Business Trading Customs [Nihon no torihiki shūkan]*, Tokyo, Yukaikaku.

Miyashita, Masafusa (1992) *The Modern Wholesale Industry [Gendai no oroshiurigyō]*, Tokyo, Nihon Keizai Shinbunsha.

Mori, Kazuo, Toshihiko Taniguchi and Shigeru Noma (1989) The Large Store Law's 15 years of bad influence: deregulation is just a word [Daitenhō 15 nen no hizumi: kisei kanwa mo na bakari], *Nikkei Business*, 5 June: 6–23.

Morishita, Kaoru and Keiji Otake (1993) Toys'R'Us forces new game plan in Japan, *Nikkei Weekly*, 22 February: 9.

Morita, Akio, Edwin M. Reingold and Mitsuko Shimomura (1987) *Made in Japan*, London, Fontana/Collins.

Mouer, Ross and Yoshio Sugimoto (1986) *Images of Japanese Society*, London and New York, Routledge and Kegan Paul.

Mukoyama, Masao (1990) *The Japanese Distribution System*, Working Paper,1 June, Kobe, University of Marketing and Distribution Sciences Research Institute.

Murata, Shoji (1961) The Japanese consumer: a profile, *Journal of Retailing*, 37: 6–9.

Murata, Shoji (1973) Distribution in Japan, *the wheel extended*, 3(2): 4–11.

Nagura, Koji (1993) Wage negotiations with wives pay off for salaried workers, *Nikkei Weekly*, 26 July: 14.

Nakane, Chie (1973) *Japanese Society*, London, Penguin Books.

Nakanishi, Masao (1985) Rethinking the concept of retail catchment area [Kouri 'shōken' gainen saikō], *Kansai Gakuin University Journal*: 59–85 (author's files).

Nakaoka, Nozomu (1989) Editorial: trade problems and consumers, *Tokyo Business Today*, June: 5.

Nakata, Shinya (1982) The applicability of overseas products in the Japanese market [Gaikoku shōhin no Nihon shijō he no tekigō], *Ryūtsū Seisaku*, 11, July: 52–8.

Nakata, Shinya (1988) Retailing: variety of means and the conglo-merchants, *Japan Update*, Summer: 18–20; reprinted from *Sumitomo Quarterly*, Winter 1987).

Nakauchi, Isao (1989) The yoke of regulation weighs down on distribution, *Economic Eye*, Summer: 17–19.

Nakauchi, Isao (1993) Deregulation a long term proposition, *Nikkei Weekly* 27 September: 7.

Nichii (1989) *MYCAL Honmoku Guide [MYCAL Honmoku Annoi]* Tokyo, store literature.

Nichii (1992) Company reports and literature, Tokyo.

Nihon Keizai Shinbun (1988) *Reading the Nikkei Ryūtsū Shinbun [Nikkei Ryūtsū Shinbun no yomikata]*, Tokyo, Nihon Keizai Shinbunsha.

Nihon Keizai Shinbun (1990a) Store opening regulations: a maximum of 1 years [Shutten chōsei: saichō de 1 nenhan], 25 May.

Nihon Keizai Shinbun (1990b) Leaders questioning ban on rice imports, *JEJ* (*Japanese Economic Journal*), 28 July: 5.

Nihon Keizai Shinbun (1990c) Toys'R'Us applies to open Niigata store, *JEJ* (*Japanese Economic Journal*), 4 August: 19.

Nihon Keizai Shinbun (1990d) Kokubu expands chain to fend off large stores, *JEJ* (*Japanese Economic Journal*), 1 September: 18.

Nihon Keizai Shinbun (1990e) The Day the Large Store Law Disappears [Daitenhō ga kieru hi], Tokyo, nihon Kezai Shinbunsha.

Nihon Keizai Shinbun (1992) *Distribution Company Yearbook 1993 [Ryūtsū kaisha nenkan]* Tokyo, Nihon Keizai Shinbunsha.

Nihon Keizai Shinbun (1993a) 'Compound depression' hits consumers: just what is stopping consumer spending?, *Nikkei Weekly*, 8 February: 11.

Nihon Keizai Shinbun (1993b) Clothing retailers flee to the suburbs, *Nikkei Weekly*, 8 March: 8.

Nihon Keizai Shinbun (1993c) Women graduates draw short straw: many decide to stay in college until job market improves, *Nikkei Weekly*, 12 October.

Nikkei Ryūtsū Shinbun (1988) *Distribution Economics Handbook 1989 [Ryūtsū keizai no tebiki 89 nenban]*, Tokyo, Nihon Keizai Shinbunsha.

Nikkei Ryūtsū Shinbun (1989a) *Retailing: The Age for Attack [Kourigyō seme no jidai]*, Tokyo, Nihon Keizai Shinbunsha.

*Nikkei Ryūtsū Shinbun* (1989b) The 29th consumer survey: high income consumers [Dai 29 kai shōhisha chōsa: kōgaku shotokusha], 10 September: 1–5.

*Nikkei Ryūtsū Shinbun* (1989c) *Distribution Economics Handbook 1990 [Ryūtsū keizai no tebiki 90 nenban]*, Tokyo, Nihon Keizai Shinbunsha.

*Nikkei Ryūtsū Shinbun* (1990a) MITI deregulation of Large Store Law [Daitenhō kanwa tsūsan no yōshi], 24 May.

Nikkei Ryūtsū Shinbun (1990b) *Distribution Economics Handbook 1991 [Ryūtsū keizai no tebiki 91 nenban]*, Tokyo, Nihon Keizai Shinbunsha.

Nikkei Ryūtsū Shinbun (1991) *Distribution Economics Handbook 1992 [Ryūtsū keizai no tebiki 92 nenban]* Tokyo, Nihon Kezai Shinbunsha.

Nikkei Ryūtsū Shinbun (1992) *Distribution Economics Handbook 1993 [Ryūtsū keizai no tebiki 93 nenban]*, Tokyo, Nihon Keizai Shinbunsha.

*Nikkei Ryūtsū Shinbun* (1993a) Private brand prices: sūpās on the offensive, makers on the defensive [PB kakaku: sūpās kōsei, mēkā kusen], 20 April.

*Nikkei Ryūtsū Shinbun* (1993b) Market analysis: o-chūgen what and to whom? [Shijō bunseki: o-chūgen, nani wo, dare ni], 15 June.

*Nikkei Ryūtsū Shinbun* (1993c) Market analysis: university students' attitudes towards cars [Shijō bunseki: daigakusei no kuruma kan], 22 June.

Nikkei Ryūtsū Shinbun (1993d) *Distribution Economics Handbook 1994 [Ryūtsū keizai no tebiki 94 nenban]*, Tokyo, Nihon Keizai Shinbunsha.

*Nikkei Ryūtsū Shinbun* (1993e) 44% of applications changed [Shinsei no 44%, keikaku henka], 27 May: 1–2.

*Nikkei Ryūtsū Shinbun* (1993f) Chamber of Commerce strengthens [Shōkōkai, pawāappu], 12 January: 1–2.

*Nikkei Ryūtsū Shinbun* (1993g) 1992 survey of convenience stores [92 nen konbiniensu sutoa chōsa], 7 October: 1–3.

*Nikkei Trendy* (1992a) Toys'R'Us first store opens in December [Toizarasu 1 gō ten ga 12 gatsu ni kaiten], 48, October: 24–5.

*Nikkei Trendy* (1992b) The newest ways to use department stores [Hyakkaten no saishin riyō jutso] special winter edition: 12–99.

*Nikkei Trendy* (1993a) English conversation schools: a detailed analysis of teaching materials [Eikaiwa sukūru, kyōzai no tettei shindan], June: 7–54.

*Nikkei Trendy* (1993b) A big study of men's mail order sales [Otoko no tsūshin hanbai dai kenkyū], July: 6–50.

Nishimura, Takako (1986) Marketing and consumers [Māketingu to shōhisha], *Hannan Shakai Kagaku Ronshū*, 21(4), March: 77–87.

Niwa, Tetsuo (1988) Retailing rigidities keep prices up, *Economic Eye*, September: 8–11.

O'Donnell, Peter (1982) Take a lesson (and more) from retailers in Japan, *Stores*, 6(1), January: 49–54.

Ogawa, Shuji (1984) The distribution industry in the 1980s, *Journal of Japanese Trade and Industry*, 3(3): 12–15.

Ohashi, Takashi (1989) The strengthening of department stores' gaishō and the local markets in Nagoya [Depāto no gaishō kyōka to Nagoya kinkō no machi], *Shōtenkai*, 70(4), April: 109.

Ohashi, Terue (1988) *Generation Gap Business Theory [Sedai sa bijinesu ron]*, Tokyo, Tōyō Keizai Hōsha.

Ohmae, Kenichi (1989) Planting for a global harvest, *Harvard Business Review*, July/August: 136–45.

Okada, Kenji (1988) *The Department Store Business Sector [Hyakkaten gyōkai]*, Tokyo, Kyōikusha Shinko.

Okumura, Hiroshi (1989) Wakayama Prefecture shows the worst decline in store numbers [Zenkoku de mottomo ōkina shōtensū genshō ritsu miseta Wakayama-ken], *Shōgyōkai*, June: 32–3.

Omura, Shigeo and Junzo Ishii (1987) The attitude of Kyoto people regarding the freezing of large store openings [Ōgata ten tōketsu sengen ni tai-suru Kyoto shimin no taido keisei ni tsuite], *Dōshisha Shōgaku*, 39(2/3): 163–98.

Osahi, Akiko and Minako Fujiyasu (1993) Open the Japanese rice market, *Tokyo Business Today*, December: 30–3.

Otani, Masao (1991) Arguments for revision of the large store law and retail policy [Daitenhō kaisei, kourigyō taisuku toshin no ronten], *Ryūtsū Dōkō*, March: 19–24.

Otomo, Satoshi (1993) Consumer purchasing trends, *Journal of Japanese Trade and Industry*, No 5: 14–15

Ozaki, Akiko (1989) How overseas companies in Japan challenge the Japanese market [Zainichi gaishi no Nihon shijō michaku sakusen], *Shūkan Tōyō Keizai*, 27 May: 54–60.

Ozawa, Kiyoshi (1989) In the era of the large shopping centre: Japan undergoes great change [Ōgata SC jidai de Nihon ha dai henbō], *Shūkan Tōyō Keizai*, 1 July: 10–17.

RICE (Research Institute for Consumer Economics) (1988) Modern urban consumers [Gendai no toshi-gata shōshisha] Tokyo, Nihon Keizai Shinbunsha.

*Ryūtsū Sābisu Shinbun* (1993) Estimating changes in distribution with the relaxation of the Large Store Law [Daitenhō kanwa ni tomonau ryūtsū gyōkai no henka yōsoku] No. 207: 1.

Rodger, Ian (1990) Stores group challenges retail law, *Financial Times*, 2 April: 2.

Ross, Randolph E. (1983) Understanding the Japanese distribution system: an exploratory framework, *European Journal of Marketing*, 17(1): 5–13.

Saeki, Yoshihiko (1981) Large-scale stores seek ways to improve retail business, *Business Japan*, May: 83–91.

Saeki, Yoshihiko (1982) Large-scale department stores must adjust roles to community interests, *Business Japan*, May: 75–81.

Sakaida, Jun and Hirofumi Tanaka (1993) A rebirth scenario for Seibu Department Stores [Seibu Hyakkaten, saisei no shinario], *Nikkei Business*, 17 May: 38–42.

Sakamoto, Tadashi, Shohiro Komuko and Tadanori Sakamaki (1993) Big changes on the Chūgen frontline [Chūgen sensen ijyō ari], *Nikkei Gifts*, September: 12–36.

Sano, Tsutomu (1993) An approach to international price difference problems [Naigai kakaku sa mondai he no apurōchi] *Ryūtsū to Shisutemu*, 75, March: 31–9.

Sanwa Bank (1990) The effects of rising land prices on household budgets, *Japan Update*, Summer: 1–5; reprinted from *Economic Letter*, March.

Sasaki, Toshiji (1988) Many items, small quantification and changes in consumer behaviour ['I'a-hinshu shōryō-ka to shohisha kōdō no henka], *Nihon Māketingu Jānaru*, 30: 25–32.

Sato, Yoshinobu (1993) *The Aoyama and Kashiyama affair*, UMDS working Paper, April.

Sato, Eiji and Kenichi Tsuboi (1993) Junior baby-boom vs shinjinrui jyunia: the giant market begins to move [Dankai jyunia vs shinjinrui junia: kyodai shijō ga ugokihajimeta] *Shūkan Daiyamondo*, 15 May: 50–65.

Sato, Toshio (1985) Changes in consumers' cognition of life and image of commercial space [Shōhisha no seikatsu ninshoku oyobi shōgyō kūkan imeji no hennka] *Nihon University Shōgaku Ronshū*, 54(4), March: 11–26.

Scott-Plummer, Simon (1984) A modern image, but still the country of the small corner shop, *The Times*, 4 July: 37.

Seascope (1989) Convenience stores: a typically Japanese industrial development, *Japan Update*, Autumn: 15–17; reprinted from *Seascope*, 29, March.

Seibu Saison Group (1986) *Tsukashin Guide [Tsukashin Annai]* Tokyo, store literature.

Seibu Saison Group (1988) *Tsukashin [Tsukashin annai]*, Tokyo, company literature.

Seibu Saison Group (1989) *Company Report*, Tokyo.

Seiki, Katsuo (1983) Retail outlets seek harmony with local communities, *Business Japan*, May: 48–50, 53, 56.

Seki, Tsuguaki (1993) Bar codes go two-dimensional: new applications seen

262 Bibliography

as crucial to success of next-generation information-storage system, *Nikkei Weekly*, 26 July: 14.

Sekiguchi, Waichi (1990) Toys'R'Us giant store plan hits legal mire: mom & pop outcry, *JEJ (Japan Economic Journal)*, 10 February: 1, 6.

Sekine, Misako, Rika Sakuma and Miki Ota (1983) Revolution in shopping perceptions [Shoppingu kankaku kakumei], *Across*, August: 3–21.

Senno, Nobuhiro (1993) Practical universities: a new ranking from personnel heads [Yaku ni tatsu daigaku: jinji buchō ga honnō de eranda shin daigaku rankingu], *Shūkan Daiyamondo*, 17 April: 108–24.

Seven-Eleven (Japan) (1989a) *Corporate Outline: An Introduction to Seven-Eleven Japan Co. Ltd for Investors*, Tokyo.

Seven-Eleven (Japan) (1989b) *Seven-Eleven Company Report*, Tokyo.

Shale, Tony (1990) No tin soldiers in battle over toys, *Independent on Sunday*, 18 March: 15.

Shimaguchi, Mitsuaki (1977) *Marketing Channels in Japan*, Michigan, Mass., UMI.

Shimaguchi, Mitsuaki (1993) New developments in channel strategies in Japan, in Michael R. Czinkota and Maasaki Kotabe (eds) *The Japanese Distribution System* Chicago and Cambridge, UK: Probus Books.

Shimaguchi, Mitsuaki and William Lazer (1979) Japanese distribution channels: invisible barriers to marketing entry, *Michigan State University Business Topics*, Winter: 49–62.

Shimaguchi, Mitsuaki and Larry J. Rosenberg (1979) Demystifying Japanese distribution, *Columbia Journal of World Business*, 14 Spring: 32–41.

Shimizu, Shigeru (1980) Large retail store developments and joining with regional retailing [Ōgata kouri ten no tenkai to chiiki kourigyō no torimi hō], *Chūshō Kigyō to Kumiai*, 35(10): 4–11.

Shimizu, Toshihiko (1989) Foreigner Parco takes on the three Nagoya giants [Ihōjin Paruko vs jimoto sankyō no atsi arasoi], *Shūkan Tōyō Keizai*, 5 August: 70–1.

Shioya, Takafusa (1989) Japan's distribution system is a result of economy, society and culture: MITI, *Business Japan*, August: 57–63.

Shiraishi, Yoshiaki (1991) The public retail market in the changing distribution system in Japan, *Ryūtsū Kagaku Daigaku Ronshū*, 4(1), September: 13–30.

Shiraishi, Yoshiaki and Yoshinobu Sato (1992) *Channel Strategy*, Kobe, special paper for Nōryoku Kaihatsu Kyōkai.

*Shōgyōkai* (1989) MITI's idea for building 'Hi-Mart 2000' [Tsūsanshō no 'Hai Māto 2000' kensetsu kōsō], June: 30–1.

Shōhin Kagaku Kenkyūjo (1981) *An International Comparison of Shopping Behaviour and Consumption Attitudes between Europe/America and Japan [Kaimono kōdō, shōhisha taido no kokusai hikaku: ōbei to Nihon]*, Tokyo.

Shōkuhin Shōgyō (1987) *Complete Book of Convenience Store Merchandising [Konbiniensu sutoa no māchandaijingu zen-kenkyū]*, Tokyo, Shōgyōkai.

*Shūkan Daiyamondo* (1987a) Rush to refurbish store exteriors [Tenpo gaikyo-ten kaisetsu rasshu], 11 July: 13.

*Shūkan Daiyamondo* (1987b) Strong department stores and weak department stores [Tsuyoi hyakkaten yowai hyakkaten ], 5 September: 66–71.

*Shūkan Daiyamondo* (1989a) Continuing strong growth from suburban roadside businesses [Bainai seichō tsuzuku kōgai-gata rōdo saido bijinesu], 8 April: 86–9.

*Shūkan Daiyamondo* (1989b) Is Mitsukoshi's revival just in their rivals' slipstream? [Oi kaze dake ka: Mitsukoshi no fukkatsu], 3 June: 80–3.

*Shūkan Daiyamondo* (1989c) Panic stricken Chūjitsuya and Inageya co-operate on all fronts [Gimon dake no Chūjitsuya, Inageya zenmen teikei], 29 July: 10–13.

*Shūkan Daiyamondo* (1989d) Upheaval in distribution: who will laugh? Shūwa, Daiei, Chūjitsuya [Ryūtsū dai-gesshin: warau no ha dare da, Shūwa, Daiē, Chūjitsuya], 26 August: 8–14.

*Shūkan Daiyamondo* (1989e) The 100 department stores that worked hard to rally the industry [Hyakkaten ki morikaesu ganbatta 100 ten], 9 September: 70–6.

*Shūkan Tōyō Keizai* (1981) Editorial: large stores against the approval system for store openings [Shasetsu: ōgata-ten shutten no kyoka-sei ni hantai suru], 31 October: 60–1.

*Shūkan Tōyō Keizai* (1989a) The issue of Chujitsuya and Inageya's joint attack method [Chūjitsuya, Inageya no Kyōtō sagyō seihi], 22 July: 20–1.

*Shūkan Tōyō Keizai* (1989b) Shūwa vs Nomura: the fight to the death begins [Shūwa vs Nomura no shitō ga hajimatta], 29 July: 25–9.

Sletmo, Gunnar K. and Ibghy, Richard (1991) *Distribution and Culture: the case of the Japanese retail store*, École des Hautes Études Commerciales (H.E.C.), Montreal, Working Paper No, 91-002R, November.

Sōmuchō (Management and Coordination Agency) (1988a) *Japanese Statistics 1988 [Nihon no tōkei Shōwa 63 nen]*, Tokyo, Ministry of Finance.

Sōmuchō (Management and Coordination Agency) (1988b) *Housing Statistics Survey [Jyūtaku tōkei chōsa]*, Tokyo, Ministry of Finance.

Sōmuchō (Management and Coordination Agency) (1991a) *Census of Population 1990 [Kokusei chōsa hōkoku]*, Tokyo, Ministry of Finance.

Sōmuchō (Management and Coordination Agency) (1991b) *1989 National Consumption Patterns Survey: Vol. 1: Household Income and Expenses Part 1 [Heisei gan nen zenkoku shōhi jittai chōsa hōkoku: dai 1 maki kakei shushi hen sono 1]*, Tokyo, Japan Statistics Association.

Sōmuchō (Management and Coordination Agency) (1992a) *Annual Survey of Labour [Rōdō ryoku chōsa]*, Tokyo, Ministry of Finance.

Sōmuchō (Management and Coordination Agency) (1992b) *Annual Report on the Family Income and Expenditure Survey 1992 [Kakei chōsa nenpō 1992]*, Tokyo, Japan Statistics Association.

Sōmuchō (Management and Coordination Agency) (1993a) *1991 Report of Basic Survey of Social Life [Heisei 3 nen shakai seikatsu kihon chōsa hōkoku]*, Tokyo, Japan Statistics Association.

Sōmuchō (Management and Coordination Agency) (1993b) *Statistics of Japan 1992–93 [Nihon no tokei 1992–93]*, Tokyo, Ministry of Finance.

Sōmuchō (Management and Coordination Agency) (1993c) *Annual Report on Family Income and Expenditure Survey 1993 [Kakei chōsa nenpō 1993]*, Tokyo, Japan Statistics Association.

Sōrifu (Prime Minister's Office) (1987) *Japanese Life and Distribution [Nihonjin no kurashi to ryūtsū]*, Tokyo, Ministry of Finance.

Sōrifu (Prime Minister's Office) (1989) *Smoking and Drinking among the Japanese [Nihonjin no sake to tabako]*, Tokyo, Ministry of Finance.

Sōrifu (Prime Minister's Office) (1992) *White Paper on Tourism [Kankō hakusho]*, Tokyo.

Sugioka, Mitsuo (1989) Criticising the 'deregulation' of the awful Large Store Law [Kekan shita no Daitenhō 'kisei kanwa' wo hihan suru], *Ekonomisuto*, 28 June: 50–6.

Suzuki, Chieko (1984) Revitalising the fashion business: the Parco organisation [Fasshon bijinesu no kakushin-sei: Paruko], *Across*, March: 6–21.

Suzuki, Takayuki (1990) A samurai goes shopping, *BZW Japan*, July: 28–30.

Suzuki, Yasushi (1988) How to keep the junior baby-boom quiet [Dankai junia ha kō damase], *Dime*, 18 August: 13–17.

Susuki, Yasuaki (1993) Large-scale retail store law: historical background and social implications, in M. R. Czinkota and M. Kotabe (eds) *The Japanese Distribution System*, Chicago and Cambridge, UK: Probus Books.

Tadase, Yasuhiko (1993) My theory for food safety [Watashi no shokuryō anzen hoshō ron], *Shūkan Tōyō Keizai*, 20 February: 10–20.

Tajima, Yoshihiro (1971) *How Goods Are Distributed in Japan*, Tokyo, Walton-Rideway & Co.

Tajima, Yoshihiro (1980) *Dictionary of Distribution Terminology [Ryūtsū yōgo jiten]*, Tokyo, Tōyō Keizai Shinhōsha.

Tajima, Yoshihiro (1984) Japan's distribution system: an international comparison, *Journal of Japanese Trade and Industry*, 3(3): 16–17.

Tajima, Yoshihiro (1987) Japan's distribution system: myth and truth, *Anglo-Japanese Economic Journal*, 1(3), October: 5–7.

Tajima, Yoshihiro (1988) Conclusion of a survey into makers' recommended retail prices [Mēkākibō kouri kakaku ni kan suru chōsa wo oete], *Kōsei Torihiki*, 452, June: 4–5.

Tajima, Yoshihiro (1989) Vision for the distribution system in the 1990s, *Journal of Japanese Trade and Industry*, 8(4): 56–7.

Takahashi, Jun (1991) summary of the revision of the large store law and related legislation [Daitenhō no kaisei oyobi kanren kaku hō no gaiyō *Jurisito*, No 983, 15 July: 71–4.

Takaoka, Sueaki (1984) The retail industry and Japan's 2nd distribution revolution, *Journal of Japanese Trade and Industry*, 3(3), 18–19.

Takaoka, Sueaki (1989) Retail revolution, *Journal of Japanese Trade and Industry*, 8(4): 54–5.

Takaoka, Sueaki and Shuzo Koyama (1970) *Modern Department Stores [Gendai no hyakkaten]*, Tokyo, Nihon Keizai Shinbunsha.

Takayama, Kunisuke (1989) What is the vision for distribution in the 1990s hoping for, and what direction is it pointing towards? ['90 nendai ryūtsū bijon' ha nani wo hokoe, dono yō na hōkō wo mezashisō to shite iru no ka], *Shōgyōkai*, August: 38–9.

Takeuchi, Hiroshi (1983) The old shōtengai are left behind [Torinokosareru furui shōtengai], *Ekonomisuto*, 8 March: 62–3.

Tamura, Masaki (1981) The problem of regional oligopoly in retailing

[Kouri-gyō ni okeru chiiki kasen mondai], *Kikan Shōhi to Ryūtsū*, 5(4), Autumn: 16–31.

Tamura, Masanori (1989) Winds of change in the distribution industry, *Economic Eye*, Summer: 20–1.

Tanaka, Hirofumi (1993) Japan Toys'R'Us: cheapness and profits come together, sales efficiency 'the Japanese way' [Nihon Toizarasu: yasusa mo rieki mo ima hitotsu, 'Nihon ryū' de hanbai wo kōritsuka], *Nikkei Business*, 3 May: 38–40.

*TBT (Tokyo Business Today)* (1989a) Japan's distribution system under scrutiny, April: 9.

*TBT (Tokyo Business Today)* (1989b) Interview with Isao Nakauchi, August: 64.

*TBT (Tokyo Business Today)* (1993a) From 'lifetime employment' to the expendable salaryman, May: 8–10.

*TBT (Tokyo Business Today)* (1993b) On the corporate dole: Japan's one million 'working unemployed', May: 10–11.

Thomson, Robert (1990a) Lesson in store for 7-Eleven chain, *Financial Times*, 23 March.

Thomson, Robert (1990b) Managed trade by another name, *Financial Times*, 11 April.

Thomson, Robert and Anatole Kaletsky (1990) Japanese group buys stake in Southland, *Financial Times*, 23 March: 3.

*Tokyo Shinbun* (1991) Not enough bar codes [Bākōdo ga tarinai] 9 July.

Tokyu (1992) *Annual Company Report*, Tokyo.

Toshida, Seiichi (1989) The trick of price differentials between Japan and overseas [Naigai kakaku-sa no kanokuri], *Shūkan Daiyamondo*, 16 August: 46–59.

Traeger, David (1982) *Letters to Sachiko*, London, Paladin Books.

Tsujinaka, Toshiki (1988) *How to Grab the Junior Baby-Boom ['Dankai junia' wo tsukamaeru hō]*, Tokyo, Kōshobō.

Tsujinaka, Toshiki (1989) *The Junior Baby-Boom: 15 Year Old White Paper [Dankai Junia – 15 sedai hakusho]*, Tokyo, Seibundō Shinkosha.

Udagawa, Hideo (1989) Today's trend is to the overseas '4C's [Hayare ha ima gaishi '4C' no jidai], *Shūkan Tōyō Keizai*, 27 May: 48–52.

Uno, Masao, Shigeru Ichikawa and Mataichiro Katayama (1988) *The Distribution Business Sector [Ryūtsū gyōkai]*, Tokyo, Kyōikusha Shinko.

Uny (1992) *Company Annual Report*, Nagoya.

USITC (United States International Trade Commission) (1990) *Japan's Distribution System and Improving Options for US Access,* Washington, DC, US Government printing office.

van Wolferen, Karel (1989) *The Enigma of Japanese Power: People and Politics in a Stateless Nation*, London, Macmillan.

Vogel, Ezra (1981) *Japan as Number One*, Cambridge, Mass., Harvard University Press.

Wada, Kumi (1992) Find the naughty boys of the nineties [Heisei no wanpaku bōzu wo sagase], *Across*, September: 44–53.

Watanabe, Kenichi and Yoshihisa Suzuki (1988) NEC resale price control activity [Nihon denki (kabu) no sai-hanbai kakaku kōsoku jiken], *Kōsei Torihiki*, 454, August: 90–3.

Weigand, Robert E. (1963) Department stores in Japan, *Journal of Retailing*, 39, Fall: 31–5, 52.

White, Merry I. (1993) Teens' test: trial by shopping, *Nikkei Weekly*, 18 March.

Wilkinson, Endymion (1983) *Japan vs Europe: A History of Misunderstanding*, Harmondsworth, Penguin Books.

Woronoff, Jon (1981) *Japan: The Coming Social Crisis*, Tokyo, Lotus Press.

Yamaichi Securities (1990) *Japanese Land*, International Business Department Special Report, Tokyo, April.

Yamanaka, Hiroyuki (1993) Onward Kashiyama: stops trading with men's clothing chain store [Onwādo Kashiyama: shinshi fuku ryōhanten to torihiki chūshi], *Nikkei Business*, 19 April: 38–41.

Yasumori, Akio (1993) 'Free delivery nationwide': simplification and hard cost reduction ['Zenkoku muryō takuhai': shinpuru ni, shitsuyō ni kosuto daun], *Nikkei Gifts*, September: 38–41.

Yasumori, Akio, Hiroki Fukui and Tomoya Mochida (1993) Guessing the gift market in a recession [Fukyō shita no gifuto shijō wo uranau], *Nikkei Gifts*, May: 12–28.

Yoshida, Naoko (1993a) Parallel importers play role of Robin Hood, *Tokyo Business Today*, March: 58.

Yoshida, Naoko (1993b) Idiotic policy treats every female employee as a potential scandal, *Tokyo Business Today*, July: 59.

Yoshida, Naoko (1993c) 9 to 5 dept: a woman's work is never done, *Tokyo Business Today*, August: 59.

Yoshino, M.Y. (1971) *The Japanese Marketing System*, Cambridge, Mass., MIT Press.

YRI (Yamaichi Research Institute of Securities and Economics) (1990) Large store openings accelerating, *Yamaichi Research*, March: 20–2.

# Source index

# Subject index

adult education 23, 37, 229; leisure 42
Adults' Day 52, 240
Aeon Group 212–15, 224, 230; South East Asia 215
age groups: see consumer age groups
aging population 14–19
agricultural buying co-operatives 79
Aichi Prefecture: geography 137: retailing concentration 75; Saison Group 212; Uny Group; 218–19; wholesaling concentration in 6
Akari 219
Akihabara 12
Akita Prefecture 214
alcohol consumption 100
Alpen 143
American: consumers 58, post-war occupation of Japan 107; rice 233
anti-competitive business practices and customs 59–61; manufacturers and 84–8
Anti-monopoly law 61, 87; strengthening of 233
Aoki International 142–3
Aoyama Shoji 88, 142–3, 214
Apita 219
Australia: women's salaries in 30
automobile distribution 83–4; see also cars

baby-boom generations 16; see also junior baby boom, senior baby-boom
background music 133
bakeries: decline in 78
banks 238
bar codes 99; article number codes 97; product codes 92; seasonal products and 99; two dimensional 99
Bausch Lomb 240
Benetton 186
Best Denki 138
bicycles 159
Big Boy 206
Bigi 137
birth rate 15, 37
Blue Grass 214
BMW 240
Body Shop 214, 230
Bon Belta 214
Bonn: shopping behavior in 47
bonuses 52; reduction in 227; see also incomes
booksellers 161
boxed gift sets of foods 2, 53, 189
boys: education in Japanese society 23–7
brands: cheaper 206; designer 143; consumers and 19, 25, 45, 211, 228; department stores and 2; famous 1, 8; fashion 137, 161; gifts and 54; high quality 129, 165; images 137; luxury 3, 188;